ADRIFT IN CHINA

ADRIFT IN CHINA

Simon Myers

SUMMERSDALE

Summersdale Publishers Ltd
46 West Street
Chichester
West Sussex
PO19 1RP

www.summersdale.com

Printed and bound in Great Britain.

ISBN 1 84024 217 5

The extract from *Please Don't Call Me Human* (2000) by Wang Shuo is reprinted by kind permission of No Exit Press (www.noexit.co.uk).

Although every effort has been made to trace the present copyright holders, we apologise in advance for any unintentional omission or neglect and will be pleased to insert appropriate acknowledgement to companies or individuals in any subsequent edition of this publication.

Cover design by Michelle Radford

For Céline (and the bikers)

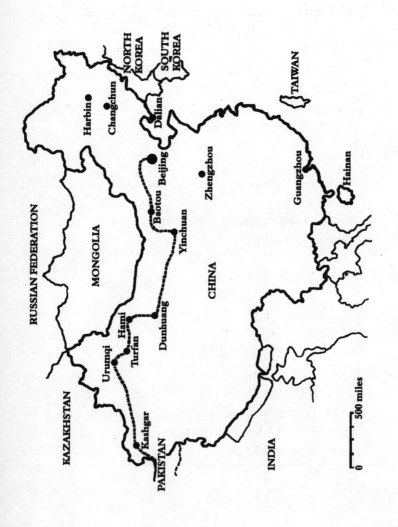

CONTENTS

Introduction

There is the kingdom of China, which they say is a very extensive dominion, both along the coast of the sea, and in the interior.
– Duarte Barbosa, AD 1518

To have an introduction these days seems somehow old-fashioned. Yet with a subject as colossal as China, a pause or brief reflection before entering such a limitless labyrinth can be a positive thing. China is the third largest country in the world, holds nearly a quarter of the earth's population and claims a recorded history going back more than 3,000 years. Foreigners' reactions to China and its people veer from one extreme to the other; the gargantuan size of the place demands a sweeping response. This is understandable. Time is needed for such a big and complex country, something most travellers today lack.

This book is about a journey in China. One that started in 1990 and finished eight years later in a daze on a Changjian motorbike and sidecar in London. I didn't think it would take that long – honest. If I had thought it would, I doubt I would have started. What began as an innocent year abroad to learn another language slipped unnoticed, like a tributary of the Yellow River, inevitable and lazy, into something bigger and more demanding.

This book is about time spent studying, working and travelling in the Middle Kingdom during a decade when much changed in China, and yet much stayed the same. It is an account that seeks to acknowledge and celebrate the country's particular disorientating appeal for the foreigner. For those readers yet to experience China, it may even provide some much needed guidance. In such an extraordinary country it is easy to get lost.

PART ONE

Prologue

People travel to escape the predators of the world, to find out what lies over the garden wall, or even to sell Coca-Cola to the Chinese.

— Eric Newby

Zhengzhou, Henan Province, 1998

I woke up sweating and feeling uncomfortable. My heart was beating at an alarming speed, breathing was difficult and my mouth was as dry as the desert. I lurched out of bed, across the small hotel room, to the bathroom. I hit my knee on the leg of the executive desk. Splashing water on my face to try to ward off a growing nausea, I looked around for the free bottles of mineral water that were fitfully placed in the rooms. *Mei you.* Nothing. I thought about drinking the tap water, but checked myself; I might have been technically drunk, but this was still one of the most polluted cities in the world. In the mirror I saw that I was still wearing my suit from the night before, and looking down I realised that my trousers were a darker and damper grey below the knees. Interesting. I stared at them until some explanation worked its way into my consciousness. Oh yes, I remembered now; the tasteful rock-pool in the middle of the lobby. Last night, I must have walked through it rather than around.

Weaving back into the bedroom, I opened the unplugged mini-fridge and found a warm Coca-Cola. With nothing else to slake my thirst, I drank Atlanta's number one product in a long series of gulps. A brief belch and with it the strong odour of last night's Red Dragon Wine. The pungent taste of alcohol made me feel faint. Putting the can down, I shuffled to the window and pulled back the thin net curtains. Another day of hazy greyness. A dried-up concrete canal full of refuse ran behind the hotel while several bulbous pipelines careered alongside. On the far side of the canal there were dusty, dilapidated brick houses, small workshops, and beyond them, large factory-like structures. Visibility was limited and smog enveloped the city. It was probably better that way as the grey haze hid the scale of the corrosive conurbation that is Zhengzhou. A city of over ten million in the heart of China. Even after nearly a year to acclimatise, it was still a depressing sight.

I gazed out while moving my tongue around a mouth made furry by the warm Coke. Just as I had suspected, the fizzy drink had provided only temporary satisfaction. It wasn't enough that I was selling the stuff; now I was drinking it before breakfast. Jesus. A headache that had earlier only threatened mild irritation was now in full progress, kicking at the back of my eyes. I stumbled into the shower. The lukewarm water had little rejuvenating effect and I felt listless and ill. How many mornings had I woken up in such a state? What was the acceptable alcoholic intake of the lone foreigner in China? At what point was one's health in danger? Whatever it was, I was convinced that the heavy drinking sessions were becoming life-threatening. I leant back on the damp tiles of the bathroom wall and let the water dribble over my head. This had to stop. It was time to leave the centre of the world.

Chapter One

City of Eternal Spring

Once you are in China, you will face not only the challenge of another educational system, but also a series of unstable emotional experiences owing to the new cultural environment.

– Study in China: A Guide for Foreign Students

I first came to China, like many others, as a foreign student. Right from the start there was confusion and misunderstanding. Our little group of six, bound for the northern city of Changchun, had been picked up from Beijing airport in a small minivan with blacked-out windows. Against the backdrop of airport, people and car commotion, we handed over stuffed rucksacks whilst staring at the offending vehicle. Hmmm . . . deliberately darkened windows, definitely something sinister here. As the first foreign students back in China one year after the bloody scenes of the 1989 Tiananmen massacre, there was a certain suspicion of anyone who represented authority. Visa officials, passport control and customs officers obviously were suspect. Now this distrust encompassed the university minibus driver and the enthusiastic pedagogue student sent to look after us. Why were the windows blacked out? Was it for security reasons? Were we already seen as a threat to stability? Why did the keen student-type have a fixed grin? Were we to be bundled out the other end into . . . something unpleasant? Despite having received a number of Mandarin lessons, our collective knowledge ran to a few set phrases: 'Hello/I'm from England/ These dumplings are delicious.' We would have found it difficult to put together a question that could have elicited a simple explanation.

Sensing our discomfort and furtive glances, the clean-cut Beijing student in the front seat turned around and pointed at the evil-looking windows.

'It is very hot outside. The dark windows keep inside cool,' he said in English.

Right. So that was it. Embarrassed smiles and nods, but one fellow-student remained sceptical, convinced there was a hidden agenda.

'They don't want anyone to see us,' she said, nodding her head in a knowing way.

This paranoia, a sense of something sinister lurking just below the surface, was a common condition amongst new arrivals in China. Apart from being in an introverted Communist state whose ruling octogenarians had just shown the world their bloody determination to hold on to power, we had drunk in the stories of older returning students. Reared on tales of bugged telephones, post being opened, read and then cunningly resealed, and all sorts of fabulous permits needed for the smallest journey, it was perhaps understandable that the mundane and the normal took on a wild significance.

We had visions of a ruthless police state intent on keeping young foreigners with crazy ideas like democracy and speaking their minds under wraps. Our very destination, not the usual exchange university in the heart of Beijing, but an out-of-the-way provincial college, seemed to confirm that the regime was somehow wary of our presence. We needed to be corralled and contained lest we contaminated the rest of the population. It would take several months before this distorted view of our own importance to the Chinese authorities and the Communist hierarchy would be punctured. That is not to say that the government of China has no totalitarian tendencies, it has; but as a foreign student one is not a primary target. One of the contributing factors to a new sense of proportion was the discovery, later in the year, that our British university had sent us out of the capital not because, as we had believed, former students had overenthusiastically participated in the Tiananmen demonstrations, but to save money.

We were on our way to Changchun, over 15 hours by train north-east of Beijing, in Manchuria. A city of nearly three million, with wide tree-lined boulevards and functional concrete housing, Changchun translates as 'city of eternal spring'. This had given it a rather appealing air back in Britain. It conjured up images of avenues with peach trees in blossom, warm days spent lying in the municipal park, and cycling to class under clear blue skies. Possibly even laughing, head back, while we pedalled alongside our Chinese classmates. I was genuinely looking forward to my time there. There was an assumption that because you studied Chinese, you knew more about what you were doing with your life and where you were going than students who took more traditional courses. This was a myth. My decision to learn Chinese had shamelessly hinged around a year abroad somewhere distant and exotic. Somewhere that held the possibility of an adventure, somewhere completely different, somewhere big, somewhere *else*. China seemed to be a parallel universe where everything was done differently and the established points of reference were no longer relevant. Dramatic confirmation of China as an attractively strange destination had come the summer before at a drinks party, in a garden overlooking the sea in Cornwall.

Amongst rhododendrons, camellias and the sound of several conversations, a handsome young man walked over with a tray of wine glasses. With a fixed smile he offered the drinks around as the whole tray shook with a low intensity. Glasses knocked against each other and white wine splashed over their rims. People pretended not to notice as they conversed. His arms were trembling and he spoke in short bursts. From the edge of the circle I heard that he had just come back from China. He had been amongst the millions of demonstrators that took to the streets of Beijing that summer. I stared fascinated at someone almost the same age as me who had returned so obviously affected by his experience in a country psychologically and geographically so far from home.

Changchun itself, however, was to be something of a disappointment. As the weather worsened the 'city of eternal spring' revealed itself as the city of eternal winter. Within weeks of our arrival the temperature plunged to below -28 °C and stayed there for over four months. This change of climate had been heralded by an invasion of cabbage from the countryside. Windowsills, pavements, concrete balconies, backyards and disused rooms were all commandeered by the green winter staple. For the local residents this was the signal needed to wrap up in layers of padded wool and cotton clothes, paste up the last of the insulation paper (old copies of the *People's Daily*) and generally hunker down for the winter. Vast quantities of snow soon fell, which in the urban environment quickly turned to slush and then limb-threatening ice. Simple daily tasks that involved going outside became hugely difficult. Going to the post office, swollen with clothing, became a formidable logistic operation; getting on and off the bus, falling over on the ice, the snail-like progress of the traffic, the crush of bodies. Inside every enclosed space hung the smell of garlic and stale sweat. I wondered if the translation of 'Changchun' had been a mistake or whether it exhibited a cruelly ironic national sense of humour. It was not until after several months in the city that I picked up the poorly printed Chinese university literature that had been handed out to us in Britain before departure. There, in the appendix, was the number of days of each season every major city in China could expect. Under 'summer' Changchun was bottom with 35 days; in case there was any doubt about it, under 'winter' Changchun was top with 210.

Not only was Changchun freezing, it was also drab, conservative and stubbornly Communist. Poorly constructed breeze-block flats lined the city roads. These were interspersed with heavy Russian-inspired buildings, porticoed and peeling, housing various government departments. A layer of soot covered the buildings, courtyards and people. Exacerbated by the wintry weather, the city exhibited a threadbare stiffness. While the rest of China was beginning to shake off its Communist past and emerge from decades of enforced boredom, Changchun remained staunchly dull. Perhaps the city, by its conformity, was trying to make up for its renegade past which saw the last emperor, Pu Yi, set up a puppet government in the city with Japanese support in 1931. Nominally the ruler of north-eastern China, or 'Emperor of Manchukuo' as the Japanese called him, Pu Yi's authority in reality ran to the end of his drive. Until the end of the Second World War he rattled around his enormous palace, venting his political and personal impotence on his wives and imperial entourage. His unwitting collusion with the 'Japanese aggressors' and his unspoken homosexuality have ensured he will remain a marginal figure in the country's collective conscience. The palace is now mostly part of a university, while some areas of it are open to the public as a reminder of China's rotten imperial past. Despite the mandatory disapproving rhetoric of the explanatory signs, a visit conjures up a strange empathy with this melancholic and lost figure from Chinese history.

There were other points of interest in Changchun. A large park, an army barracks, an enormous car plant (which had just formed a joint venture with Audi) and the national 'Liberation' (*Jiefang*) truck factory. These lumbering eight-wheeler lorries are the modern pack-horses of the Chinese economy and can be seen the length and breadth of China. They come in two colours – pastel 'hospital' green or electric 'worker' blue. The noise they make is unlike more modern designs where the engine is the primary source of sound. Instead, the whole of a Liberation rattles, shudders and shakes. There is a creaking din that is hard to pinpoint. It is as if the workers in the Changchun plant have partially unscrewed all the nuts and bolts at the end of the production line as part of some mechanical practical joke. At high speed or with a heavy load one waited for the Liberation lorry to implode.

There is also a vast film studio in Changchun belonging to the People's Liberation Army (PLA) where propaganda films were churned out about Chinese heroics against the Japanese in the Second World War. As pale-faced Europeans, we were invited to be extras in a film about the Japanese attack on Shanghai in 1941. Playing effete foreign journalists held at gunpoint by khaki-clad bayonet-toting Japanese, we shrieked in mock horror as we were rounded up and gently pushed around. The soldiers were PLA personnel dressed up in Japanese uniforms, which must have been a duty on a par with cleaning the latrines. When the director screamed 'Action!' we stared menacingly at each other across the shiny tip of a bayonet. The soldier opposite me seemed incredibly nervous, as if one split second of sub-standard concentration would see his bayonet nicking my neck, causing untold harm to Changchun's newly established relationship with the outside world.

The horror of the Japanese occupation and the doughty Chinese response is an ever-present theme in the north-east of China where the population suffered terribly at the hands of the Japanese army. This grim period saw starvation, random killings, rape and torture, the destruction of villages and complete helplessness in the face of a methodical and brutal Japanese war machine. Not far from Changchun one can visit an 'experimentation farm' where Japanese doctors carried out gruesome medical experiments on Chinese soldiers and civilians.

However, it wasn't just the PLA propaganda department who had a monopoly on creating anti-Japanese spectacles. Later in the year, at a university sports day, the athletic festivities started with a full-scale re-enactment by students dressed as the PLA battling the beastly Jap invaders. This encounter came complete with smoke bombs, shouting, blanks and Oscar-winning death performances. After a lot of noise, the PLA troops swarmed across the running tracks and chased the Japanese soldiers out of the sports arena. The two Japanese exchange students standing next to me stared on in horror.

But Changchun had also suffered at the hands of other Chinese. The Communists had 'liberated' the city by first starving the nationalist-held town into submission. *White Snow, Red Blood*, written by a former PLA officer called Zheng Zhenglong, tells the story of how thousands died of starvation, while others were forced to eat leather and rats to survive. There were incidents of cannibalism. The book was banned just before our arrival.

Just down from a commemorative concrete plinth supporting a Soviet Tupolev bomber (Soviet forces helped liberate the city from the Japanese in 1945) was the university dormitory for foreign students. Situated on the corner of Stalin Street and Liberation Avenue, this 'foreign student hotel' was our home for a year. I shared a room with a bluff ex-fireman called Dave. Blond and beefy, if people asked where he came from he would say, 'Grimsby, town of a thousand delights.'

Back in the UK I remember thinking this was a great line. It played on the unspoken prejudices of fellow, mostly southern, students. It also hinted at the existence of a self-deprecating humour which I instinctively warmed to. In Changchun, however, it was simply confusing for the people we met. Despite Dave taking a large amount of time to translate the phrase into Mandarin, frozen grins remained when these words were spoken to a group of Changchun students and embarrassingly, Dave was forced to explain. The conversation went something like this:

'Hello, I am Zhang, from Changchun.'

'Hi, I'm Dave from Grimsby, town of a thousand delights.'

'Town . . . of a . . . thousand . . . delight.'

'Yup.'

'What so delight about this town?'

'Nothing. It's awful.'

'So not delight?'

'That's right.'

'Then why call it town of a . . .'

'Thousand delights. British humour. Actually gritty northern humour. The place is so awful that we play on this and say it is like a fairytale city.'

'What is so awful about Grimsby?'

'It's cold, grey and there's nothing to do.'

'Oh, like Changchun!'

'Exactly.'

To help smooth our way into Chinese society, we were given Chinese names. This was an exciting moment as not only did we feel it necessary for our entrée into polite society, but they were also generally more interesting than the ones we already had. My name was *Ma Shi Min*, three characters all with positive meanings that sort of sounded like a Chinese person saying my surname and Christian name together: *ma* (horse) *shi* (world) *min* (people). If the *shi* was pronounced with the wrong tone though I ended up introducing myself as Mr Horse Shit. Dave realised after six months that he had been introducing himself as Little Red Fire Truck. Surely someone was playing a joke?

Other foreign students were thin on the ground and we were the first group from the West. There were a few Japanese, a large contingent of bored Africans from Gabon, Mali and Zambia, a gang of North Koreans, and homesick Russians who cheerfully lived up to their national stereotype by drinking large amounts of vodka and singing maudlin folk songs while becoming increasingly emotional.

The Africans had arrived on 'socialist scholarships' and some had been in the frozen wastes of Manchuria for an incomprehensible three years. After an initial language course they learnt about computers in Chinese. All in all they were expected to stay for five years and many did not return home during this period. They survived by organising weekly parties to meet any available single women, smoking marijuana, and watching a steady stream of pirated action videos. The Chinese viewed them with a mixture of fear and barely disguised disgust. While we may have been ignorant foreigners, they were viewed as primitive barbarians. The Africans rewarded this xenophobia with an outright contempt for any rules and regulations that they encountered. For example, travelling without a ticket on a train became de rigeur. When cornered by the ticket inspector, brazen lying and stonewalling tactics were used ('I lost it.') For some reason, they never got into serious trouble. The local authorities were not used to such barefaced cheek. Perhaps there was also an unspoken fear. A few months earlier, African students had rioted at Nanjing University over the treatment of one of their colleagues accused of raping a Chinese girl.

The North Koreans (all male) were the only ones who

seemed genuinely happy and content in Changchun. Singing, laughter and general alcohol-fuelled merriment could be heard most nights from their rooms. They were all ferocious table tennis players, and despite a year of effort none of us ever beat any of them. They seemed uninterested in anything but table tennis, homework and beer. They certainly remained supremely aloof from the handful of female students. This may have been as a result of their desire not to do anything that could get them into trouble and subsequently sent back to the crazy socialist paradise over the border. We had learnt, for instance, much to our student horror, that in Pyongyang, beer was rationed! No wonder they were on their best behaviour. That they showered together in groups of three amidst much laughter was perhaps another reason for their disinterest in the opposite sex. This was certainly Dave's interpretation. He felt his suspicions were confirmed when one of the Koreans grabbed his left buttock in the lift and told him that he had the looks of a filmstar. Red-faced and furious, he recounted the incident in our room. My interpretation was that the Korean student in question had overenthusiastically interpreted an Asian tradition of developing good relations with anyone who someday might influence any sort of decision; this included Dave.

They all had to wear badges of Kim Il Sung, 'The Great Leader', that were never removed. Dave once offered cash for one of these emblems of egocentric mania, but was severely reprimanded, 'Some things are not for sale, David.'

A Korean student later told me that if he went back home without his badge he would be in severe trouble.

'What sort of trouble?'

He shook his head with a short shudder to indicate that this was not an appropriate subject for further discussion.

There was a tracksuited minder who hung around with the Korean group. Much older, he had a little wiry moustache and was fastidious about his appearance. He wore a tight, pressed tracksuit all the time apart from Workers' Day, when he changed into a black suit. He reminded me of the archetypal fascist PE teacher from my schooldays. While for us he was a figure of sinister fun, for the Korean students he was a permanent reminder that although we were all in China, they would be judged by another set of rules.

During our time in Changchun, Mrs Thatcher was pushed from power. There was general merriment amongst the small British contingent. We started drinking earlier than usual, playing some music and generally jumping about. I bumped into one of the Koreans in the corridor. He asked what all the celebration was about.

'Our leader has stepped down.'

'Why are you so happy?'

'She had been there for over eleven years and was going a bit crazy . . .'

There was a pause and a frown.

'Well, I don't understand. Our Dear Leader, Kim Il Sung, has been there for over forty years . . .'

'Maybe it's time he stepped down as well then,' I said, emboldened by the beer.

'Our leader will never step down. That is why he is our leader.'

The mean-looking minder suddenly appeared from the showers in a short towel and plastic flip-flops and glared in our direction. The Korean student slipped back into his room.

The thin chaperone gave me a long blank look before walking away.

Yi . . . er . . . san . . . si. One, two, three, four. We were woken every morning at 6.45 by the workers of the town-planning authority going through their morning aerobics en masse. Our cracked concrete balcony overlooked a dusty yard where about sixty people exercised in formation. A loudspeaker counted out time while a large grey-haired lady led from the front with a fluorescent pink and green fan. At the same time, just across the road, students were put through their morning exercises, which since the Tiananmen crackdown had taken on a distinctly martial flavour. One, two, one, two, halt! About turn! The military drill routine was meant to toughen them up against unnamed 'counter-revolutionary forces'.

While we were still swept up in the newness of it all, there was a concerted attempt to discover the city and its inhabitants. This included explorations by bicycle in several layers of clothes, a short stint at piano lessons and numerous attempts to meet local fellow-students and 'hang out'. This last activity was more challenging and precarious than we realised.

We made few local friends. This was not through want of trying. There were several barriers in the way as well as differing expectations. There was very little common ground on which to build a relationship. Economically, socially and politically we were from a different world. Despite all being students, it was difficult to connect. They were very serious; we were not. 'Hello, Mr Ma, I would like to talk about Marx and why your capitalist society will collapse,' was a not uncommon starting point. We had travelled abroad; they had not. Secluded in the backwaters of the north-east, their only points of reference were China and its great history. Within months though we had visited more places than they had in their lifetimes. They began to ask us about places in China, which they felt by right we should be asking them about.

Their earnestness about everything, unleavened by any irony, was cloying. Patriotic and defensive about China, at the same time fascinated by all things European, they embodied the country's contradictory attitude to the West.

They were easily shocked into embarrassed silence; we were not. Raised in a society that placed the communal before the individual, discussing personal passions, hopes and dreams was something deemed inappropriate and selfish. A natural reservation placed potentially interesting but complex subjects off-limits. As well as this, we were foreigners, to be treated circumspectly. This was not Shanghai or Beijing with budding avant-garde scenes where young people of all nationalities had begun to mix freely. In the streets of Changchun people still said '*laowai*' ('foreigner') in whispered intakes of breath as we walked past.

On top of this, hanging out with your friends was a new concept that had yet to arrive in the city. Life revolved around the work unit (*danwei*) and the family. Personal leisure time had yet to break down the rigid routines of the city. There were few comfortable restaurants, no cafés, no bars and no teahouses. The cold weather meant outside rendezvous were impractical. As for socialising with foreigners, there was no neutral space in which to meet. Locals were barred from the lobby of the two hotels in town, and if any student wanted to come round to our rooms, they had to sign in and adhere to a curfew, which understandably made people nervous.

Back on their own turf, private space was non-existent. Chinese students slept ten to a room in a space reminiscent of crew quarters on a World War II U-boat, while the university dining hall was the size of an aircraft hangar, draughty and uncomfortable. There was a smattering of restaurants where we could go out and eat together unmolested, but this was complicated by a financial imbalance. By local standards we were impossibly rich; the vast majority of students had no money, least of all to throw away on a restaurant meal. While we were happy to pay on every occasion, it became apparent that despite being the same age, the relationship was distorted, unequal and even unfair. Unable to play a reciprocal role as the host, many local students felt a loss of face. A wall of unspoken embarrassment rose between us.

At one social event, hosted by local students in an empty classroom, we were asked to perform a song. Chairs were stacked up against the hospital-green walls in anticipation. The day's mental exertions on the blackboard had been wiped clean and replaced with a line of characters welcoming the foreign students. A performance was demanded. After one of us had sung a terrible 'Mull of Kintyre', a bespectacled girl with pigtails announced that she would like to see us dance. With that she pushed down hard on the play button of an enormous black plastic tape deck and Michael Jackson's 'Billie Jean' echoed tinnily around the classroom. Embarrassed, we shuffled and grinned foolishly. The girl with pigtails, who reminded me of a class prefect from an earlier life, stood there smiling and staring straight at us. My God, she was serious. Feeling honour-bound to do something – anything – I tentatively took to the floor with an American called Ami. I jerked an arm, then a leg. Ami responded with the same and we were greeted with a short burst of applause. We looked at each other in disbelief – were they serious? Twenty pairs of eyes followed our every disco move around the classroom. With every shower of applause our confidence increased until we were swinging each other around in dynamic, complex moves. With the end of the song there was an eruption of rhythmic clapping and we turned, breathless and red-faced, to a sea of beaming faces.

As the next Michael Jackson number spilled across the classroom floor, we were asked to dance again, but this time all the students joined in. I noticed that several were mimicking exactly our every uncoordinated move. Ami, unable to resist the temptation, made ludicrous hand and leg movements that were more appropriate to someone drowning than dancing. When her every jerk was religiously copied by two boys in tight stone-washed jeans and feeble moustaches at the other side of the room, I couldn't help but laugh. The scene under the neon strip lighting was too ridiculous. Visitors from another planet. Despite a certain eagerness, only a superficial connection was made.

Various other forms of excruciating social interaction took place, each time leaving one or both sides confused or let down. At Christmas I was asked by a teacher friend to be Father Christmas for her English class. I dutifully spent time preparing an impressive Father Christmas outfit complete with white beard and paunch. Dressed up as Santa, I waddled down the snow-filled streets attracting enough attention from passing cyclists to cause several minor accidents.

In front of the class I talked about the meaning of Christmas and traditional activities back in Britain. Someone asked about the 'London fog'. At the end, after polite applause, the teacher whispered, 'You can hand out the presents now.' I looked at the expectant faces in front of me and the smiling teacher to my left. I had none. I was a presentless Father Christmas. The class was dismissed. While students clambered past me, I explained to the teacher that I hadn't realised I should have brought presents as well.

'Are you or are you not a Father Christmas?' she replied, eyes narrowing.

I have since discovered that Changchun now has the first Christmas theme park in China, complete with Santas, reindeer, elves and sleighs (nothing religious obviously). Apparently it is very popular and I like to think that maybe, presentless as I was, my Santa had a seminal influence.

I made friends with a young art teacher called Hong Fu. We would hang out in his freezing studio, each wrapped in enormous army greatcoats, smoke and drink tea. He shared the studio with two others. It was a tiny room with easels set as deliberate obstacles. We would discuss art, although this subject was severely curtailed by my language ability. I asked Hong Fu if he had ever had an exhibition.

'Of course not. Where would we do it?'

Changchun had no space for showing paintings. Art, apart from traditional mountain and river scenes in ink, was still regarded in China as something dodgy and bourgeois. It smacked of unspoken personal emotions and individual desires. The mere use of oils as materials was in itself something revolutionary and daring. It was something the conservative Changchun authorities were in no rush to encourage. No doubt they were wary of repeating the surreal scenes that had taken place in Beijing a mere twelve months earlier. Several artists had put on a provocative show at the Central Academy of Arts involving huge inflatable breasts and penises, and a woman firing a gun at her sculpture of a telephone box. The authorities responded by sending in police armed with machine guns to close down the exhibition.

So Hong Fu had all the trappings of the aspiring artist; long hair, existential pauses, paint-encrusted fingertips and cigarettes, but few had seen his work.

Staring at the ceiling one afternoon as snow swirled outside the window, I resolved to help out.

'Dave, I think I'm going to organise an exhibition.'

'I'm only coming if there's going to be a party with women, alcohol and music.'

Two months later, in a large white classroom cleared of tables and chairs, Africans, British, Chinese, Russian scientists and American Baptist missionaries mingled together and sipped sweet white wine. Paintings hung from the four walls and jazz played from the tape recorder. Dave met a Russian woman. Hong Fu's mate Ju, sold five of his paintings. Hong Fu didn't sell any. We didn't meet for a while after that.

When feeling guilty about not exploring the city more thoroughly, I would venture out into the icy maze of streets behind the dormitory. I traipsed past mountains of cabbage and coal briquettes that lay dotted around like strategic arms dumps while people cycled past in slow motion. I wore a hat with earflaps that tied underneath the chin, gloves, long johns, trousers and a thick army greatcoat

Trudging around one mid-winter afternoon I turned down an alley and came cross a large, skinned Alsatian dog hanging by its hind legs from a tree. Its flesh was a translucent white and I could see the blue veins underneath the skin. An enormous black tongue lolled out of its mouth. Underneath its nose there was a small patch of discoloured snow. Presently a man came out of a nearby restaurant, hacked off pieces of meat with a large chopper and threw them into a big metal container. Eyes wide, I shivered with cold and fascination. 'They eat cats and dogs you know,' my grandmother had said when I told her of my intention to study in China. Here was the first glimpse of Chinese eating-habit mythology made real. All those yucky children's stories made flesh. In the north-east, eating dog is extremely popular and those averse to canine cuisine should make a point of asking what type of meat is in each dish.

Grey, dusty, cold and bleak, we never warmed to the city and after a while gave up all pretence of interest in our immediate surroundings, retreating to the unhealthy beery fug of our rooms. We spent most of our days sitting around talking, smoking and drinking. This was interspersed with table tennis, writing begging letters back home for chocolate and cheese, watching local TV, and staring at pages of Chinese characters. I silently cursed the university professor who had sent us to this arctic outpost.

Those reading this may wish to accuse me of an insufferable lack of curiosity. However, years later I felt a sense of vindication upon learning that the famously sympathetic travel writer, Colin Thubron, didn't even leave the station when he came through Changchun by train 'as it was too cold'. The backpacker bible, Lonely Planet, merely advises travellers that there is 'little reason to visit Changchun except to use it as a transit point to somewhere else.'

Chapter Two

Foreign Guests

Some Chinese may watch, surround and even talk about them [foreigners] in public because of the different appearance, colour, costumes and decorations from the Orientals, or because of some other reasons. In that case, no one should have the least fear, nervousness or anger. He just acts lightly, naturally and easily and the onlookers will soon disappear.

– Study in China: A Guide for Foreign Students

We sat near the back of a large bus, one of those long tinny ones with a squidgy black rubber bit in the middle, rather like an accordion. The bus, which was full by European standards but not by Asian, headed through the streets of the port city of Dalian (known to an older European generation as Port Arthur). Dave, Jane (a female British student) and I were on a journey to Qufu, the birthplace of Confucius, China's conservative and influential philosopher-civil servant. We were to be part of the million-plus domestic tourists that visit this small town of 60,000 every year. To get there we had to take a passenger ferry from Dalian to Yantai, about ten hours' sedate steaming across the Gulf of Bohai.

We were here because of conversations earlier in the month in Changchun during which the need for a break from the city of eternal boredom became apparent. Dave had paced up and down our tiny room smoking furiously in his Yves Saint Laurent leopard-skin Y-fronts. He was quite obviously preoccupied with some burning issue and was maybe even having one of those 'unstable emotional experiences' that the foreign student advice book had warned about.

'Have I got two heads or what?'

'I'm sorry?'

'Have I got two heads or what?'

'What do you mean?'

'Well, I've been here six weeks and not had so much as a hint of a shag.'

'Perhaps we should get out of here for a while,' I ventured. 'Go on a trip.'

After days of discussion it was agreed that we would head to Dalian (sixteen hours south by train) and then take a boat to Qufu. The itinerary was a compromise between Dave's desire to meet available local ladies (Dalian is a port city used to the lax moral ways of foreigners) and our desire to seek inspiration from a visit to the home of the Middle Kingdom's most famous son.

Behind us on the bus were a couple of drunken local lads. They made several references (in Mandarin of course) to Jane.

'Blonde hair.'

'Yeah, blonde hair!'

'Quite pretty.'

'Yes, but her nose is enormous.'

Dave was unable to resist the challenge, even one as harmless as this. Turning sharply, he pointed a gloved finger at the pair and said (in Chinese) a variation on: 'You are being fucking rude and if you don't stop talking about my friend there'll be trouble.'

With that he turned back to the front of the bus. They stared back open-mouthed. Actually, I thought the lads were being extremely polite. Blonde hair is naturally fascinating in this homogenous nation and the bit about the nose was quite accurate. She did have a large nose. To a Chinese person unused to the general size of European noses, it must well have been 'enormous'.

Following Dave's warning there was an awkward silence, then some rustling movements followed by a scream. One of the lads, smarting at having been effectively 'told off' by a foreigner, in Chinese and in front of a lot of people, decided to displace his anger by hitting the woman sitting next to him. Even his mate looked a bit surprised by his violent reaction to this loss of face.

The woman clutched her cheek and moaned. Every single passenger on the bus turned around and stared at the woman and the two lads. The woman didn't move, neither did the men. It was as if they were actors on a stage waiting for their next cue.

They didn't have to wait long. Dave stood up, stepped up to the lads and, as one of them got up to face him, he punched him hard in the stomach. As the unfortunate youth doubled up, Dave swung his fist again and hit him in the face. The youth screamed and fell to the floor clutching his nose. Blood trickled out from underneath his fingers. The bus erupted. 'The foreigner hit the hooligan! The foreigner hit the hooligan!' I looked on in open-mouthed amazement at the bloodied youth writhing on the floor and back to Dave who was now squaring up to the second lad.

The bus lurched to one side and Dave lost his footing. The second lad needed no encouragement to move. He scrambled over behind the back seats and pulled out the wooden broom, which every Chinese bus carries. He waved it violently at Dave, while fellow-passengers clambered out of the way. He swung heavily just as the bus lurched again, missing Dave but making contact with a window. Shards of glass sprinkled the seats and people started to scream. Other passengers shouted encouragement, instructions and warnings: 'Grab his hair!' 'Kick him in the shins!' 'Calm down, someone will get hurt!'

This last bit of advice was too late for the youth on the floor; it seemed that Dave had broken his nose. While Dave and the second youth wrestled with the broom handle, I noticed a sudden increase in speed as the bus driver, sensing a real crisis, headed for some emergency destination. We hurtled through the streets, leaving people stranded at bus stops in a storm of dust and diesel fumes.

With no warning, the bus came to a sudden halt. There was an eruption of noise and movement as people were thrown about, and as the doors opened there was a stampede to get out. Dave and the youth both looked up from their Olympian struggle to see not only people streaming off the bus, but the peaked caps of the police waiting outside. Disentangling themselves, they moved back from each other, breathing heavily, faces filled with a resentful awkwardness. Green-uniformed police swarmed onto the bus. The bus driver, sensing a complicated international situation, had driven straight to the city police station.

We were all marched inside.

'This could be a very big problem,' said one of the police officers.

The youth that Dave had knocked to the ground was in a dreadful state. His face was bloody and his shirtfront was also covered in blood. He still clutched his nose and kept his face fixed on the floor while wailing intermittently. His friend, perhaps emboldened by Dave's forced restraint, gave his version of events in a loud angry voice.

A policeman sauntered over to where the three of us sat on a bench.

'We will need to take statements from you to find the truth.'

We were taken, one by one, to tell a fierce-looking lady with a notepad and pen what had happened. Behind her stood a large senior policeman, cigarette in hand, who asked the questions. So, Mr Ma, tell us what happened. I described to the best of my ability what had taken place. While the broken face of the youth outside was unfortunate, he had hit a female passenger with no justification other than that he felt humiliated after a petty verbal exchange.

The large policeman seemed particularly interested in the fighting. Imagining that Dave's immediate future now hung on these fateful moments, I stood up and recreated his movements. Fat cop asked me to show him again, slowly this time, how Dave had felled the youth. I recreated Dave's swift knocking down of the lad. I realise now that it looked rather professional. Fat cop later asked the same of Jane and finally, of Dave himself. Indeed, he asked Dave if he had knocked any other people down.

'Not in China, no.'

Dave, without worrying about incriminating himself

further, gave a rather fancy two-step shuffle and threw his arms like pistons.

'Good, good,' said his interrogators.

We all waited in a hallway for the police to make a decision about what to do with us. We saw the two lads being frog-marched into the back of a van and taken away.

'No papers,' said a policeman standing next to us. We all inwardly grimaced at their fate. Salt mine? Labour camp? Huge fine? Sent back to the countryside?

The large cop from the interrogation room appeared and announced that we were free to go. I felt a sense of relief and all of us moved towards the main door. The senior-looking cop asked us where we were going.

We told him that we were on our way to catch a ferry to Yantai. Shouting instructions to his colleagues, we were ushered outside and two motorbikes with sidecars noisily appeared. Both had flashing red lights and were ridden with style by two policemen wearing the latest in authoritarian chic. Politely manhandled into the back of a blacked-out Toyota jeep, we were driven at speed, complete with screaming sirens, to the docks.

We came to a halt just by the gangplank, at the front of a very long queue of passengers. The chief of police shook our hands and wished us well. We thanked him for his reassuringly brief hospitality. He saved his warmest words for Dave.

'Great pleasure to meet true English prizefighter!'

With that he clasped both hands over Dave's and looked him square in the eye before turning and climbing back into the jeep.

Was that my imagination or did I see Dave's feet do a sort of boxer's shuffle?

Dave was, of course, cock-a-hoop. He felt this lavish praise vindicated not only his recent behaviour on the bus, but his general refusal to compromise in any way with accepted local practice. Much light relief in a grey year was provided by Dave and his titanic clashes with the conventions of Chinese society. In a culture which implicitly and explicitly rewards the patient and those who compromise, Dave's direct style coupled with an alarmingly high testosterone level meant that 'incidents' were inevitable. The cloak of cultural empathy could at last be thrown aside as his way of dealing with the Chinese had been proved right.

'Simon,' he said after yet another amateur discussion on Chinese psychology, 'you've just got to tell 'em what's what. Call a spade a spade. All this *guanxi* stuff is a load of bollocks.'

Guanxi is a word often heard in China. It roughly translates as 'personal relationships' and has become shorthand for the web of reciprocity that every person in China lives in. *Guanxi* is the natural outcome of a Confucian heritage and reflects some of the central tenets of Chinese life: keeping on good terms with people, not causing offence, and the importance of nurturing good relations. Shouting, arguing or causing a scene could lead to you insulting someone who could be of use to you later. This is part of a survivalist culture, a mentality that is the result of a tumultuous history where people have had to rely on their own personal network as they couldn't trust the state.

One disadvantage of this intensely practical approach to life is the inevitable politicisation of personal relationships.

As the sinologist W. J. F. Jenner noted, 'This calculation of obligations owed to you and by you leaves little room for spontaneous acts of generosity to strangers or the community except at times of great crisis.'

Another side effect of *guanxi* is that it provides a fertile breeding ground for corruption, especially for the 60-odd million Party officials who believe themselves, and are perceived to be, above the law. The cultivation of relationships based on tangible favours, the giving of gifts, dinners and karaoke entertainment, easily becomes a bribe or a marker placed for future reciprocation. Hospitality becomes a means to an end.

Dave didn't bother with any of this. Taxi drivers that argued over the fare, peasants that failed to queue up properly at train stations, surly waitresses, unhelpful receptionists, people who pushed, Dave took them all on. No compromise. Arguing, swearing, shouting, pushing and occasionally punching, this was a man who single-handedly seemed to want to slap the Chinese nation into shape. While he often seemed to get his way, the personal toll must have been huge. Such activity comes at a price and in provincial China where one can expect daily incidents, it called for an incredible mental stamina.

This was intensified in our situation as the 'foreign student hotel' we lived in was run by a particularly ferocious band of *fuwuyuan* (literally, 'service person'. Always female, a sort of chambermaid, security guard and room service all rolled into one). In fact, it would not be too much to say that they ran the hotel for their own benefit. The best food, the hottest water, the shortest working hours – the ladies of the *liuxue bingguan* (foreign student hotel) had taken over. If one dared to complain too much about the food, the water, the cleaning or the archaic telephone system, one was placed in a sort of 'service-free zone', a Manchurian Coventry. Calls were misplaced, bed linen remained unchanged, requests in the dining room went unheeded. This of course happened to Dave on numerous occasions. During particularly hard psychological tussles he would sit on his bed and throw a tennis ball at the opposite wall for hours. Changchun's own Steve McQueen.

Despite this, and perhaps fortified by a string of romantic conquests, Dave remained jaunty and upbeat until the end of our time in Changchun. I remained in awe.

As students with time on our hands we gradually explored the region. In between the big cities of the north-east, Dalian, Shenyang, Changchun and Harbin, flat brittle fields stretched across the horizon. The distances were huge and we travelled everywhere by train. The only way out of Changchun in any comfort was to buy tickets 'by the back door' from a small room up a flight of dark stairs near the station. Allocated tickets by the railway authorities, underpaid bureaucrats supplemented their income by flogging them to the highest bidder. While they were normally twice the price, we were happy to avoid several hours of scrummaging with hundreds of others in front of the ticket counter. There was no certainty that having finally reached the counter there would be a ticket available anyway. The brusqueness of the harassed female ticket-sellers was a further hurdle and required special mental strength. Forced to communicate through a three-by-three-inch hole, plaintive questions and barked requests met with an increasingly ferocious response. Until the paper stubs appeared at the bottom of the metal dish one was never sure as to whether this particular encounter would yield positive results. At one provincial station we came across two Swedes who had been stranded for four days because of their inability to make headway with these 'angels' of the state railway system.

These small stubs of cardboard covered in characters were passports to a comfortable journey – a bunk bed. Failure to secure one would lead to hours sitting on a wooden bench or on the floor in the unheated 'hard seat' compartment. Here, China's huddled peasant masses competed for a few square inches of space. The neon lights were never turned off and at every stop there was a rush of activity. Newspaper, fluorescent sausage skin, sunflower seeds and peanut shells littered the floor. Garlic and the smell of unwashed bodies hung in the air. One hundred strangers stuffed together, swaying through the night. Just as one was getting comfortable and building up a pocket of warmth, a woman would appear and start sweeping the floor, setting off a slow chain reaction of movement from previously inert bodies.

As foreign-looking people, our views were sought out by new travelling companions. Away from home, people talked more openly: 'How much does your father earn?' 'Why does the rest of the world gang up on China?' 'Have you tried spicy tofu before?' Answers to questions were broadcast to the rest of the compartment. The time of night was no impediment to these random interrogations.

Some foreign students would brag about the length of journey done in a hard seat compartment.

'Twelve hours? Nothing, mate. Guangzhou-Beijing, thirty-six hours.'

A badge of just how much discomfort you could take. Failure to have experienced the hard seat phenomenon for any length of time was an immediate disqualification from being a true China traveller. When I was forced to take it, I always arrived at my destination cold and exhausted. While there is a warm feeling of solidarity with China's poorest, this is not enough to outweigh the discomfort. Nor is it something that would survive repeated long-distance journeys.

The tickets we were after were for the next class up, 'hard sleeper'. Sixty to a carriage and six to a space open to the corridor. Here we read, chatted, ate pistachio nuts and slurped tea from jamjars like everyone else. No one stared too much. This was where we got to practise our Mandarin and talk to strangers about everything and anything to do with China. Unlike in hard-seat class, there was conversation rather than interrogation. The personal space afforded by a bunk meant that one could drop out at any time. Lights were turned out before midnight by uniformed *fuwuyuan* who patrolled the length of the train. A real travelling dormitory. 'Soft sleeper' (first class) was out of our student budget and anyway, we felt ill at ease as the compartment (four beds not six) was completely enclosed and more often than not contained self-important party officials on their way to some invaluable meeting. This forced proximity to dull officialdom plus the embroidered net curtains and flowery pillows made for a claustrophobic journey.

Tickets to Beijing on the overnight train were highly prized. Things happened there. Power and politics, temples and palaces. International hotels, luxuries such as croissants, pizza, wine, ham, chocolate and cheese. Foreigners with cool-sounding jobs, 'cultural attaché' and 'foreign correspondent'. We based ourselves at a dilapidated government hostel just south of the Temple of Heaven, since demolished. One of only a handful at the time, it was host to a disparate bunch of foreign nationals, keen American students, bored Russian professors and partying Africans. On one trip I shared a dormitory with 38 Bangladeshi construction workers who were stranded on their way home from the Middle East. They had run out of money. It was during the Gulf War and thousands of migrant workers had been expelled from Kuwait. We stayed up all night together writing a petition in formal English to the then UN Secretary-General, Boutrous Boutrous Gali.

The crowds were bigger in Beijing and we learnt to walk with everyone else. We discovered that if you tried to go faster than the average speed you would arrive at your destination tired and bothered. If you went with the flow you were carried along and there was no friction. A neat metaphor for life in China.

On another trip to Beijing I was invited to a party with a mixture of Chinese and foreigners in a spacious flat. These young Chinese were very different from the ones I knew in Changchun. Here they were relaxed, fashionable and enjoying themselves. No one stared and no one asked how much your trousers cost. The combination of Western food (smoked salmon! Camembert!), sophisticated conversation and red wine sent me into an intoxicated spin. I hung on the edge of conversations and contributed in short bursts of English, weak French or even worse Mandarin. My overexcited provincialism was obvious.

One smart Italian woman asked me what I was doing in China.

'I'm a foreign student studying Chinese in Changchun,' I replied enthusiastically, knocking over a wine glass.

Picking up the glass, she smiled and began talking in fluent Mandarin to a Chinese man in a black polo neck and sharp glasses to her left. I loitered uneasily before resuming my near conquest of the buffet table.

The host, a well-known journalist, ignoring my insightful comments on the upcoming Communist Party plenary session, hinted that it might be time for me to leave. His Venezuelan girlfriend frowned when I said goodbye. I left with my pockets stuffed with expensively wrapped chocolate mints, souvenirs for the others back in Changchun.

Cheese became an obsession. We were prepared to travel for hours if there was any possibility of buying the stuff. It was rumoured that Harbin, five hours to the north by slow train, had a shop that sold a local Chinese cheese. Someone had met someone else who had met one of the eight American students studying there in sub-arctic conditions (the temperature drops below -40 °C in January). Apparently, they had a regular local cheese supply. Also there was general agreement that Harbin, 'Paris of the North' (not to be confused with Suzhou, 'Venice of the East') with its long trading history with Russia and large former White Russian population, would yield up cheese.

As a result of this now-vanished community, the city has a faded architectural charm with onion domes, cobbled streets and turn-of-the-century housing. Once a year it is invaded by hundreds of thousands of people who come to see the annual Ice Sculpture Festival. Huge and fantastic sculptures of ice are lit up at night and families, wrapped up to the point of immobility because of the cold, slip and slide merrily amongst them.

We wandered in Stalin Park along the banks of the Songhua River and traipsed through the melancholic streets with their disused Orthodox churches, elaborate ironwork and pointed roofs. Amidst stares and cries of 'Ruski! Ruski!' we explored the city in search of cheese.

'Apparently it's like cheddar.'

'I heard it's more like mozzarella.'

Department store after department store. In through the strips of heavy frosted plastic that keep out the cold and into a maze of display cabinets, shelving and white-coated assistants. Some stores didn't know what cheese was. In other stores they simply said, *'Mei you'* ('We don't have any'). But in one, the tired woman behind the glass counter said yes, she thought they did but she wasn't sure where. She shouted at her colleague across the room and we were pointed up the stairs. We charged upwards. We asked again and were directed to the other end of the room.

'Mei you.'

We were directed up another flight of stairs. Another counter.

'Mei you.'

And so we went from one section to another, spurred on by a sense that we were extremely close to cheese success. We were told to go down again. We arrived at a counter selling pigs' trotters and dry biscuits.

'You.' ('We have it.')

'You!' we shouted back in surprise.

The white-hatted assistant disappeared and re-emerged with a yellow block. Cutting off a slice, she held it out.

'Cheese.'

Dave grabbed it and took a huge bite. He coughed it straight up, catching it in gloved hands.

A strangled cry: 'Butter!'

Chapter Three

Cultural Exchange

During the Spring Festival break we all headed south like migratory birds in search of warmth and sunlight. 'China's Hawaii', the island of Hainan, sits 20 miles off the bottom of south-east China in the South China Sea. With a relatively remote interior and unspoilt beaches, Hainan was talked about as a semi-mythical destination in Changchun – if only for its warmth. One of the local students we knew had a picture of a palm-fringed sandy shore above his bunk bed and he would point at it, saying, 'Hainan,' in breathless tones. Later we discovered that Hainan's reputation rested as much on its easygoing attitude to acquiring wealth as its sandy beaches.

We travelled down on a bus from Nanning. Four geese sat trussed up amongst boxes on the roof. Only their necks and beaks could move, and they bit one of their number almost to death on the long journey. Each time we stopped for a break another great tuft of feathers had been removed from his long neck. By the time we reached the coast the bullied goose looked like a defeated boxer at the end of the fight, his head covered in cuts and bruises, and swelling around his beak.

Hainan is the most lazily corrupt place in China in terms of column inches devoted to corruption scandals, money involved (although this is now being challenged by another offshore island, Xiamen) and historical activity. The Hainanese got started before everyone else, smuggling untaxed foreign goods onto the mainland with the help of the Chinese Navy. Having been granted a lighter tax regime to facilitate foreign investment, the Hainanese promptly imported millions of washing machines, cars, TV sets, video recorders and computers at next to no duty and then sold them straight on to the mainland. Many people became very rich very quickly and ploughed their money into property development, restaurant ventures and building new office space. Large parts of the island became construction sites while people from neighbouring provinces flocked to work as builders, waiters, prostitutes and hairdressers. It became a place to make money and where anything went. With a balmy climate, frontier atmosphere and good seafood, Hainan became the destination of choice for those seeking a new life.

We were heading for Sanya on the south side of the island where the fabled beaches lay. In 1991, Sanya was still a delightful place, relatively unspoilt by speculative property development. It did have a palm-fringed beach, though it wasn't quite as picturesque as the poster back in Changchun. The water was clean and much of the area was covered in brilliant green foliage. There was a beguiling laziness to the place and it seemed free of the suffocating conservatism of the north. Above all, it was warm. It didn't really feel like the China we knew at all. We lay on the beach as Han tourists strolled along the water's edge fully clothed, surreptitiously staring at the semi-naked foreigners.

In the room next to ours at the beachfront guesthouse was a Welshman who dressed in black ninja-style clothing, with a leather bandoleer to hold several knives. I sat fascinated each morning as he emerged to throw several large ornamental Uighur knives around. Sunburnt and with large glasses, his hair was tied back in an unimpressive ponytail. He looked as though he was training for some mission. An attractive young Uighur woman with long black hair and flared jeans accompanied him. Uighurs come from the remote north-west of China and are of Turkish origin with their own language. The only Uighurs we had met to date sold kebabs and changed money outside the Number Two Friendship Store in Changchun. The young woman sat on the tough wiry grass and repaired a shirt while he practised. What was she doing with this slightly manic figure? Maybe it was the knives. Maybe he had pledged himself to fight for Uighur self-rule against the Han oppressors in Xinjiang. In one of his black pouches he carried a stash of marijuana which he smoked nonchalantly. I wondered if he did his smoking after his morning knife display or before. He looked confident, but not so confident that you didn't keep an eye on how he was getting on.

Under the unspoken hierarchy of travellers in China I didn't ask him what he was up to. He was older, had the appearance of an experienced traveller and had a local girlfriend. I was a mere language student.

Two years later, however, I found out. In a brief report in *The China Daily* it was announced that a British national with the same name, and from Wales, had been sentenced to four years in jail in Shanghai for selling drugs.

At the end of the year the foreign students took an exam. In the weeks running up to the test, there had been much revision and late-night memorising of thousands of characters. This formal test could be unkind in its exposure. There was a general realisation that our classroom Mandarin only allowed for the most basic conversations. Months of tedious rote learning under the benign gaze of our teacher, Grandma Wu, had failed to generate the necessary amount of enthusiasm for the language. We had all improved since our arrival at Beijing airport eleven months earlier, but for many the necessary step-change in Mandarin had yet to occur.

Learning Mandarin is a slow and laborious process. A tonal language with thousands of characters, only those who are keen and committed will make progress. The difficulty lies not so much in the grammar, but in the need for constant curiosity, a good memory and clear and proper pronunciation. Above all, practise.

Grandma Wu's preferred teaching methods had us chanting characters out loud in class over and over again in a sort of Buddhist prayer. Coupled with her beaming countenance and unwillingness to engage in any conversation, this was a recipe for a gradual freezing over of the brain. Our critical faculties became dormant. Gradually this regime took its toll with the thought of cycling through falling snow at 7.15 in the morning to reach class proving too much for many. The class size rose and fell in tune with the severity of the weather. '*Ta bing le*' ('he/she is ill') was a phrase we all knew by heart.

To his credit, later in the year Dave attempted to remedy this unproductive situation by forming his own personal language exchange. Alone in the room one day drawing out a list of characters for the sixth time, there was a faint knock at the door. I opened it and in walked a young woman wearing a thick coat with Hello Kitty characters emblazoned on the front.

'Where is Dave?'

'I'm not sure, maybe at the post office.'

'Please tell him I came to see him for his lesson.'

'Oh, you must be his language exchange student,' I said.

'Yes, my name is Wang Li and my English name is Fanny.'

We looked at each other, but I only received an innocent stare back.

Dave refused to acknowledge any underhand role in her English name or that the relationship was anything other than professional. I almost began to believe this, until returning one frozen Sunday afternoon I found the room locked. Twisting the handle produced rustling movements from inside and a muffled shout from Dave, 'Fuck off Simon, I'm busy! Come back in half an hour.'

I looked out of the corridor window. It had started to snow and was already dark. After sitting around in one of the Russians' rooms ('Ah, Dave, he is big man! Big man!' chuckled Alexei), I returned a couple of hours later to find Dave sitting upright on his bed, reading a Chinese text and smoking.

'Good lesson?' I asked.

'Yup. But a bit exhausting. Unfortunately Fanny is going to Shanghai, so we had to cram a lot into the last session.'

After the final exam, Madam Wu personally handed out the results with a sympathetic smile and a pat on the arm. Opening the folded results slip, I stared in disbelief at the 99 per cent written at the top. Looking around, I realised that others were staring at their papers in a similar fashion; every person in the class had a near perfect score. No one quite knew how to react to the officially fudged response to our mediocre linguistic efforts. Madam Wu had taken the importance Chinese attach to 'face' to a marvellous degree. By giving several of us low marks, or heaven forbid, failing one of us, the unmistakable air of failure would hang over our class. This would not be good for her standing as a teacher or the university. At the same time, the fact that we were foreigners had pushed this tradition into the absurd. We were the guinea pigs for an expected influx of dollar-waving foreign students from all corners of the Western world. How would foreigners, or anyone else for that matter, know Jilin University was a great university if people got bad marks? Would they still come if students (who had paid good money) failed to gain superb results? Where would the attraction be in that?

Afterwards, some of the harder working students felt cheated, while those who hadn't done a stroke of revision were giddy with relief and wonder. The realisation that unless you were a complete degenerate you were bound to pass your exams with flying colours was something that I wished I had been told at the outset of the year.

As it was, my own last-minute revision had been disturbed. There had been a knock at the door and one of the North Koreans, Kim, entered, clutching his crotch and walking with a limp. Apparently Dave had kicked him in the testicles during a heated argument over a girl at a dance and he now wanted to claim damages – 'in US dollars.' Kim informed me that the local doctor had told him he would be unable to have children.

I had been chosen as the middleman to convey the news to Dave that unless he paid up, the North Korean group would be making a formal complaint, en masse, to the Dean of the university. We discussed the exact sequence of events on the evening in question and when I expressed some scepticism as to the seriousness of the injury, Kim stood up, and shouting, 'Look! Look!' began to pull off his trousers. I assured him that there was no need for me to inspect the damaged testicle.

In the run-up to the exam, valuable study time was spent in the offices of the university authorities seeking a suitable compromise between the two parties. I represented Dave while the North Korean minder represented Kim. (Having once called him a 'fascist cunt', Dave and the minder could not be in the same room as each other.) This was a role at which the university bureaucrats excelled, and after several days of cigarettes and jasmine tea, a suitable rapprochement was made which satisfied the honour of both parties, and there was a formal shaking of hands. Both were to apologise to each other but with no acceptance of responsibility, much like the resolution to the forced landing of the US spy plane in Hainan. Apologies were accepted. As one would expect in a country where the language has no direct 'yes' or 'no' the art of compromise is a virtue to be practised on a daily basis.

The university authorities were personified for us by Mr Yang. He had an office on our floor and cultivated the tired look of someone with enormous patience. He would have needed a fair amount; as we were the first Westerners the university had ever hosted, misunderstandings and confusion were rife. Mr Yang was, however, more prepared than we were. There is a whole reference library of material for officials of all ranks on how to treat resident foreigners. In imperial times it was called rather bluntly, 'barbarian management' (yiwu) but now continued under the more politically correct term '*waishi*' – foreign affairs. Bureaucrats, translators, policemen and hotel workers all received some training in the correct way to handle these pesky outsiders with their annoying questions. One of our teachers, after a discussion that took us dangerously close to a debate on democracy, offered an insight into the mentality expected.

'With some issues, the more you talk about them, the more confusing they become. In the end it is best not to talk about them.'

We were guests of China and should behave as such, doing nothing that might embarrass our hosts.

Fortunately for the authorities, like all guests, we were temporary. After nearly one year in Chanchun, we climbed back on the train to Beijing and a flight west.

Back in the UK, we discovered that the next batch of fresh-faced Mandarin students had not been sent to the city of eternal spring, but to Beijing. The professor who had sent us to Changchun mumbled an apology. He explained that the idea was that we would learn so much more in Manchuria because there were so few distractions, unlike in Beijing say, or Shanghai. My scepticism at this flawed theory was evident. He put a hand on my shoulder.

'It's the real China,' he said.

Maybe it was. But it was still only a part. I felt I had been part of some experiment that had gone wrong. Indeed, that the Changchun experience had fundamentally affected a previously stable equilibrium.

Final year revision in the UK was interrupted by severe headaches that started the moment I woke up and grew like a tidal wave until any concentrated activity was impossible.

Concerned at their near permanent status as part of my life, I visited a doctor who told me to take more headache pills. I was already popping pills on an hourly basis. Dissatisfied with the advice to consume yet more, I pressed to be able to see a specialist. I think I sounded quite dramatic.

'You don't understand. I've been in China. In remote parts of China. I might have picked something up there. Like travel hero Bruce Chatwin. Something that you may have never seen before! I was an explorer. I could be seriously ill!'

Eventually, I was allowed an appointment with a leading head specialist. I wore a tie and jacket. I sat on a chair in a white room while a tall man looked at me. Without saying anything he walked over and tapped my knees, then felt my head. He went back to his desk and wrote a cursory line.

'So, you've been in China.' Not a question but a sort of opening statement, as if in court.

'Yes.'

'I understand that you now have a problem adjusting to reality.'

We looked at each other. I felt as if a bucket of cold water had been thrown over me and I stared at him in silence. The specialist then explained that the headaches were because of exam-induced stress and had nothing to do with China.

'Really?'

'Really.'

Adjusting my tie I stood up. I left relieved, slightly embarrassed but also a little disappointed. I knew my time in China had somehow affected me – perhaps I wanted some scientific proof. Despite the difficulties of chilly Changchun, an ambiguous relationship had started. China intrigued me. I felt we were just getting acquainted. The sheer scale of the country with its massive population, different linguistic universe, alien mindset, tumultuous history and its love/hate relationship with the rest of the world demanded more time. I knew I would return.

Chapter Four

Boomtime!

I am on the back of a whining high-pitched motorbike, weaving in and out of dense traffic, holding on to number three salesman, Ai Ding. I am wearing a smart tailored suit for my first day of work. The city is hot and humid. A red plastic helmet one size too small rests uncomfortably on top of my head. The plastic chinstraps flap and scratch in the wind. The helmets, a recent phenomenon in Guangzhou, all seem to have been made by the same company that produced plastic buckets and spades for British holidaymakers in the 1970s. In any collision, they would offer similar protection.

Amidst the beeping, honking and snorting of engines, I hang on to Ai Ding as we descend a flyover in the fumes to visit yet another Carlsberg outlet. We pass old blocks of flats and villas crumbling under dirt, damp and the thunder of traffic. Washing is strung out and there is a pervasive smell of fried tofu. I pass a sleeve across my face and it turns black from the fumes. I realise I must look ridiculous, but no one is looking. Everyone is too busy getting on with their lives, making money. I am back in the People's Republic of China, but it is a different country from the one I left.

The whole place was in a state of noisy revolution.

Two years earlier Deng Xiaoping, China's then paramount leader, had visited Guangzhou, Shenzhen and Zhuhai in

Guangdong province and famously urged the authorities to be bolder in their reforms. While his comments that the country should open up to the West and embrace market reforms were enthusiastically received by the whole nation, nowhere were they taken more to heart than in Guangdong. Bolstered by the apparent blessing of the most powerful man in China, previously suppressed capitalist desires burst forth from officials and ordinary citizens alike. Confidence soared and Deng's comments triggered a frenzy of economic activity that was to propel this part of southern China into becoming the wealthiest province in the country. Within a few years Guangdong's high-speed capitalism had created an area with the highest personal income, the highest consumption of consumer goods and the largest concentration of light industry anywhere in Asia.

It was now official: it's OK to make money!

Strong connections between local and overseas Cantonese and a proximity to the capitalist enclave of Hong Kong ensured a headstart on the rest of the country. Foreign investment flooded in through Great Britain's wealthiest colony and local officials encouraged (and took part in) any scheme with a commercial benefit. In Guangzhou, the provincial capital, the streets were choked with mopeds, minivans, trucks and foreign cars: Mercedes-Benz, Audi and VW saloons. The city shuddered to the sound of a thousand hammers as whole streets were encased in bamboo scaffolding.

New residential suburbs were built on former rice fields and fish farms while daily press conferences showcased new high-rise office space available soon for rent. At night the city just carried on. Smart restaurants, discos, bowling alleys, fast-food joints and shopping malls, all lit up in bright neon. Canto-pop blared out from stalls selling the latest CDs (counterfeit of course) as couples strolled the streets in the latest Hong Kong fashions. On their belts hung pagers, mobile phones and leather pouches for cigarette lighters. Pierre Cardin ties and Playboy socks, tasselled loafers and high heels. People had money to spend for the first time, and something to spend it on. And they didn't mind showing it off either. Eat, drink and be merry! Guangzhou revelled in its role as national champion of a new high-spirited consumerism.

An hour's drive south towards the Hong Kong border was Guangzhou's wild little brother, Shenzhen, the city that grew faster than any other. More has been written about this city in the last decade than any other in China. It holds a fascination for economists, anthropologists, political scientists and urban planners alike. Probably because a decade ago it didn't exist and now it's a glitzy glass, marble and concrete shrine of more than four million people from all over China. Its residents speak of the intoxicating atmosphere of instant modernisation. Companies making everything from plastic flowers to computers employ thousands of people in their smart offices. On the streets, women wearing lipstick, short skirts and high heels try to wrestle passers-by into nearby brothels. In the surrounding area, millions of former peasants live and work in factories where Dickensian conditions prevail. Shenzhen exists as a gaudy urban testament to the power of new money. Everything is new. It is on the edge of China, Beijing is a long way away and one can almost touch Hong Kong. Anything goes.

For many people not enthralled by the rapacious capitalism on offer, there is an emptiness to Shenzhen that is unnerving.

'There are no cathedrals. There is nothing to do but buy sex and do business' wrote sinologist Orville Schell. For many peasants though, it is still better than farming.

The one hundred or so miles between Shenzhen in the south and Guangzhou in the north are now home to an estimated 20 million people.

We pass Guangzhou railway station. It spews forth a torrent of humanity from all over China, intent on joining in the revolution. Squat Hunanese, Sichuanese, people from the north-east rustbelt, Uighurs, unemployed peasants and workers temporarily united in an attempt to survive and prosper in the new economic order. Part of the hopeful diaspora of millions that now flock to the Pearl River delta in search of a better life. Scores pass through the station's dark mock-Stalinist halls every day and emerge blinking into the sunlight. They look as though they've landed on another planet. Which they have.

'*Waidiren*,' said Ai Ding dismissively. Outsiders.

In front of the main entrance, people camp out in their hundreds waiting for something or someone. A group of peasants with thick spiky hair and khaki plimsolls, an aspiring salesman adjusting his glasses in a pressed white shirt and tie, a young woman in a pleated skirt and red high heels with a white handkerchief pressed to her nose. The lucky ones are met by friends and colleagues, the rest will have to fend for themselves. Some head off with construction foremen looking for unskilled labour. A group of women surround a production manager looking for new recruits. Some wait for buses to Shenzhen. Some stay and just stare at the city skyline, overawed by the noise, the heat and the pace.

Western companies based in Hong Kong sensed something was up and sent people over the border to ensure that any opportunities were firmly seized. As a foreigner with a smattering of Mandarin and an interest in China, I was now one of the advance party. Overdressed, on the back of a motorbike. I was hired to sell beer, Carlsberg beer.

Ai Ding and I have lunch at a seafood restaurant that stocks Carlsberg. The manager squeezes out from a small office filled with a giant black leather sofa. We exchange formalities and grumble about the price of beer while behind us ugly fish thrash around in murky tanks. The floor is wet with water from a leaky rubber hose that trails through the restaurant. There is a continual clatter of plates being stacked loudly and the harsh quick sounds of the local dialect.

'Cantonese only like two foreign beers, Carlsberg and Heineken. Out of these two they prefer Heineken as it is imported, and therefore has a higher status. We have a couple of good sales people – the manager is a playboy and crook though.'

With that rousing introduction to the local alcoholic beverage scene, Ai Ding returned to the crab and ginger in spring onion sauce. He handed me the bill when it came.

'I believe you can expense this.'

Guangzhou residents didn't need to be taught anything when it came to Western business practices.

The Carlsberg office was a small room above a shopping mall in the city centre. It was opposite a hotel where foreign businessmen would stay and which had the highest concentration of prostitutes cruising the lobby of any hotel in China. In the morning we would zoom about on the bike visiting wholesalers and restaurants; in the afternoon I would study Chinese characters. In the evening I would visit new bars and nightclubs and wake up with a headache.

Ai Ding suggests we visit a bar in a nondescript Guangzhou backstreet. The area is dark and quiet. There is a hole in the wall where money is handed over. Next to the hole is a door that swings open and one squeezes past a bear of a bouncer. Inside, a wooden bar, balconies and a small dancefloor. The place is full of Chinese with a sprinkling of foreigners. As the night wears on, the crowd thins. Ai Ding heads off to the opening of a new karaoke venture. Early in the morning, the door crashes open and a dozen blonde Russian women sweep in to loud cheers and wolf whistles. Dancers from a nearby fantasy floorshow, they have just finished their shift. They spray each other with beer and terrify the few remaining Chinese men with their outrageous dancing. One athletic woman leaps on the bar and mimes to the music while three others indulge in a rhythmic formation bump and grind.

'You see,' said the nonplussed barman, 'we get outsiders from all over the place at the moment.'

After my crash course in Chinese capitalism in the south, I moved up to Beijing. For three years I sold beer in the capital and the north-east. It was an exciting time as business was an adventure and routine had yet to be established. Everything was a novelty and no one quite knew what to expect.

Beijing is a city of bureaucrats rather than businessmen. It is the centre of political power and headquarters to an enormous state apparatus. This is where the decisions get made. Bulky brick ministries dominate the centre. Yet despite its size and relative importance, it is a more conservative and parochial place than the coastal cities of Shanghai or Guangzhou. It is traditionally an intensely political city where one can feel the hand of government everywhere. For many foreigners this has been part of its appeal; the illicit thrill of being close to the heart of a dictatorship.

I am at birthday party in a park behind the Friendship Store. On a raised stone dais, a banner is strung between two trees with 'Happy Birthday' written in English. The gathering swells, people talk in Chinese, French, English and Italian. Three grim-faced policemen arrive. They are concerned that it is a political gathering. They point to the banner and ask what the unauthorised demonstration is calling for. It is explained that it is a birthday greeting. Much discussion follows. There is a compromise; we can stay if the subversive banner is taken down. The 1989 Tiananmen demonstrations may be five years ago, but they linger on in the scarred official psyche.

Yet even in stuffy, uptight old Beijing things were moving.

The reforms pioneered by Zhao Ziyang at the end of the 1980s had given the first inkling of change in the air. One day, pool tables appeared on the dull streets of the capital. An explicit rejection of the puritanical, proletarian selflessness previously expected. It's OK to enjoy yourself! When there were politburo tussles over the pace and direction of reform, the tables would disappear again, only to reappear later when the reformers had won their argument. The state was signalling its willingness to retreat from private areas of people's lives. What you ate, whom you slept with, what you did for a living. We don't really care. There were still many restrictions but one could see a personal space to inhabit.

Temporarily traumatised by the bloody end of the

Tiananmen demonstrations, Beijing residents left their southern countrymen to get on with the cutting edge of capitalism until they felt comfortable enough to believe that this was not just another passing political fashion.

Soon Beijingers themselves began to test the new atmosphere. Here was a chance to change one's circumstances. A private bar opened, a mini-supermarket, a new hair salon, a karaoke joint, an art gallery, a new restaurant, a new apartment complex; each new venture adding momentum to the last. And each new venture was slightly more professional than the last, thousands of unchoreographed individual steps creating a new pattern. Local connections were still crucial, but the first question was no longer, 'Which work unit are you from?' but 'What is your plan?'

Whilst the pace of change lacked the frenetic air of the south, there was a tangible sense of expectancy. The status quo was shifting. Everyone had a project or knew someone that had a project. People were optimistic about the future for the first time in a long time. China and Asia were on the up! Not only was everyone in China talking about China, but also everyone outside China was talking about China. Double-digit growth, a dragon wakes, foreign investment up by 110 per cent, Communism to consumerism, Mao suits to Moschino. The media turned its gaze on the Middle Kingdom. China was the centre of attention again, something that hadn't happened for over forty years.

Amidst the storm of hyperbole Beijing remained a paradoxically provincial place, a collection of random villages rather than a modern city. It had yet to experience the wholesale change of the south. At the beginning of the 1990s there were still few private cars, local nightlife was non-existent to extremely limited, and shopping as a way of life had yet to take off. People still washed in communal bathhouses, bicycles ruled the roads, and rag-and-bone men with tired horses trudged between houses. As a city of bureaucrats suggests, it was a conservative place. The foreign population of less than 3,000, mostly diplomats, long-term journalists and language students, lived in officially sanctioned ghettos just as their predecessors had at the turn of the century. Many parts of the country were still off-limits. Until 1993 there was only one Western bar in a city of 11 million. Entertainment retained an almost Victorian feel as people were forced to improvise for themselves. What was available was eclectic and unpredictable and spread by word of mouth. The leisure corporations had yet to arrive.

With the economic and physical changes came the realisation that it was all right for Chinese and foreigners to mix. This was an exciting novelty for both sides. At the time, if you were a foreigner you had VIP status. You were still an object of curiosity and genuine interest. People listened to what you had to say and wanted your opinion on life in China. At any gathering you were up there with the bosses and leaders, toasting and being toasted. Now though, there was an opportunity to be more than just a 'foreign friend' of the Chinese. As representatives of mature Western capitalist states that force-fed consumerism to their young from the playground on, you could make yourself useful and get involved. Please, just how did this business thing work?

For a short period, young Mandarin-speaking foreigners living in China were the recipient of all sorts of business opportunities, hinted at and explicit, the fanciful and the prosaic. Gold concessions, import licences, export licences, land-development rights, nightclub propositions, partnerships of every kind. Over green tea and cigarettes in hotel lobbies with heavy armchairs, savvy foreign language students vied with disoriented Western businessmen over grandiose schemes. Whilst few came to fruition, they served to highlight the opportunities available for the committed. A scene was being played out just as it had at the turn of the century as a reclusive regime let its people come into contact with Western elements. For a hustler, China at the beginning of the 1990s was a good place to be. In Shenzhen, one friend who had arrived to study rapid urban change in the raw ended up with a five-minute TV slot teaching English. Despite being only 25, he also advised a local company on success in business by teaching *The Seven Habits of Highly Effective People* by Stephen R. Covey, a preposterous book that had achieved cult status among the ambitious. At the same time he coached would be emigrants on how to get past the Canadian immigration services. The company he worked for claimed a higher rate of entry success for those who took his course than those who didn't. His services were advertised under 'Top Tips for Entry'. This mainly consisted of shaking hands firmly, looking people in the eye, and speaking the required phrases of English.

In Beijing, there was soon a new army of entrepreneurs, adventurers and romantics to join the sinologists and political junkies. Of the foreigners that I knew at this time, one friend ran a bar, another advised Beijing TV on programming rights, another had a duck farm, another ran a research company, another imported cheese, another wine, and one ran a recruitment venture for the nascent foreign operations. For a magical moment everything was new and almost everything seemed possible. For those involved, the fact that work didn't conform to the traditional concept of business was part of its appeal. The large multinational giants had yet to arrive. Gradually though, word spread that China was ready for business.

After the pioneer corps came the corporate professionals. From 1995 onwards things became more serious as trade turned into investment. Hotel companies, media players, fast-food chains, mobile phone manufacturers, beverage giants and entertainment groups set up base. Big shiny Western brands appeared around town on billboards and in neon: Marlboro, McDonalds, Heineken, IBM, KFC, L'Oreal. The foreign population swelled from a couple of thousand to over 90,000. Foreigners settled in selling planes, cars, mobile phones, computers, alcohol, cigarettes, biscuits, cheese and bubblegum. The politicians came as well: the French president, the British prime minister, the German chancellor and Fidel Castro. A whole host of lesser players, all intent on doing their best for their country's interests: the Zimbabwean defence minister, the Czech deputy foreign minister, the Moroccan justice minister. Beijing was the place to visit. There was a feeling that if one met the right person, the right economic, military or political door would magically swing open.

A third wave appeared to service and offer advice to all those here in the first place: estate agents, consultants, doctors and cooks. No one said 'laowai' anymore, and people had stopped staring. Foreigners, by their increasing ubiquity, had become less interesting.

This large foreign influx mirrored a domestic migration

of millions of peasants into major cities across the country. By the end of the 1990s China had a floating population of over 120 million people.

The Carlsberg sales team consisted of young Beijingers; a mixture of the educated, the street-sharp and the rough. None of them had experience of a successful, professional sales operation, but then neither had I. At the first sales meeting everyone sat around waiting for something to happen. There were only a few established accounts selling small amounts of beer. There was no sales system. The most stable account was that of the Danish ambassador, who would place an order for kegs of Carlsberg once a month. Eventually, we took a map of Beijing and divided up the city with a pencil. Together we sectioned off the streets that each individual would be responsible for. The sales effort would be done restaurant by restaurant, karaoke joint by karaoke joint. There was some bargaining and much laughter. The serious part of the day over, the discussion of sales plans drifted off into unrelated areas.

'Mr Ma, why did the British burn down the Summer Palace?'

'Are your parents not concerned at your being so far away?'

'My cousin is opening a country-and-western bar and would like free beer.'

These were the young, urban middle class. On the up. Earning more in a month than their parents in a year. Some didn't even live at home any more, preferring to rent their own rooms. Patriotic but not political, they were ready to enjoy the benefits of China's reforms. In the absence of any ground rules or established paths to follow, there was instead a chaotic enthusiasm and enterprise. The office grew from four people in a hotel room balancing files on their knees to a large operation with desks, computers, promotion girls, warehouses and smart gift pens.

Liu Feng, a well-connected salesman, had managed to get half the Beijing football team along to a dance club we were sponsoring. Holding aloft cans of Carlsberg in front of an excited mêlée of nearly 1,000, one of the players was asked by a petite hostess what he thought of probably the best beer in the world.

'It's the cow's cunt!' (In the UK the nearest translation would be 'the dog's bollocks'.)

The hostess looked embarrassed, the crowd roared its approval and the DJ turned up the volume. The players took this as the cue to hurl newly opened cans into the jumping mass. Trajectories of alcohol flew across the cavernous room to great applause. The dancing youth of Beijing where thrilled by the use of local slang by celebrities on a public stage. Things threatened to turn ugly when a couple of overexcited youngsters threw their own cans at the soccer stars on the podium. Security guards waded into the crowd. The players beat a hasty exit while everyone else carried on grooving. Liu Feng was beside himself with the celebrity endorsement. His eyes shining with excitement, he clapped and jumped up and down on the spot.

'Ma! Isn't this great!'

Yes it was. This was a magical period of opportunity as society changed. The barriers were falling away and by virtue of being a Mandarin-speaking Westerner in Beijing, you were first over the bamboo wall. Given a jeep with 'Carlsberg' emblazoned on the side, a flat and a mission to sell beer, I lived happily, taking part in something that was revolutionising China.

Hand in hand with the economic boom went corruption of every sort. As one hard-pressed official put it, economic crimes rose 'uncontrollably' during this period. With little legal oversight, poorly paid party officials embraced the market reforms as long as they got a slice of the action. How to police and prosecute economic crimes in a new era? The government issued edict after edict primarily aimed at its own party members who were enjoying the economic fruits of powerful political positions. Not only were thousands of officials trying to avoid being left out of the boom, many were sufficiently confident to show off their new-found wealth. The PLA itself opened an expensive nightclub in Beijing with guest DJs from the UK and scantily clad female dancers suspended above the dancefloor in theatrical cages. Campaigns tried to rein in 'feasting and seeking pleasure' but to no avail. It was difficult, as everyone knew that the guys at the top were at it as well.

The symbol of official excess in Beijing during this period was Chen Xitong, the Beijing party boss. Chen was arrested in April 1995 after the mysterious suicide of his deputy, Wang Baosen. Wang's body was found on a hillside near a remote village in Huairou county outside Beijing. He and Chen are reported to have squandered 4.5 million US dollars of public funds on lavish lifestyles that included building two luxurious villas in the Beijing suburbs and frequenting them for 'extravagant wining, dining and entertainment'. A permanent monument to his discredited rule was the unfinished underground extension opposite the China World Trade

Centre. A suitable location in fact to remind everyone that any large investment project in the capital needed his seal of approval, which was always available at a price.

Chen Xitong's sentencing to sixteen years in jail more than three years later marked the beginning of a series of never-ending national campaigns to put a stop to officials on the take. Despite the imprisonment and execution of thousands of cadres, bribery and corruption involving officials at all levels have become more and more daring in their size and scale. Prime Minister's son implicated in a futures fraud case, Shenzhen deputy mayor arrested for corruption for embezzling over 200 million yuan, 1,000 corrupt officials persecuted in Jiangxi province, senior Guangdong official arrested in corruption case involving 100 million yuan.

The latest to surface is a billion-dollar smuggling ring based in the port of Xiamen involving more than 200 officials, including the wife of a politburo member, Jia Qinglin – the very person chosen to replace Chen Xitong as Beijing party leader.

I returned, in a suit and selling lager, to cities that I had visited as a student. This included Changchun. I had been invited to the wedding of a Chinese colleague. Apart from the novelty of flying into a city I had always associated with the train, Changchun appeared much the same. The same unforgiving greyness, the industrial architecture and the conservative air (the reception was in a hotel on Worker Peasant Boulevard). There were, however, subtle signs of change. A few neon signs, an international hotel, the more colourful clothes of the city's inhabitants. The one thing that had mushroomed since my student days was the growth of the local wedding industry. The bridegroom, Wang Shuo, seemed to have picked a day when all the other couples in Changchun were also getting married. Every fifth car was a black Audi with darkened windows and plastic figurines of the bride and bridegroom in tuxedo and white meringue dress on the bonnet. Following each wedding chariot, squeezed into smaller cars, were relatives, friends and colleagues hooting horns.

The taxi driver noted my interest in the darkened bride carriers, modern versions of the covered 'happiness' sedan chairs that carried bewildered teenage brides from village to village. While approving of marriage, he wondered where all the money was coming from to pay for these flamboyant displays of marital harmony. As another large car rolled past with a bride inside he shook his head. 'It's too much,' he said, 'too much.'

Despite decades of official discouragement of lavish weddings, the old traditions of throwing a large party and letting the whole town know your son or daughter was getting married are back with a vengeance. As in former times, the cost of these weddings is prohibitive. Whereas in the past you would invite the whole village to celebrate, now you invite everyone you know. Whilst everyone is encouraged to bring little red envelopes filled with cash donations, these rarely cover the cost involved.

It is a very public affair and there is little privacy for the happy couple on their big day. Indeed, one of the more annoying traditional wedding customs in China is for the guests to charge into the bedroom as the bride and groom are preparing for their first night of wedded bliss, dance around and generally irritate them.

> Soon after the newlyweds have entered the nuptial
> chamber, all the wedding guests, male and female,
> follow. To win the smiles of the bride, people wilfully
> tease her with all kinds of ridicule and jokes. This
> practice of foolery and frivolity by adults in the nuptial
> chamber is intended to embarrass the bride and the
> bridesmaid. The guests crack vulgar jokes in bawdy
> language and make flippant remarks about the bride's
> appearance . . . They do not stop until they have had
> their fill of wanton fun and foolery.
>
> – Xue Ke, *Anecdotes of the Qing Dynasty*

While perhaps not as wilfully intrusive as the past, the teasing
of the bride and bridegroom is legitimate and part of the fun
of the marriage day. The joy of the couple seems subordinate
to the enjoyment of everyone else. Free food, wine and
cigarettes for all! The size and random nature of the guest
list make intimacy difficult and hinder any communal feeling
of sharing a personal and special moment.

A wedding I went to in Henan confirmed a suspicion that
for most young couples, the wedding banquet is an
uncomfortable rite of passage that has to be borne with stoic
good nature. The young bride and groom sat together in
silence while male guests challenged each other to drink
themselves under the table. At my table such a ferocious spirit
was displayed in the attempt to get everyone drunk that after
just over an hour, two men had left, another sat there looking
extremely ill, and a fourth lay slumped forward with his head
in his hands. I felt sick myself and only avoided displaying
any outward loss of control by arriving late and therefore
missing out on the first twelve rounds of toasts. The bride in

white (a colour that used to be reserved for mourning) flicked imaginary specks of food from her dress and looked at her watch.

The flight back to Beijing was delayed at the departure gate. The reason, passed like a relay baton from the front of the aircraft to the back, was the late arrival of fellow-passengers. Everyone waited with admirable patience. Along with my neighbour I assumed it was some provincial official. I leant my head on the plastic bulkhead and closed my eyes trying to ignore the delay.

I was woken up by a rush of whispered noise from the front of the plane.

Three Africans had boarded. I wondered if they were Changchun-based students on an upgraded 'socialist scholarship'. It was obvious that they were the late passengers. As they made their way slowly down the aisle with their cases, there was a rush of conversation.

'Black people?'

'Yes, black people!'

'We are waiting for black people?'

A man leapt up to my left and shouted: 'But who do you think you are? I can't believe we have had to wait for these people!'

It seemed that waiting was not the source of agitation, but waiting for non-Chinese, and more specifically black people, sparked an angry chorus of resentment and denunciation. Soon everyone was in the aisles shouting and gesticulating. The plane could not take off.

While the three Africans cowered in their seats, the hostesses stood transfixed before the baying crowd.

The Captain came through over the intercom: 'Please, can everyone return to their seats! Please can everyone return to their seats!'

He was ignored and it seemed as if the angry momentum of the crowd would lead to the Africans, now visibly alarmed, being attacked.

Eventually, the Captain entered the cabin and a hush descended.

'We cannot go to Beijing as we cannot take off!'

Silence, then another groundswell of aggrieved voices: 'But of course we are going to Beijing!' 'What are you saying?' 'Who says we aren't going to Beijing?' 'On my ticket it says Beijing!'

A chorus of '*Zou ba! Zou ba!*' ('Let's go!')

'What are you waiting for?'

The Captain turned and entered his little cabin. Everyone sat heavily back in their seats and muttered about the standard of China's airline staff. The man sitting next to me tapped his forehead with a finger.

'Why on earth wouldn't we be going to Beijing? The Captain's crazy!' he said with a look of innocent astonishment.

Consumerism is an unforgiving creed. Gradually the face of old Beijing disappeared under steel, concrete, and blue and gold glass. A horizontal city became vertical, like every other one in Asia. While the great city walls had been torn down in the 1950s to make way for a ring road, Beijing had managed to hang on to enough distinctiveness to intrigue. The small pleasures that had made the capital a delight until the mid-1990s were snuffed out. Markets pushed to outlying districts, old landmarks and quiet corners obliterated, the warren of *hutong,* which until recently most Beijingers had lived in, systematically destroyed.

The car overtook the bicycle. The traffic worsened. Luxury housing appeared. You could buy everything you could possibly need. There were people at parties you didn't recognise. At work, systems were put in place. Work became routine and the unexpected nature of life in Beijing disappeared. While (an older) Cui Jian, the Chinese Bruce Springsteen, might still be playing, everyone in the audience was over 30. The youth were no longer listening. They were too busy trying to earn money, like everyone else in the country.

Not content with a comfortable existence in Beijing selling beer amidst the trappings of expatdom, I felt the need to strike out. After three years I was restless, impatient. I needed a change. I wanted to head for a tougher and more challenging place. A part of China remote from the superficial Westernisation of the capital. Away from the swelling foreign community and the familiar, the traffic jams, the inhuman gargantuanopolis that is modern Beijing. Frontier stuff, that's what I needed. A wider horizon. A latent puritanical streak asserted itself. Beijing wasn't the real China. It had changed too much over the last couple of years. There was another side that I was missing, that wasn't to be found here amongst the tennis, the tourists, the overpriced new blocks of flats and the endless socialising. All these recently arrived foreigners who couldn't even string a sentence together in Mandarin! People who claimed to know all about China revealing their recent arrival. All those five-star hotels with their Sunday brunches. Beijing's shops even had Mother's

Day cards now. Where was the adventure that China had promised?

Offered a position in Henan, a place that no one ever seemed to go to, I had simply said yes. By choosing a province at the centre of China there was the unconscious hope that I would get closer to the essential nature of the country and its people and have a 'real' experience, undiluted by bread, cheese, foreigners and pubs. It was time to regain some of that initial pioneering spirit.

Chapter Five

A Mouthful of Happiness

A yellow country streaked here and there with red. Everywhere startling terraced hills of loess, grotesquer than the most outlandish ant-hills . . . the ochre earth had, for so ancient a place, a strangely brittle air, and was in fact most easily eroded. There was a kind of prehistoric look about this land . . .

— Peter Fleming, *News from Tartary*

The Beijing evening air rushed in through the back window as we headed along the third ring road. I lay slumped in the back seat taking in the warm fumes that have made the city the most polluted capital in the world. We were on the way to the airport and I was on my way back to Henan. It was a Sunday evening and I had a sinking feeling, as if I was heading back to school.

'Where are you going?' asked the taxi driver as he offered me a Hilton, the cigarette of choice for the capital's cabbies. 'London?'

'No, Henan.'

'Aiya! What on earth for?'

'I live there, in Zhengzhou.'

He chuckled and shook his head. 'That's too bad, too bad.'

Zhengzhou is the capital of a province in China called Henan.

With a population of over 90 million, Henan, geographically and culturally, lies at the heart of Chinese civilisation. The name for China in Mandarin is '*Zhongguo*' which means 'middle' or 'central kingdom'. One could argue that as Henan lies at the centre of *Zhongguo*, it therefore lies at the centre of the world. As every local will tell you, Henan was where it all began. The beginnings of Han Chinese civilisation over 3,500 years ago can be traced back to the crumbling, ochre-yellow earth of this province. People are forever digging up bits of ancient pottery and implements that constantly remind one of the enormous age and depth of Chinese culture. One telling statistic that highlights Henan's role as the cradle of Chinese civilisation is that 73 of the 100 most common Chinese surnames originate from this province. In Taiwan, the four most common family names, Chen, Lin, Huang and Zheng, all have their roots in Henan. The regular unearthing of prehistoric animal bones reinforces an even older connection. Recently, police in Henan arrested four men who were caught trying to smuggle 59 fossilised dinosaur eggs out of the province. The eggs in the three cases were all over 150 million years old. Henan's local history is uniquely intertwined with national history and as such demands to be taken seriously by all those interested in the early development of China.

An ancient and important past has not, unfortunately, seemed to have bestowed any modern favours on the Henanese. Its people are infamous in China for hard drinking and, there is no sensitive way to say this, cheating. They are the rough kids on the block. There is no Shanghai sophistication or the studied politeness of Beijing in Henan. It is a rough, conservative and ugly province.

In the airport lounge I sat with a crowd waiting for the plane to Zhengzhou. I found the airport a chance to dream. The list of possible flights encouraged contemplation of other more desirable destinations. As a result of some unaccountable computer error, I imagined that the flight to Henan would end up flying to Hawaii, Holland or Helsinki. The announcement of an hour's delay was accepted by the waiting passengers with the usual equanimity. I chatted with a young woman who sat next to me and asked her where she was from. She lowered her eyes and scratched the back of her hand.

'Zhengzhou, but I don't like to tell many people that as they think we are all uncouth and not to be trusted.'

As well as being labelled ruffians by their kith and kin, the Henanese are viewed by the more cosmopolitan parts of China as having been left behind in the enormous socio-economic changes that have fundamentally altered Chinese society over the last ten years. Stuck in the middle of China with little or no exposure to the West, either as a result of commercial exchange or through tourism, it is undoubtedly true that Henan lags behind the modernisation that is apparent in the south and east of the country.

One reason for this state of affairs is geography. Henan is a long way from the coast and access to any port. However, this cannot explain everything. There is an innate conservatism in this part of China, perhaps as a result of a too glorious past. China has a claim to be the oldest continuous civilisation in the world. Its traditions of historical narrative are unsurpassed; twenty-five dynasties recorded their histories from around the twentieth century BC to the collapse of the Qing Dynasty in 1912. With a general consciousness of the length and depth of Chinese civilisation, coupled with Henan's physical position at the heart of Han China, it is perhaps not surprising that the Henanese have an inflated view of their importance in world history. Communism with its rigid certainties has compounded this essentially conservative, and some would say arrogant, mentality. Yet Henan is not some bucolic backwater, but a large province with millions of city dwellers, much industry and some of the best farmland in the country. There are also huge problems with alcoholism, unemployment (an estimated 50 per cent of the urban population is out of work), pollution and poverty.

There is a love of generalisations amongst the Chinese, possibly as a result of trying to comprehend a country of 1.2 billion inhabitants. This is borne out by the widespread use of idioms. Their continued popularity in everyday conversation stands in contrast to European languages where such expressions tend to be used only for cliché effect. Their survival in China can be seen as connected to the impossible task of trying to make sense of a vast and ancient society. Better to leave it to these accumulated pearls of wisdom, passed down from generation to generation. On the whole they have pleasant or innocuous things to say about each region. So people from Shanghai are clever and commercially minded, people from the north-east are honest and friendly, while those in the south will eat anything (contrary to Western opinion, not all Chinese love to eat dog, chaffinch or turtle penis). Even China's ethnic minorities, Tibetans, Uighurs, Mongolians and others who are not really viewed by the Han Chinese as being on the same level as themselves, receive warmish comments. 'Very colourful' or, relentlessly practical as the Chinese are, 'foreign tourists love them' (i.e. a useful source of foreign currency). Such mild generalisations do not seem to apply to Henan, the heart of ancient China. Despite claiming the first capital of a more or less unified kingdom and a starting point (or ending point depending which direction you were coming from) of the famous Silk Road, the Henan people lost the respect and goodwill of their fellow-countrymen, who generally have nothing good to say about them, somewhere along the line.

'They are all black-market boys down there', 'You can't trust them', 'Rough' or just simply, 'Country gangsters' with its hint of violence and botched amateurism. When I told a Shanghai friend that I would be moving to Henan, there was an incredulous silence at the end of the phone line.

'Are you serious?'

In recent years many Henanese have flocked to other more prosperous parts of China, where they take on the work that no one else wants to do. This has not helped their image. In Beijing, the rubbish-collecting operations consist of thousands of Henanese who would rather collect and sort the detritus of the capital's population than live in their home province. Many of them live in chaotic Bajia, otherwise known as 'Henan village' in the north-west of the capital. Many do not posses the right documentation for living in Beijing and police raids are frequent. Not frequent enough for many Beijingers, who view the influx of migrant workers as the main reason for an increase in crime. Living and working, sometimes illegally, on the fringes of Beijing society has done little to correct the general view that nothing good comes out of Henan, unless of course it took place over a thousand years ago.

The one thing that does come out of Henan on a daily basis, and about which others are presumably fairly positive, is a mass of bamboo for the pandas of Beijing Zoo. Urban sprawl and agriculture have destroyed the bamboo forests around the capital, and the zoo is now reliant on truckloads of bamboo driven up from Henan. It seems appropriate that a province which boasts the first ever capital of China should now be engaged in feeding one of the recurring symbols of China's pride. (Did you know an adult panda eats more than 45 pounds of fresh bamboo per day?)

Despite Henan having been at the centre of Han civilisation for thousands of years, tourists are not really encouraged to visit. Tour agencies and other Chinese will point you towards trendsetting Shanghai, Beijing with its palaces and temples, Xian with its army of terracotta warriors and maybe Chengdu, or the idyllic countryside of Yunnan. Henan has ceased to be a destination of choice.

It was in this unlikely, and for a foreigner inhospitable, environment that I found myself selling that symbol of the West and Progress, Coca-Cola. Those millions of mouths needed sweet relief. Ke Kou Ke Le, 'a mouthful of happiness' (the phonetic translation of Coca-Cola) was to be put within reach of everyone in China; every town, village, nightclub, restaurant and corner store. And that now included the backwaters of Henan. WITHIN AN ARM'S REACH OF DESIRE! was the battle cry from Atlanta, Coke HQ. At a senior level the sense of mission, augmented by daily faxes, was palpable. On arrival I was packed off around the province on a ten-day fact-finding mission with driver and jeep. I felt like a newly arrived colonial commissioner on his first tour of duty. Only now you were supposed to sell something as well.

A polluted expanse of opaque grimness, traffic-choked streets and railway tracks, Zhengzhou squats on the sandy southern banks of the Yellow River. The Coca-Cola factory is situated in an ubiquitous International Business Development Park, a wind-scrubbed area of concrete outside the city centre. Amidst several factories, brick walls enclose derelict open spaces. On the main road that leads to the first oversized roundabout is a line of the most improbable buildings. They had all been erected at the same time, but all represented different architectural heritages. There was a crenellated castle, a Corbusier-inspired construction, a South Carolina mansion, Swiss wooden chalet, Queen Anne townhouse, mini New York tower block and several other stylistic examples. On closer inspection many of the constructions were abandoned, with windows broken or boarded up. The castle had been turned into a restaurant but the rest were devoid of human activity. The buildings were less than a year old.

Every day as I drove past these fantasy monuments to a better life, it occurred to me that their position at the investment park entrance was a subliminal warning for potential investors. A piece of municipal folly serving as an entirely appropriate metaphor not just for doing business in Henan, but for the wider investment environment in China. A lot of show up front, impressive from a distance, but on closer inspection nothing much substantial going on. Is this too harsh a judgement? Of course. But it does hint at the gap between business reality and expectation in China.

I once had lunch in the castle, a gaudy Louis XIV-style restaurant complete with waitresses in corsets and black hooped dresses, plush velvet fabrics and 'gold' fittings. I cannot remember any more about the dining experience because it was one of my first business lunches in Henan and I had yet to master the art of staying sober. At the end of the meal I had to be carried out, draped across the shoulders of two colleagues.

The plant itself, all blue glass and white tiling, had about 350 employees, was wonderfully inefficient and mired in political in-fighting. In such an atmosphere, corruption flourished. Many of its sales team were in the pocket of Zhengzhou's powerful wholesalers, product was disappearing from the warehouses unrecorded, and most of the staff were not on speaking terms with each other. A Byzantine pricing policy made life unnecessarily complex and encouraged anomalies. Signatures (easily faked) were needed for everything. The director of the plant was an authoritarian Taiwanese, Mr Liu, who was often hoarse from shouting and ill from stress. Amiable enough in private, he attempted to rule the factory from behind his desk with a fierce countenance.

Our first conversation revolved around what was to be a central theme of life in Henan.

'Can you drink?'

I hesitated.

'You have to be able to drink. It is the only thing they respect here. That is why I agreed to have you as you used to sell beer. It will have been useful training.'

So much for selling soft drink.

Mr Liu was a manager in the classical Chinese tradition. This meant adopting an authoritarian front, making all the important decisions, and assigning tasks to subordinates, all the while striving to be kind and considerate to those led. This pattern of leadership may work well in small-scale family-run operations, but in larger, more complex organisations, it is a recipe for inefficiency on a grand scale.

I was given an airless room with no telephone across the corridor from the director. All attempts to get the logistics manager, Madam Wei, to find a chair and phone failed. Rumour had it that she had pocketed thousands of yuan from the opening of the plant.

My sales manager was a large man with hooded eyelids and skin like porcelain. He hardly spoke in front of colleagues, not out of shyness, but as a means of fostering an image of great wisdom. Every action had been decided in advance, everything was done with a calculated deliberateness. However, natty red clip-on braces hinted at a self-consciousness that belied his ostentatiously reserved behaviour. He reminded me of the rotund and manipulative Chinese magistrate in George Orwell's *Burmese Days*. I never really trusted him and he reciprocated. Our discussions quickly took the form of crabs circling each other.

Every morning I stood up in front of thirty salesmen, and after a few brief pleasantries in Mandarin, we would launch into the company song, which had a martial flavour ('We are the soldiers of Coca-Cola, we are the hope of Coca-Cola'). At the end we would punch the air en masse. Then the eager salesmen, caught up in the excitement of selling this global elixir, would rush out to the trucks, climb aboard and disappear in a cloud of dust to sell, sell, sell. Unfortunately it never happened quite like that.

There was normally a desultory singalong which no matter how forcefully and loudly it started, always dribbled to a halt with the words *'Jia you!'* repeated three times in a lifeless manner. *Jia you*, literally 'add oil', is a common phrase that can be translated as 'Let's do it!' or 'Come on!' At this point the salesmen were all supposed to raise their fists in a purposeful fashion. I only managed to inspire a feeble raising of right and left hands varying from a subtle upward sweep of the lower arm to assorted finger movements. It seemed quite obvious that the morning ritual was a perfectly useless staff motivator. I also felt slightly ridiculous standing at the front of this mass display of apathy.

The sensitive subject of dropping the morning singalong altogether was broached with the plant director, who unfortunately refused to countenance such a radical move. Such a sweeping change could be taken as a sign of weakening authority. I struggled on for several weeks, but eventually found a compromise whereby we would sing the company song at a ridiculously fast speed – like a 33 rpm record played as a 45. This not only rendered the meaning unintelligible, but also shortened the sales hymn to about six seconds, just about bearable.

Perhaps it was this early failure to whip the sales team into a focused selling fury each morning that sowed the first seeds of doubt as to my suitability for the position of sales director. However, nearly a year later I was pleased to note that my successor, another authoritarian-inclined Taiwanese and a successful salesman in his own right, failed to elicit much more response than my efforts had. This was despite taking the song back to its original length and getting everyone to parade about outside on the concrete forecourt. (In the thousands of small Taiwanese-run factories that have mushroomed in southern China one can catch a glimpse of this militaristic, almost fascist approach to organising the workforce. It is an uncomfortable sight as one is aware that behind the regimentation lie some of the worst abuses of cheap labour in the country.)

If the truth be told, they were not the best sales force in the world. Daily records of the previous day's activities were read out at the morning meeting, and hinted at some hidden distortion.

'Little Liu, three cases, Big Wang, one and a half, Wang Zhou, five thousand six hundred and fifty-two.'

With the wholesale system it made more sense to hang out with the leather-jacketed wide boys, smoke Red Mountain fags, drink tea and get one of them (perhaps a relative) to place a large order near the end of the month. Quota reached, job done.

Changing such a system, however, meant a delicate balancing act between encouraging the laborious process of opening more outlets while avoiding a sudden haemorrhaging of sales due to angry uncooperative wholesalers.

Chapter Six

Business Lubricant

Maotai looks crystal clear. Though a potent drink, it is never burning to the mouth or to throat, nor does it go to the head or upset the stomach. Since ancient times it has been a favourite drink with poets and other people of artistic penchant. They believe that when setting their writing or painting brushes to paper, they find inspiration from a cup of Maotai more than anything else.

– *Things Chinese and Their Stories*, China Travel and Tourism Press

Please not another toast. I sat around a large circular dinner table in a city called Kaifeng. In the eleventh century Kaifeng was the greatest city on earth. As the capital of the Song Dynasty its population was close to a million and it produced a flowering in ceramics that has not been equalled since. It took the Europeans another seven hundred years to achieve anything close to the porcelain that came out of this part of China. At one point the French even sent missionaries to spy on production techniques. To the casual visitor today, its former glory is hard to spot. It has become like thousands of other concrete cities the length and breadth of China.

I am drunk and struggling to hold myself together at the table, another business dinner. I am the only foreigner present, and as such, a legitimate easy target for the other eleven people at the table. Their unspoken goal is to get me drunk on the local *baijiu* (literally 'white' or 'clear spirit'), the preferred drink in Henan. They were succeeding. An innocuous phrase from my Changchun student days swam into my head: 'Chinese hospitality is fully expressed at banquets.' I had never sought to dig further as to its true meaning. Now I was finding out and it was an overpowering experience.

There is a ritual to drinking with business partners and colleagues that Western sinologists and some Chinese would like to call 'elaborate' but quite simply involves getting the honoured guest wrecked while avoiding too much damage to oneself.

In a country as large as China there are of course regional variations. In the south for instance, alcohol does not play such a prominent role at the dinner table. In the north-east it is beer rather than spirits that is the drink of choice earlier in the evening. In Henan, however, a tradition of drinking *baijiu* has been developed to a ferocious degree. Perhaps this is to be expected in a province whose population manages to consume just over one-third of all spirit products produced in China.

The honoured guest, someone senior in business terms (more money, higher position and/or a foreigner), has to become extremely skilled to survive the long hours at the restaurant table. There is very little escape as the honoured guest has to fend and parry numerous offers to drink a shot with others around the table. One can refuse now and then, but this must be done with good humour and grace. For those who cannot speak Chinese, this becomes an impossible task and one is left saying 'no' every five minutes, which does not give the best impression. Even when speaking Chinese, you need all your wits to stay one step ahead of the rest of the table. Too defensive a position will leave you looking ill at ease and ungrateful; too quick to join in and you will be on the floor before the plates of fruit arrive. All you can realistically hope for is that you drag enough of the others down with you, thereby slackening the pace of the alcohol intake.

All this forced drinking is justified as a way of making both the hosts and guests 'happy and relaxed'. The hosts have visible proof that you are enjoying yourself, and if a guest refuses to drink, may legitimately take offence. The idea is to loosen everyone up as a way of getting to know each other better, a sort of debilitating version of Victorian parlour games. All sorts of elaborate rules have been concocted to ensure everyone drinks as much as possible. They are adhered to with fascist zeal. Dinner becomes a protocol minefield and it is easy to trip up, at which point others will shout with glee. Only the nimble survive. Arguing over the desired alcohol intake makes no impression. Drinking is something that has to be done; a monotonous and regular group affirmation of masculinity. Just as the insistence is exaggerated, so your protestations are treated as part of the game.

While the honoured guest is never explicitly identified, if you are one, you will soon know about it as several others congregate around you and start pushing you towards a chair. Lightly manhandled to your seat, it is common for there to be several minutes of hand-to-hand combat between the guests as one is encouraged to sit down. It is polite to resist this friendly mauling and push other people to their seats. However, no one will sit down until the guest of honour is seated. The pushing and shoving continues until a decent amount of time has elapsed, and the guest of honour reluctantly takes his place. This charade is repeated at the end of the dinner when there is another battle to propel the honoured guest out of the room first. When several of the dinner party are inebriated, this is a potentially dangerous affair. I witnessed several end of dinner routines that finished with men in suits shouting loudly and roughly pushing each other around just in front of the entrance to a private dining room. Hapless waitresses clearing away plates and cutlery were knocked to the ground by the brawling guests.

At this particular dinner I was the first foreigner that the people around the table had ever met, let alone done business with. I was an emissary, a representative of a foreign and strange culture, an alien beamed down from another planet. A spokesman for the rest of the world. With such significance attached to my every utterance, I was without doubt an honoured guest – and there would be no mercy.

I looked nervously at the twelve glasses on the table and it was with relief that I saw they were tiny, thimble-sized. I smiled and thought to myself that I might just get through the evening relatively unscathed. I engaged the most senior of the people seated around the table in conversation about Kaifeng's development.

Then, a strange thing happened. The waitress appeared and walked slowly around the table removing each of the thimble-sized glasses. It was too good to be true! We were not going to have to drink the vile stuff after all! I couldn't help but frown; no *baijiu* in Henan? Home to China's heaviest drinkers? This was headline stuff.

Then, horror as Mr Wang spoke: 'In Kaifeng we do not use such small glasses. They are for little girls.'

With that he grabbed the bottle out of the waitress' hand

and proceeded to pour the *baijiu* into my saucer-like plate. He did this, it must be said, to everyone. I stared down at the clear spirit gently lapping at the edges of my plate, looked at the others around the table and realised he was not joking.

'Here in Henan we like to drink like this before we start eating.'

With a slight nod of encouragement, I was invited to take the saucer, lift it to my lips and down the fiery liquid with a loud slurp. As it burnt its way down my throat and made my eyes water with its pungent smell, I realised that my chances of getting back into my hotel room unassisted were non-existent.

Cigarettes and liquor are the lubricants of the Chinese business scene. They are consumed in such quantities that one's health cannot fail to be affected. The Chinese have been brewing potent alcohol for over 4,000 years. They are the experts. *Baijiu* is the common name for Chinese-produced spirit made from fermented maize, rice or sorghum. The lowliest *baijiu* is around 48 degrees proof, while I have drunk spirits of 72 plus. Most foreigners' initiation to the world of *baijiu* comes with consumption of Maotai, the most famous brand due to its prominence at official banquets. This dangerous alcohol is named after a small town in Guizhou province, southern China, where it is produced.

Marco Polo described Maotai as 'the finest wine in the world.' Along with his failure to mention the Great Wall or chopsticks, this comment is enough to make me agree with Dr Frances Wood, author of *Did Marco Polo Go to China?* that the great traveller never really made it to China at all.

Despite drinking large quantities over the years my palette never quite grasped the intricacies of the clear liquid. My main concern on seeing a bottle produced at the table was to ascertain the alcohol level. If it was under 50 per cent I felt reasonably certain of lasting the evening, but anything over this made me sink into depression. I was drunk with sickening regularity.

Many Chinese have no qualms about getting completely smashed at dinner, and indeed it is to be encouraged. In the work environment, where nearly all banquets take place, being seen to enjoy oneself freely by drinking liberally is a positive sign. It shows that you have no airs and graces, and are prepared to let your guard down amongst friends and colleagues. In Henan this would be taken to extreme lengths; not only were you encouraged to drink, but if you didn't, you spoilt the whole evening for everyone else. The proffered toasts would go on and on throughout the meal until you showed signs of drunkenness. Swaying in your chair, smoking with your elbow in a rice bowl or dribbling in silence are all acceptable indications that you have reached a satisfactory limit. If you leave the table showing no signs of drunkenness, some hosts take offence. After one business dinner I made the mistake of bouncing down several steps outside a restaurant, pleased to be heading for bed without the usual nausea. My host, spotting this sign of vitality after a large banquet, pointed at me and said in an aggrieved voice, 'He hasn't drunk enough.'

He would have been much more satisfied if I had fallen, rather than skipped down the steps. He felt somehow cheated. When I had refused several cups of *baijiu* during the meal, insisting that I had already drunk more than enough, it was quite plain in his eyes that I had been lying.

Perhaps he felt annoyed at having failed to deliver the knockout blow with the established Henan 'fish head' routine. A steamed fish dish is placed on the table with the head pointing at the honoured guest. This is the cue for others around the table to ask the guest to down anything from one to three glasses of *baijiu* – on their own. This has to be done before anyone will think of touching the fish. Sometimes one can escape by spinning the table server slightly before anyone has realised, so the fish head points at some other unfortunate, but there is usually some clever dick who will spot you and raise the alarm.

The tyranny of the Chinese dinner table is unrelenting. Circular in shape, there is no opportunity to chat casually with one's neighbour; everything must be directed to the whole group. There is no private space, no room for intimate bilateral relationships to develop and form. It is completely group-oriented and consequently there is no cover, no hiding place and no subtlety. Only one conversation is possible and with ten other people around the table, all on their best behaviour, this can only result in the most superficial discussions. There is no excuse for not listening intently to the table bore or when someone challenges you to another glass of 63 per cent alcohol. Any flirtation is carried out under the gaze of the group. Food and drink are usually ordered by one person only; individual requests are rare and are greeted with raised eyebrows. One's personal desires are subordinated to the group.

The fishbowl atmosphere is heightened by the fact that many formal dinners take place in private rooms. Sealed off from the life of the restaurant, there are no distractions to divert attention away from the food and drink. It was on occasions like this that I could see the evening stretching out before me; I felt like a marathon runner before a race.

The food is commented on endlessly and everyone is generally encouraged to eat what he or she wants. However, some particularly keen hosts insist on serving you themselves, which can become a particular form of torture if the food on your plate is not to your liking. As the rest of the table stares, there is no room for a subtle and whispered, 'No, thank you.' It was in such a way that I came to eat my first sea slug, bull's penis and snake. (It should perhaps come as no surprise that the success of Western fast-food outlets in China, McDonalds and KFC, is in a large part due to the fact that for the first time children get to *choose* what to eat. Everyone cheerfully admits the food is '*mama huhu*' – 'so-so'.)

Western fascination with Chinese eating habits centres on the exotic and 'inedible'. Food is the most fundamental aspect of Chinese culture. Yet it is not entirely accurate to say that 'the Chinese will eat anything.' The trend towards the exotic is more pronounced in the south of the country (where nothing seems out of bounds) and during banquets on formal occasions. Southern food is daintier than in the north and puts clearness, blandness and freshness above all else. The search for freshness can be seen at its most gruesome in the markets of Guangzhou where animals of all sizes are cut up whilst still alive.

Apart from taste and flavour, it is perhaps the delight in texture that marks out the Chinese view of food. Many of the rare and expensive animals, or parts of animals, are sought after not for their taste, which is often non-existent, but for their texture. It is this obsession with the textural nature of food which explains why Chinese eat so many things that Westerners consider tasteless (shark's fin), inedible (bird's nest), or plain revolting (sea slug). T. C. Lai in his book, *At the Chinese Table*, explains it well:

> The texture of each ingredient is sensed by the tongue, the teeth and the throat: abalone is rubbery, smooth and chewy; bird's nest is tender and delicate; liver is grainy and gizzards are fibrous. To people who are not attuned to the appreciation of textures, many of these qualities are classified under the epithet 'slimy'.

One can view this different approach to food at any formal banquet. Here, pieces of food are selected according to textures that please the most and are offered to the guest. Fish eyeballs, chicken feet, duck's tongue, pickled scorpion or sea slug are amongst the more common.

There is, however, an undoubted snobbery to eating the rare and the exotic. This extravagance with food is not a central part of Chinese cuisine, it belongs to a social environment that seeks to flatter the guest and raise the stature of the host. One of China's earliest celebrity chefs, Yuan Mei, who lived in the eighteenth century, noted the trend to cook for social effect rather than flavour and taste. He criticised those who cooked to impress others, using obscure delicacies, the rare and exotic, to display their wealth rather than the staples of chicken, fish, pork and duck.

> I was once asked to a party given by a certain Governor, who gave us plain boiled swallows'-nest,

served in enormous vases, like flower-pots. It had no taste at all. The other guests were obsequious in their praise of it. But I said: 'We are here to eat swallows'-nest, not to take delivery of it wholesale.' If our host's object was simply to impress, it would have been better to put a hundred pearls into each bowl. Then we should have known that the meat had cost him tens of thousands, without the unpleasantness of being expected to eat what was uneatable.

– Arthur Waley, *Yuan Mei: Eighteenth-Century Chinese Poet*

It was now nearly the end of the evening. We were surely the last guests in the restaurant. The glass placed before me was filled with a curious caramel-coloured viscous liquid. From the top I could see a reddish patch. I guessed immediately what lay in store from the expectant look on the faces of my neighbours. It had to happen sooner or later, especially in Henan – the ultimate macho drink: snake's bile mixed with Maotai.

'Come on Mr Ma, bottoms up! It's good for your health!' shouted a large wholesaler to my right.

I froze in front of the evil-coloured glass. It was late and the table was littered with the remains of dishes and cigarette ends. The room echoed to the raucous shouts of '*Gan bei! Gan bei!*' (literally, 'dry glass'.) The drinking and discussions had exhausted me and I couldn't find the energy to argue this one. Lifting the glass and swiftly chucking the contents down my throat I gave a forced smile. I could feel the heavy texture of the snake bile as it rolled its way down.

'I think I have to go to bed,' I said before stumbling into the foyer and throwing up in a waterless concrete fountain.

Most evenings involved some sort of business function. Why invest so much time and energy you might ask? Because personal relationships hold the key to business in China. In Henan, to my growing dismay, this was clearly impossible without large amounts of high percentage alcohol. There was one group in particular that I had to spend more time with than any other: the wholesalers.

Nothing can be understood about the workings of the Chinese economy and the failure of many foreign companies to make a profit without understanding the crucial role of the wholesaler in China. While recent developments have tempered some of their might, it is they who hold the key to the distribution of consumer goods in China. How did this come about? The state used to have a monopoly on distribution and many large entities were created to store and transport goods around the vast country. Often these large wholesalers were departments of city or county authorities. With the gradual dismantling of the planned economy and the creation of a more market-based environment, many wholesalers realised they wielded large and formidable powers. While retaining their links with local government, they were encouraged to go and make money from this position of dominance. Operating in the half-light of a semi-reformed economy, many large wholesalers, often the sole distributor in a given area, started to make substantial amounts of money. They used their monopoly position to make a profit and also to set the ground rules. If they did not agree to carry your product, there was little hope of you getting on the shelves of the thousands of stores in your area, let alone any sort of national penetration. Local officials were kept sweet with brown envelopes stuffed with cash or free cases of spirits.

The growing success and power of the wholesalers was turbo-boosted with the arrival of hungry foreign companies in China, eager to sell their goods to potentially 'the biggest market in the world.' The large wholesalers were flooded with smartly suited men offering special terms, incentives and dispensing large dinners. Stiff competition amongst rival consumer-goods companies only further enhanced the position of the big wholesalers who could happily play a brand of foreign beer, toothpaste or soft drink against each other.

Many companies found themselves being driven down a path of giving more and more away just to stay in the game. A bizarre one-sided poker that for many companies ended in humiliating failure. Having handed over large amounts of product on credit, when the time came to pay up, many wholesalers subtly resisted, citing a host of reasons. There was never an outright refusal. Poor transportation and harsh climates compounded the situation as many months of sales had to be sent and stored with the distributor all at once. Once in their warehouse, the wholesaler had a useful leverage tool. Unwilling to lose a potentially important distribution ally or disrupt a nice sales curve, foreign companies would negotiate for months and months before finally resorting to a legal remedy. However, by then either key wholesale personnel had moved on, the appropriate authorities had been paid off, or the documentation was so weak as to be useless in a court of law.

It was in such a way that foreign consumer-goods companies were forced to write off millions of US dollars in bad debt in the 1990s and many Chinese became very wealthy.

The cleverer wholesalers applied subtle psychological pressure on the company representatives sent to negotiate with them and to whom they invariably owed money. This was a combination of playing on fears of competitors and stressing their own powerful connections, all the while assuming a generous posture and emphasising the possibility of reconciliation. There was a wholesaler in Shaanxi city who would have me picked up in a white imported Cadillac that belonged to the city government and was normally used for visiting dignitaries. On the way from the airport I had sufficient time behind the blackened glass to reflect on this seemingly warm and spontaneous welcoming act. The message was two-fold and unambiguous: (a) I show you a lot of respect by sending such a beautiful car to pick you up, you should show me some. (b) The fact that it belongs to the city government and I can use it shows that I have friends in high places, so don't fuck with me.

In Harbin, in the far north-east, another wholesaler would welcome foreign business partners with police outriders and flashing lights. Foreign executives were flattered.

In Zhengzhou, the beverage wholesalers stood at the centre of a maze of railway tracks and from such a convenient position had grown into large and powerful distributors. Aided and abetted by sales personnel who wanted to see ferocious sales growth, a small handful of wholesalers dominated the distribution of Coke in Henan through lucrative volume discounts. By threatening to stop ordering for a few weeks, thereby making a severe dent in the sales figures, these tough wholesalers wielded enormous influence over the sales team, who lived in a state of fear and awe. The plant had unwittingly put itself at the mercy of its own customers. Timid attempts to curb some of their influence were met with a show of defiant unity. While they quite happily schemed amongst each other, the Zhengzhou wholesalers were capable of putting on a united front if they felt they were not being given their due.

In my second week in Henan, I came into the plant to be greeted by a group of leather-jacketed people sitting in the middle of one of the main corridors. Zhang Ye, one of the senior salesmen, was standing amongst them looking despondent. When he saw me arrive, he ran over. The people on the floor were the top ten wholesalers in Zhengzhou and they had a grievance against the company for what they saw as unfair pricing arrangements. They were angry with the director and insisted on a meeting. They were going to sit there until their concerns were addressed. Zhang Ye was in a state of high agitation as between them they accounted for 90 per cent of all the Coca-Cola shipped out of the factory gates. The wholesalers had chosen their day of protest well: a senior foreign manager was coming to inspect the plant. Not wishing to meet the enraged wholesalers, but quite rightly judging that his career would be over if the top executive's stately progress was interrupted by the mutinous mob, the plant director delegated the task of dealing with the situation to me. I asked him what was I supposed to do.

'You are a foreigner, they will be honoured if you spend time with them.'

'Spending time' meant a three-hour lunchtime banquet in a gaudy restaurant being lectured on the hurt feelings and lost profits of the wholesalers. Vast amounts of high-octane *baijiu* were consumed in polite toasts with each and every wholesaler as an acknowledgement of their concerns and my interest in a resolution. After drinking several bottles between us and having promised to look into the matter, I returned to the plant without the wholesalers, which I suppose was a victory of sorts. But I was forced to take the first of many afternoons off to lie in a darkened room incapacitated by the alcohol.

There are now many books about working in China, even some about being a foreign manager in China. I bought several in the hope that they would help. I found them all well-meaning, but hopelessly impractical. Nothing in writing can prepare one for the chaos that is the day to day reality; the relentless tidal wave of small practical problems that threatens to overwhelm an operation; the complexity of relationships, that if mishandled, can bring an organisation to an effective standstill, and the importance of all the while preserving an outward display of normality.

The difficulties of making a profit in China were compounded by the skewed strategic assumptions of overexcited corporate executives. Optimistic and unrealistic foreign assessments of the size of the Chinese market, something the Chinese have been delighting in for years, led and still leads to impractical and unrealistic targets.

China has always been a fantasy land for foreign businessmen. The sheer size of the population and the vibrancy of the cities have overwhelmed even the most cynical and hard-bitten. The dream of tapping into China's vast domestic market has been present ever since foreigners first arrived in numbers to buy and sell off the coast of southern China at the beginning of the nineteenth century. It was the determination of British businessmen to open up the country to trade (albeit a lucrative trade in opium) that first led to war with the West. In the last decade, a growing economy and the tremendous physical changes that have taken place as a result, particularly along the coast, have provided concrete proof of the efficacy of the Chinese market. 'China fever' touched a new generation of normally level-headed businessmen.

Just days before the Communist regime celebrated fifty years of one-party rule, *Fortune* magazine organised a gathering of the world's chief executives in Beijing. Ostensibly to look at future investment in the Chinese market, the Fortune Forum, described by one delegate as 'a great corporate kowtow' represented the triumph of hope over reason, hype over reality. Delegates praised the economic reforms undertaken and waxed lyrical about the future. This was despite the fact that many delegates represented companies that had yet to make one dollar of profit from their operations in China.

For some reason this deeply conservative Communist country is the Never-Never Land of capitalists. Corporate strategists masturbate over the huge population and the potential profits. 'The last frontier of significant growth', 'a land of unparalleled opportunities', 'the world's largest market', 'a market no one can afford not to be in' are characteristic of phrases bandied about by senior executives. Yet sales strategies were really an 'if only': if only we could get every Chinese male to wear our condoms; if only each family would buy our car; if only we could get every Chinese child to buy our bubblegum; if only they would use our toothbrush to brush their teeth. Such hopes are no different from those at the turn of the century when foreign traders dreamed of the scale of the Chinese market – Land of a Billion Pairs of Trousers! In 1898 people would compare Argentina with its 6,000 miles of railway to China with its 340 and conclude the potential was enormous. And people are still at it. Here is an extract from the 1999 Coca-Cola Company annual report: 'To put our opportunity in perspective, moving China to the same per capita consumption level as the Philippines would increase our Company's unit case volume by almost 40 per cent.'

Ah, the size, the size! At many consumer-goods companies the corporate dream often conflicted with reality with dire results for the bottom line. Nowhere was this more spectacularly seen than in the so-called 'Lager Wars' of the mid-nineties. During this time there was a flood of foreign entrants into the Chinese domestic beer market. The world's leading brewing operations – Budweiser, Carlsberg, Bass, Fosters, Tiger, San Miguel and others – all poured into China, established joint ventures to make and market their own brands, and then set about making their dreams a reality. Five years later when I left China, all of these operations had yet to make a profit.

How were such assumptions about the wonderful Chinese market substantiated? Here is how the market-size, and hence projected sales, was calculated for one particular beer company.

Work out how many units of lager are drunk per head per annum on average in different countries. For example, the Czech Republic, Germany and the United Kingdom all had over 100 units per head per year. In China it was about 11. Then times this by the size of the population. Despite the fact that the beer intake was far lower in China per head, the size of the population, on paper, yielded up a market of fantastical size. Even taking away around 30–40 per cent for women and children, hey presto, here was a potential market-size of awesome proportions.

Now, if one could increase the intake by just one or two units on average per person per year, surely not a difficult task, the size of the population would ensure a massive leap in market-size. I can still see the presentations where such claims were treated as gospel.

It soon became quite obvious that such calculations were wildly inaccurate, not least because they did not differentiate between the type of beer drunk or the dramatic difference in spending power between regions. For instance, China does produce and drink enormous amounts of beer, but in general it is of the extremely cheap variety. Full of chemicals, sometimes unpleasant to the taste, but costing as little as ten pence a bottle. The market for expensive 'premium' foreign branded lagers was a tiny fraction of the overall market.

Obviously, starting with skewed assumptions will lead to financial disappointment and this is precisely what happened not only to this beer company, but also to several others. Some had to retreat or sell out as the costs of the operation in China multiplied while sales and revenue forecasts remained stubbornly static. The difficulty of extracting any meaningful statistics from China compounded the situation.

Even when it became apparent that the market was not as easy to penetrate as had been assumed, there was a conspiracy of silence among the top executives on the issues. In the macho world of beverages where size is everything, to have admitted the truth could be interpreted by others as a sign of corporate weakness. There was an unspoken agreement not to mention the difficulties of making a profit in China. At one marketing meeting in Hong Kong where the very real difficulties were alluded to, the whole room descended into an embarrassed silence as if someone had uttered a terrible blasphemy. People refused to believe that a country with a population of over a billion would not yield itself up to the marketing nous of the West. The sheer size of the population had cast a spell over these corporate businessmen.

Instead, blame was laid at the door of poor operational factors, and the weather was often mentioned as a major reason contributing to yet another dismal year. Despite losing millions of dollars, many felt unable to leave as this would be an admission of defeat, as well as perhaps barring them from returning when China *was* a profitable place.

A journalist friend once interviewed a senior Budweiser executive on a visit to Beijing. He complained loudly, before the interview formally started, that he sold more beer in St Louis than he did in the whole of China. He was furious when this comment appeared in an article, and denied ever saying it. In Guangzhou, formerly Canton, where the first foreign traders had been allowed to operate over two hundred years ago, I met a senior Fosters executive. Exhausted after a visit to the region's wholesalers, he admitted things were 'tough' and quoted De Gaulle's comment on Brazil as applicable to China: 'A country with a lot of potential and always will be.'

He resigned a few months later.

Billions of dollars have been written off as 'an investment in the long term.' You would not know from the business community or politicians that at the turn of the millennium, the vast majority of foreign enterprises operating in China were failing to make a profit. This does not mean that money cannot be made, but that the hyperbole and the talk bear no reality to the size of the market. It also obscures the very real difficulties of running a successful business in China.

An industry has been built up around the 'enormous opportunities' available in the Middle Kingdom. Presidents, civil servants, captains of industry, analysts, investment bankers, academics and journalists enthusiastically participate. Encouraged by books with titles such as *The Last Great Market on Earth* and *The Dragon Rises*, commentators and business circles are enraptured by the potential of China. One man who saw through the hype was the late Gerald Segal, until his death the director of the International Institute for Strategic Studies in London. Here is what he had to say in an article in *Foreign Affairs*:

> Let us begin with some harsh realities about the size and growth of the Chinese economy. In 1997 China accounted for 3.5 per cent of world GNP, while the share for the US was 25.6 per cent. China's economy ranked 7th in the world, ahead of Brazil's and behind Italy's. But its per capita GDP ranking was 81st, just ahead of Georgia's and behind Papua New Guinea's. Taking the most favourable of the now dubious purchasing power parity calculations, in 1997 China accounted for 11.8 per cent of world GNP, and its per capita ranking was 65th, ahead of Jamaica and behind Latvia. Using the UN Human Development Index, China is a miserable 107th, bracketed by Albania and Namibia – not an impressive story. China made up less than 3 per cent of world trade in 1997, about the same as South Korea and less than the

Netherlands. Despite the hype about the importance
of the Chinese market, exports to China are tiny . . .
China accounts for 0.5 per cent of British exports,
about the same level as exports to Sri Lanka and less
than those to Malaysia.

The recent downturn in recorded foreign investment in China
is perhaps a reflection of a creeping disappointment after several
years of losses and little immediate prospect of profit. Perhaps
people are also aware of the vast amounts of Chinese money
moving out of China. It is doubtful that this more mature
strategic approach from the corporate HQs of the US and
Europe will last. The same beer company that was highlighted
earlier noted in its 1999 annual report that 'the development
in sales did not meet expectations' yet ends with, 'a number of
improvements have been initiated, including a change in the
distribution structure. The positive results of these initiatives
are expected to take effect in the year 2000.' In a country the
size of China there is always hope.

What explains this strange love-in between capitalists and
Communists? Why China in particular? Apart from the
dream of an infinite market, maybe the answer is to be found
in the long-standing mercantile culture of Chinese society.
Mao Zedong's reign in China has obscured a vibrant
commercial heritage, a market economy of millions of small
entrepreneurs. For thousands of years they have been buying
and selling, and there were no social barriers to taking part.
The urban centres were hives of activity and industry. At the
same time the Chinese are an extremely practical people.
Everything has a price. The upheavals of the Maoist years

have perversely reinforced this. Everything can be bought or sold. This is music to the ears of capitalists the world over.

We seemed to have been driving for hours in the hot sun through dry fields and dusty poplars when the company driver, Mr Zhu, pulled into a truck-stop restaurant, between Xinyang and Zhengzhou. A sordid strip of brick buildings perched close to the road with rubbish strewn about. Inside was a gloomy warren of small private eating areas and off the other side of the corridor were what looked like bedrooms. We sat down at a table with a greasy plastic tablecloth and waited for the waitress while flies buzzed around in the midday heat.

The waitress arrived and took our orders. I stared out of the window at the yellow land. Turning round, I was surprised to see a woman in a red frilly nylon dress flounce into our room and stand next to the table. She was a young peasant of sturdy build, unattractive, caked in garish make-up and swaying as if drunk.

'*Ni hao*,' ('hello') she cooed unconvincingly. I looked at Zhu who just grinned back. I thought she might break into song when the food arrived, but instead she plumped herself down next to me.

Her rough hand gripped mine under the table. I slipped my hand out of hers and drank some tea. Hunger, the heat, the desperate surroundings and now this depressing encounter. I felt uncomfortable. When the food arrived, this pathetic lady of the road attempted to feed me with her chopsticks. I refused to play and after several minutes of eating, she put down her chopsticks and asked if I would like to 'retire' with her. I must be tired after the long journey on the road and in need of a rest. Zhu encouraged me to take up the offer.

I declined the transparent attempt at a sexual transaction and for the rest of the meal she sat in a sulk. I glowered at the driver who ate heartily and seemed to revel in my discomfort. A truck thundered past outside, releasing a cloud of dust.

As we left, the girl whispered something to the driver, who grinned.

'She wants to see your thing,' he announced cheerily.

'Yes,' she said in a sing-song voice, catching my arm as I walked to the car. 'I would like to see your foreign thing.'

I shrugged her off and climbed into the car. Afterwards I primly berated Zhu for stopping at such a place and encouraging an awkward situation.

'What's the big deal? She liked you. She is poor and you are rich – a good transaction if you ask me.'

In China, everything is for sale if you have the money.

Chapter Seven

A Need to Believe

All that is left is the comfort of the past: pride in the ineffable superiority of Chineseness; in Confucius, Lao Zi and the rest of them; in the world's most subtle and complicated writing system; in a literature that is inexhaustible; in those high moral standards that, when all is said and done, mark the difference between civilised people and barbarians; in the world's longest recorded tradition of autocracy; in the Great Wall and everything it stands for.

– W. J. F. Jenner, *The Tyranny of History*

Luoyang, and another business dinner. Like Kaifeng, Luoyang has a glorious past. It was founded in 1200 BC and was the capital of ten dynasties, including the first capital of a unified China. The first Buddhist monastery in China was built here in AD 68 and the city once held over 1,200 temples. Luoyang was rich, cultured and the starting (or finishing) point of the Silk Road that linked West with East in an economic and cultural exchange of immense significance. But like Kaifeng, the traces of a glorious past have been concreted over. There are no buildings more than fifty years old in present-day Luoyang. The 'new' constructions are already disintegrating, cheated of supervisory attention and quality materials at birth. The surrounding countryside is as Peter Fleming describes, brittle and fragile. Centuries of concentrated cultivation and excessive grazing have resulted in weak topsoil that can be blown away by wind or washed away by rain. This has led to steady soil erosion and steep-sided gullies criss-cross the landscape where the elements have cut up the plateau. In some places the abused land has the texture of wet sand, in others fine granules of dust. In this loess landscape live millions of cave-dwellers who have hacked out a subterranean domesticity from the clay and silt.

Keen to avoid more drinking, I engaged the man next to me in conversation about the realities of foreign investment in Henan. Our modest conversation was interrupted by a shout from the other side of the table where Mr Zhang, the company chairman, wanted to ask the foreigner a couple of questions.

'Mr Ma, what do other foreigners, no, let me rephrase that . . . what does the rest of the world think about Luoyang?'

I was speechless. What to say? It was an extraordinary assumption that anyone outside China would have heard of this grey and polluted city. Most people had not heard of the province, Henan, which has a population of over 80 million.

I did not feel like playing along. I told him that not many people had heard of Luoyang.

It was his turn to be dumbstruck.

'But we are a very old city. We were once the capital of China!'

'When was that exactly?'

'771 BC!'

It struck me as strange, this obsession with the past. Can one imagine a visitor to a provincial city in Europe being regaled with such a distant claim to fame? Maybe; but the genuine bafflement at the lack of recognition from the visitor is something else. Perhaps it is because recent history and present reality are so depressing that the locals have decided to immerse themselves in a distant past, a glorious past, one that cannot be sullied by today's pollution, corruption and dead-ends. For the casual visitor there seemed to be little justification for such municipal pride in an ancient past. Luoyang has the same dreary architecture and unimaginative urban landscape as thousands of other cities in China. Mr Zhang had taken to an extreme a noticeable feature of Henan and Chinese culture in general: an obsession with its own glorious history.

The list of discoveries claimed to be from ancient China is as impressive as it is daunting. These include: paper money, kites, printing (the first book), the magnetic compass, gunpowder, fireworks, the brush, and toilet paper. Recently the discovery of a 2,000-year-old toilet complete with running water, a stone seat and an armrest have confirmed what many Chinese knew all along; the Chinese, and not Great Britain's Sir Thomas Crapper, invented the toilet. (While many Chinese will add pasta to this long list, much to Italian irritation, Dr Frances Wood suggests that it was the Iranians, conveniently sited between both countries, that produced the first pasta. In Henan this was seen as a ludicrous suggestion.) These inventions or 'firsts' for China are lodestars that confirm the innate superiority of all things Chinese and remind everyone of a continuous civilisation that is older (and better) than anyone else's. But it is hard not to feel that today such an illustrious past has become a refuge from the present and its worship is more debilitating than positive. It shapes attitudes towards other countries, other peoples and hinders innovation of any kind. (How else to explain that thousands of years after the Chinese teapot first appeared, they still dribble when poured?) It has produced a rigidity of mind that closes off avenues unknown. As W. J. F. Jenner wrote, it is 'the comfort of the grave.'

In Henan, the desire to boast and brag about China's civilisation was witnessed through an intense local nationalism that often had very little relation to modern reality. It was a compensation mechanism for a life of unremitting struggle amidst dust, concrete and the stares of your neighbours.

Later that night, there was a knock at the door. I opened it to see a young woman standing there in make-up, earrings, a black top and skirt. She looked slightly uncomfortable.

'What's up?'

'Wholesaler Zhang sent me,' she said, walking into the room.

'Please come in.'

She sat down on the corner of the bed with her hands in her lap. We sat in silence for about a minute.

'I can't do it.'

With that she smoothed her skirt and left the room.

Lying in the darkness I wasn't sure which was more discomforting. That (a) Wholesaler Zhang had ordered a woman to my room to sleep with me, (b) she had turned me down, or (c) that I didn't really mind either way. I contented myself with the knowledge that if we had had sex I would have been beholden to him and everyone would know. Still, navigating the murkier depths of Henan life was taking its toll.

Mr Zhao, the gruff sales manager for the south-eastern part of Henan province had only managed to sell 280 crates of Coca-Cola in three months. Believe it or not this was not a lot; in fact it was so little that I had come to find out what was wrong. Even by the low productivity standards of the salesmen of the plant this was an impressive effort. I also wanted to ask why all but one of his staff had left. After a five-hour journey by car, I arrived. He insisted on lunch, preferably somewhere expensive. I refused, knowing that I would have to sit through a long monologue of self-explanation that I could not immediately disprove. He knew that I knew that his sales were an astonishing testament to his lack of activity. As a compromise, the next day we ended up in the flat of one of the town's wholesalers, who was also a government official. Zhao insisted on the need to convince him to take Coca-Cola if sales were to be kick-started again. He waxed lyrical about his influence. The official was polite and distant.

The official's wife, wearing an apron, round and red-faced, briefly appeared before heading back into the kitchen where industrial noises could be heard. The banging of metal on metal, hisses of gas, whooshes of flame and the clattering of china. The obligatory shot of *baijiu* was drunk – I had given up arguing now – before a plate of sliced cucumber was placed on the table.

'Ah ha!' said the official. 'This is one of Xinyang's specialities. Xinyang cucumber. Please eat.'

The cucumber in question looked no different from any other cucumber that I had seen, in China or anywhere else. I took my chopsticks and picked up a slice, dipped it in the soy sauce and then munched away. The official stared at me with a great big smile, expectant. While it was a fine cucumber, I could not taste the defining element that made this a local speciality. Both Mr Official and Mr Zhao were, however, waiting for something – an endorsement.

'*Hao chi*,' ('very good') I nodded with a fixed grin.

This was the correct and expected response.

'Manager Ma, you know these cucumbers are peculiar to Xinyang. In fact, you cannot find them anywhere else.'

Unique? Really? I looked again at the cucumber. It was a cucumber. No more, no less.

'But this is a cucumber . . . I don't see why it is unique to Xinyang.'

The official looked at me with incomprehension.

'This is a Xinyang speciality dish. Of course it is different. Of course.'

I ploughed on.

'Yesterday, I was in Nanyang and they have cucumbers like this as well.'

'But they are not the same!'

I could see that I had offended my host. He was agitated and flushed and I let the matter drop. We clinked glasses for another shot of Gu Yue Long Shan *baijiu* to clear the air.

I tried to move the discussion away from the food, which was arriving in a steady stream – huge plates of tofu, pig's knuckles, green beans and sliced ginger.

We talked of his business. All officials have some sort of business, and he, of course, was a wholesaler, which explained why Zhao had brought me to his house. Mrs Official brought in the pièce de résistance, a steamed fish in soy sauce with fish head and eye intact. Relieved that the usual 'fish head' routine didn't seem to be on the agenda today, I congratulated Mrs Official on her cooking.

'You haven't eaten any yet!' She rolled her eyeballs and walked off.

I took a piece of fish after the others; it was indeed delicious.

'Where do you get your fish from?'

Henan is a landlocked province, and the surrounding area seemed quite dry.

'Guess,' said Mr Zhao. I named a couple of rivers that I had seen on the map, but they both shook their heads with a smile.

'No, no, no . . .'

'This is from Lake Nanwang. This is a very big lake not far from here. In fact, it is the biggest lake in Henan.' He sat back, taking a nip of *baijiu*, folded his arms and stared at me.

'Really?' I said.

'Oh yes, it's the biggest lake in Henan. In fact, I think it's the biggest lake in central China.'

'If not the whole of China,' chirped in Zhao. They both nodded at me and we drank again. They both waited for the endorsement. Actually, not so much of an endorsement, more of a kowtow. A submissive subliminal acknowledgement of the many wonders and delights of China. There are indeed many fantastic elements of Chinese culture, but I refused to be complicit in this vast provincial conspiracy to talk everything up, to find uniqueness where there was none, to acclaim a 'specialness' that they knew and I knew did not exist.

I couldn't let it go unchallenged, this piling up of myth upon myth of local pride.

'Really? The biggest in China, are you sure?'

'Why, of course. It has 540 metric tonnes of water in it. That's pretty damn big.'

'Sure, but I don't think that makes it the biggest. There are lakes in Tibet . . .'

'Of course it's the biggest, that's why it's famous!' They both looked at each other as if I was crazy.

'Anyway, how would you know? You've never even seen it!'

At this they both laughed and I smiled weakly. Their logic and the unspoken assumption that as a foreigner I did not really 'get it' defeated me. I slumped in my chair and offered up my glass as a toast.

'To the glories of Henan!'

'To the glories of Henan!'

On a personal level, the human desire to believe in something other than a glorious Chinese civilisation or the size of China's lakes is becoming more and more apparent. Many Chinese have turned to religion – Protestantism, Catholicism, or semi-spiritual movements such as the Falun Gong, a sort of quasi-Buddhist aerobics – for answers. Despite periodic crackdowns there is every sign that such 'cults', as the Beijing authorities like to call them, are flourishing. The desperate need for something to believe in, a source of new pride, can also be viewed in the urban populations' reaction to the national football team. The hapless squad has become the lightening rod of nationalist aspirations and their repeated failure to date to beat any teams of note was a source of national embarrassment.

I was at the first match between another national side, England, since the Tiananmen demonstrations of 1989.

Thousands had crammed into the Workers' Stadium in Beijing to catch the historic moment. Millions more watched on television. At last the Chinese team would be playing someone worth playing. There were high hopes.

The festival atmosphere remained unharmed by Paul Gascoigne's drunken comments to a local journalist at the airport.

'So, Mr Gascoigne, what are your first thoughts on being here in China?'

'Fook – *belch* – we're only here for the fookin' money . . .' (scuffling as Bryan Robson appeared and dragged him onto the team bus.)

The Chinese politely ignored these comments and all hopes were concentrated on the big Wednesday night game. Football has a huge following in China, and over 80 million people regularly watch English Premiership matches on TV. In Beijing, the capital's taxi drivers are famous for the fanaticism with which they follow the sport. Taking a taxi to the game, we were regaled with the name of every club in the Premiership and their key players. There were people on the streets in large numbers, singing, blowing trumpets and banging drums – an unusual sight in modern-day China. The government's fear of large numbers of people congregating to chant slogans on the street is self-evident. The last time anyone tried this in Beijing, the tanks were brought in. Inside, the Workers' Stadium was packed to the gunnels. The roll of noise was impressive and quite thrilling; a passion that no authority could hope to compete with. The game began.

One-nil, two-nil . . . the carnival atmosphere gradually ebbed away to be replaced by a stadium seething with indignation at the Chinese team. And then the final humiliation . . . three-nil to the English team. The Chinese national team were quite simply out of their league. The English supporters, not numerous, gradually lapsed into silence as the enormity of the local disappointment and sense of grievance became obvious.

'*Si bi ling!*' ('four-nil!') screamed the crowd, urging the English players on.

Streams of vile invective fell on the Chinese players' heads. If a player hesitated, passed the ball back, or lost possession, a fury of noise erupted. Faces in the crowd were contorted with rage. Fingers were pointed, voices raised and cheeks flushed. Whenever an England player won possession of the ball there was a loud cheer. When Paul Gascoigne (known as Gazza even in Beijing) dribbled past his opposite number, and then another player, an enormous cheer swept around the stadium, then furious shouting. Their own players had let them down.

After the game, people went home quietly. No shouting, trashing of cars, or breaking of windows. People were, in football-speak, 'gutted'. The English fans furled up their flags and pointed their painted faces at the ground. Who could celebrate such a comprehensive defeat of such well-meaning foes?

A couple of days later, after passions had cooled, I broached the subject of the match with some colleagues. It was not a light matter, and the game was approached with a heavy sigh and lowered voices, as if discussing a death or some terrible natural disaster.

'So humiliating!'

'Pampered lazy playboys!'

'Feeble cowards!'

'Wankers!'

This was combined with comments about their expensive and inappropriate private lifestyles, limousines, the best restaurants, call girls and nightclubs. In opinion polls the country has consistently voted the men's soccer team China's most hated institution, along with China Telecom.

'They don't care whether they win or lose!' ventured one friend.

I found this hard to believe, having seen the crowd's visceral reaction to a lost fixture. A continual theme was the lack of mental and physical preparedness of the team. They were viewed as just not tough enough to take on the bigger, more aggressive and fitter Western sides. Whatever the reasons offered, everyone agreed it was a source of national shame and humiliation.

'China is such a big country, but we can't produce a halfway decent football team!'

Maybe next time, I ventured optimistically.

Asked about the possibility of the national side qualifying for the 2002 World Cup, a former assistant coach to the Chinese team, Keith Blunt, was brutal.

'I don't think they have a cat-in-hell's chance.'

Luckily for millions of rapturous Chinese and bruised national pride, the Chinese team proved him wrong, beating Oman 1-0 to qualify for the Cup for the first time in history. As one local paper wrote, 'It is time to cry happy tears for the long-awaited triumph national football fans deserve.'

So why did it take so long? One answer, according to the current South American coaching assistant, was the puzzling paucity of matches with good international sides despite many interested teams' desire to play the PRC. There was a fear of losing. When asked why they played so few international games he was told, 'We are Chinese and we don't want to lose face.'

The Chinese reverence for statistics also contributed. There was an obsession with how many times each side had won or lost against the other. This was, of course, to the Chinese team's disadvantage – they had only ever lost.

Chapter Eight

Not the Real Thing

A chaotic society riddled with corruption and stultification, a society racked by the politics of enslavement, perverse morality, an overly self-centred world view, and the worship of power and money, a society where normal human intelligence has become so ossified that little of it remains intact.

— Bo Yang, *The Ugly Chinaman*

Under the heading 'City That Dances The Night Away' the *Independent*'s former correspondent in China visited Zhengzhou and found formation street dancing in the evenings, under a flyover. When asked why this seemed a popular phenomenon, Ms Chai, the dance instructor replied: 'People want to make a more colourful life, especially older women.'

The search for a brighter time and some respite from a life of grinding routine is not a phenomenon confined to the elderly population of Zhengzhou. For many people in China, temporary relief from day to day concerns is near at hand in the thousands of karaoke houses that stretch from north to south, east to west. They often provide the only source of entertainment. From two-roomed holes in the wall to glittering temples of hedonism, from urban yuppies to provincial officials, from those seeking illicit pleasures to those who just want a night out with friends; there is something for everybody. Even President Jiang Zemin has the need for the odd karaoke session now and then. At a meeting of Asian leaders in 1996 Jiang finished the evening by serenading the wide-eyed dignitaries with a rousing rendition of Elvis Presley's 'Love Me Tender'. (Asked later why he chose this song, Jiang said he knew Bill Clinton was an Elvis fan.)

In the more sophisticated cities such as Beijing, Shanghai and Guangzhou, multiplex centres combining karaoke, restaurant and disco have emerged. Wood panelling, frosted glass and leather seats provide an upmarket environment where fashion conscious youths spend their monthly salaries on drinking, talking, singing, eating and dancing. Expensive, and pulsing to the latest in Western and Hong Kong dance music, these places are a new and very different variation on the more established variety.

Traditional karaoke haunts, often the only entertainment after dark in provincial cities, rely on gaudy glitz and an army of 'hostesses'. Their customers are exclusively groups of businessmen and officials spending someone else's money. As well as a warren of snug, private rooms, there is often one main room for dubious 'fashion shows' to keep the guests entertained. These often start with garish ballgowns and towering headdresses, and finish with women skipping around on stage in a state of undress. Sometimes there are embarrassing attempts at modern dance, which involve an awkward semi-nudity, frozen frowns and a lot of rolling around on the floor.

After the show one can disappear back to a private room, where a procession of young women will visit you until you have chosen several to sit and sing with you for the night. Plates of sculpted fruit, cigarettes, beer and brandy are ordered. While there is much holding of hands, adolescent cuddling and singing of sentimental love ballads, that is as far as it goes for the majority of guests. Here the tyranny of the group in China exerts a mildly restraining effect as it is considered impolite to disappear until the party has broken up or the honoured guest has retired. By this time the majority of guests are either too drunk or too tired to take matters further, even if they wanted to.

While undoubtedly seedy and sometimes sordid, for the most part there seemed an air of artlessness about the whole thing. There was nothing remotely sexual about the experience. On many lost nights of karaoke and drinking, most of the guests I saw got so drunk that they were incapable of moving, let alone disappearing with a woman and embarking on a night of passion.

At the end of the evening, one would walk past rooms where three or four men in suits lay sprawled on the sofas, asleep, snoring or staring with glazed eyes at the television. The girls had all long since disappeared. It seemed a ritual whereby at a price, privacy was obtained. In these dark cocoons of red carpet and plush sofas, men could talk more openly with each other while getting fantastically drunk. They could bond. The hostesses seemed an afterthought. Not surprisingly, they appeared bored to death. I was amazed by their capacity to put up with the atrocious nightly singing, not to mention the lecherous middle-aged men.

'It must be boring,' I ventured to my neighbour, a quiet woman with a false smile. Her colleagues were leading others in the room in a lusty singalong of 'Take Me Home Country

Roads'. (Other all time favourites include 'Top of the World', 'Sha-la-la-la' and 'You Were Always On My Mind'.)

'It is not as boring as my home town.'

'Do you have a boyfriend?'

'Yes.'

'Doesn't he mind you working here?'

'Yes, but it is good money and besides he is a layabout – he can't complain.'

'It must be boring to sing all those songs again and again.'

'It's OK, I like singing . . .'

With that she keyed in a number on the console and minutes later we were singing a sickly duet while on screen a Chinese couple frolicked on a sandy beach.

The karaoke capital of China is undoubtedly Dongguan, a city that more than any other promoted the social acceptability of getting drunk and singing badly in front of friends and colleagues whilst holding hands with a complete stranger. In Dongguan, a new city close to Hong Kong, the karaoke experience is as close to singing in a brothel as is allowed.

Huge neon temples to bawdy behaviour with marble, mirrors, grandiose rococo decorations, smoked glass and thick carpets. Suitably subservient waitresses hovered at every elbow, directed by fierce female sergeant-majors with walkie-talkies. The difference in the Dongguan karaoke experience is its disconcerting size as much as its decadence. Dongguan's proximity to Hong Kong means the karaoke scene is flush with the salaries of lonely Hong Kong businessmen. Hundreds of young women in cocktail outfits wait to entertain behind glass walls in the lobbies. There is a murmur and movement as a group of businessmen enter; someone recognised, someone new. Some of the women push themselves forward. A Madam tut-tuts them back. They retreat slightly, jostling, like a group of runners on the start line before a race.

The traditional culture of the hostess in China is fuelled by poverty and the lack of opportunities for today's provincial women. No longer content to stay at home and wait to get married off, many want the chance to make some money and have some independence. Short of outright prostitution, options are limited for the unconnected or those without higher education degrees. (Only 2 per cent of people attend university in China.) In Beijing, Guangzhou and Shanghai, the majority of women who work in the karaoke industry come from inland secondary cities, such as Xian, Zhengzhou and Shenyang. In the secondary cities they come from smaller towns, and in the smaller towns from the countryside; a neat hierarchy of desperate ambition. With generous clients who tip, however, many can earn far more than in a more respectable environment.

I first stumbled upon this world of purposeful personal economic progress as a pathetically naive businessman in southern China.

In a hotel disco a woman approached and sat down.

'You are . . . very . . . beautiful,' she said in English.

'Er . . . thank you.'

Switching to Mandarin, we managed to skip the more self-conscious standard lines and talked about her and her life. She was from Xian and her parents owned a hardware shop. It was taken away from them in the late 1950s and her parents were put to work in a steel factory. Now the steel factory had shut down, and they had decided to open a store again. But they didn't earn much and that was why she had come to Guangzhou, to make some money.

'What do you do during the day?' I asked.

'Hairdresser,' she said, rearranging her dress. 'Do you like to dance? I love it! Come on!'

We walked hand in hand to the dancefloor and I moved amongst other self-conscious Western and Hong Kong businessmen.

She was an atrocious dancer. She shifted her weight from foot to foot in an attempt at moving with the music, with an occasional skip or hop. What was more disconcerting was her obvious lack of interest. Her eyes wandered over the other dancers and gradually her movements became more and more listless. I felt embarrassed and foolish. I mean, did she want to dance or not? Hadn't she asked me? The song finished, the feeble dancing stopped and everyone headed back to their darkened corners.

Back at our table, I drained my drink and made 'I'm-getting-ready-to-leave' movements.

'Canyoupaymenow!' It came out like a bullet.

'Er . . . I'm sorry?'

'Canyoupaymenow!'

From the intonation it was obvious that this was not a request, but a demand. A verbal printout of some transaction that had taken place.

'But, I mean . . . we haven't done anything!'

'Incorrect. I have talked with you, danced with you and had a beer with you, in short, I have kept you from being alone.'

Right. Um. OK. I thought for a moment before choosing a reply that would not offend, but would try to seek a common ground; we were after all roughly the same age. Patronisingly, I explained that in the West it is possible to have a drink with a girl and a dance, and not have to hand over any money.

'People do this because they like each other's company . . . maybe they are even attracted to each other,' I added somewhat optimistically.

'Ah. Not in China. China is a developing economy. Now pay up.'

It was in karaoke joints that I spent a disproportionate amount of my life in China. It was here that business relationships were formed, problems ironed out, objectives agreed and terms and conditions made clear. It was a place where intimacy (not always welcome) between two parties was encouraged; the sharing of hopes and concerns. Company team evenings out would always incorporate karaoke at the end of the evening. Drunken singing exercises in team building. As drink flowed it was a chance to view people's characters in a less inhibited environment. Was that earlier suspicion justified? Was he a bully? Could she be trusted? Could we really work together in the absence of any legal redress in China? Gradually the drinking takes over, the girls seem more attractive, the singing gets worse and several people in the room fall asleep. Trays of Heineken, 555 cigarettes and fresh fruit cut into animal shapes are replaced. The music and alcohol encourages an emotional exhibitionism which, for a naturally reserved people, is not easily glimpsed during the day.

On occasions the alcohol fuelled resentment. In one karaoke joint in Shenyang a wholesaler I was with, denied his favourite singing companion, went on a rampage, smashing doors and throwing glasses and bottles around. The girls fled from the room. His colleagues gradually restrained him and he was led away. My own exit was blocked by several hostesses demanding payment for the evening and compensation for the wholesaler's threatening behaviour. One by one they broke into mournful, loud wailing. I hurriedly handed over crumpled 100 yuan notes. The protestations abruptly stopped. A strip of textbook paper with a pager number was pressed into my palm.

'See you tomorrow night?' said a high sweet voice.

The Coca-Cola saga continued. I criss-crossed Henan county in a low-slung maroon VW sedan with the monosyllabic Mr Zhu. Luohe, Nanyang, Zhumadian, Xucheng. Dots on the map but containing millions of people living out their lives. In Anyang I stood on the pavement in front of a new white-tiled office decorated with red banners and large gold characters. I gave a short speech while to my left four local girls in red *cheongsam* and sashes stood erect. They all looked distinctly uncomfortable at being at the centre of attention. Two Coca-Cola dispensers were lined smartly up and after some polite clapping, free plastic cupfuls were handed out to a scrum of children. A crowd of onlookers had formed behind the seated VIPs.

Later at lunch, one tipsy wholesaler confided that it had taken him a while to work out what I was saying.

'When you opened your mouth I thought I wouldn't understand you because you would be speaking foreign words. But then I realised you were speaking our language!'

We toasted the prosperity of the office. On the long drive back I wondered if this was an elliptical statement that referred not to my language capabilities, but to the exhortations to future wealth and prosperity in the speech.

In Xucheng, salesman Wang and I lunch on *guotie*, fried dumplings, in bowls of vinegar. A hundred faces in the cheap restaurant turn to face us. Wang goes red. It is a long time since I have been stared at in China. The last time was probably in Changchun. A sign that this part of Henan is definitely off the tourist map. I ignore the stares. Wang is embarrassed and slurps nosily on his dumplings. Later he tells me that he felt very uncomfortable.

'It is not healthy to attract so much attention,' he says. 'I am glad I am not a foreigner in Henan.'

On the way to a muddy wholesale street market we leave an alley and turn right into a maelstrom of people and noise. Wang and I are pushed together. Horns blow, children shout. I stick my head over the crowd and am confronted by a giant looking down on me. A masked face juts forward to cymbals clashing. Stick-like arms shake. I am momentarily disoriented by the sudden burst of colour in this grey city. I can't tell whether this mannequin is real or not. The face looks real but the body is distorted. The tall puppets pass by, and from behind I catch sight of a small boy standing on the shoulders of a man wielding sticks as limb extensions. I ask Wang what it is.

'I don't know. Peasant stuff.'

We received reports of fake Coca-Cola on the market. Hundreds, maybe thousands of bottles. Salesmen brought bottles of the stuff back as proof. The company lawyer was put on the case and after several weeks was ready for a visit to the offending establishment which had been located with the help of the police. I was invited along. We drove in a small convoy with policemen to a warehouse complex near a railway junction. Inside the gloom of one of the warehouses was a huge humming vat. At the bottom beneath a tap was a line of plastic Coke bottles waiting to be filled. A man was bent over the tap, filling the bottles one by one. Brown frothing liquid filled the bottle in seconds, then he handed it over to a boy who inserted it in some sort of carbonating device rather like the ones many families had in the late 1970s in the UK. Between swigs, another man screwed the tops on.

A large man in a stained vest emerged from a door in the wall, putting on a shirt.

'What do you want?'

'Lu Ying Wei! You are under arrest!' said the senior policeman.

'What for?'

'For selling illegal counterfeit products.'

'This isn't fair! How can I make real Coca-Cola when the recipe is a secret?'

This was a rhetorical question aimed at all of us. Our silence in the face of such clear logic served to embolden Mr Lu.

'You see! They keep it locked up tighter than a cow's cunt in Washington!'

'Atlanta,' said Little Liu, the keen salesman to my left.

'Atlanta, Washington, New York, Ningxia. What's the fucking difference?' growled Mr Lu.

The senior police officer tried to pull the proceedings back into line. The conversation was taking on a surreal edge.

'You are not allowed to sell imitation products. Besides, your liquid could be dangerous.'

'Dangerous? It's delicious! I am willing to do the Pepsi challenge with anyone – you pick the time and place!'

With this challenge to the new economic order he thrust a sticky bottle into the hands of the police officer and stuck out his chin. The lawyer made as if to confiscate several bottles for analysis. Lu screamed abuse at him, and he jumped back as if scalded. No one wanted a violent scene. There were regular stories in the local press about police, lawyers and company employees attempting to close down counterfeit operations and being beaten up by mobs of angry locals, furious at the loss of a profitable business.

'OK. Let's all calm down. Why don't we go into your office and talk about this?' said the senior cop.

'OK,' said Mr Lu. The lawyer and two police officers wandered off into the gloom of the warehouse.

As cigarette smoke and the sound of arguing voices wafted out, I wandered around with Little Liu and chatted with other members of the illegal operation. We were invited to inspect the bubbling vats and climbed up a metal staircase that led to an aerial view of the warehouse. The vat was open from the top. A large pipe swung in from the left. ('That's where the ingredients enter,' explained a helpful employee.) A sea of dark liquid bubbled below. There was a strange smell. On one side of the room was a mountain of second-hand Coca-Cola bottles and next to them thousands of red screw tops. Next to that were hundreds of stolen Coca-Cola crates filled with the offending drink.

Following my gaze the helpful employee pointed out that far from creating trouble, they were recycling for the benefit of the community.

'What do you put in it?' I asked.

'Oh, the usual stuff. Water, colouring, sugar, but we also have our own recipe. But I'm not allowed to say.'

'Why don't you create your own name?' I asked.

'How can we compete against a huge company like Coca-Cola? Everyone knows 'a mouthful of happiness'!'

We climbed down and waited outside by the cars with the drivers, smoking. At length the police officers, the lawyer and Mr Lu emerged. Everyone shook hands and we drove off. There was a general sense of relief.

The lawyer explained the deal that had been struck as we bumped along a dirt track. Mr Lu would cease production immediately, but would be allowed to sell what was left in his warehouse. There would be no prosecution, but there would be a ceremonial destruction of his equipment in the presence of local journalists the following week for the county campaign against fake and shoddy goods. Mr Lu would apologise in public and promise never to engage in similar activity again. If he did, said the lawyer, he would be thrown in jail immediately. The Coca-Cola plant would be happy at closing the back room operation and getting its destruction publicised as a deterrent against other Mr Lus. The local government would be happy at avoiding an expensive and tedious trial, and Mr Lu would be happy at avoiding prison and keeping most of his profits.

'A good resolution of this problem,' I volunteered.

'Very good,' said the lawyer.

There was one part of the province that none of the drivers or salesmen were keen on visiting at all. This was Wenlou and the surrounding area. Towards the end of my time in Henan a story that was only a rumour began to appear in the local papers. Later it made national headlines. From the mid-1980s thousands of poor peasants in the province became in effect professional blood-sellers to the local health authorities. Paid nearly 40 yuan a time to donate blood, it became a profitable and respectable way to earn some money.

'I sold my blood at the state-owned hospital in 1992. We sold the blood to pay the local taxes and also to help support our kids through school and make a living,' said one woman when interviewed by a regional paper. She was from Wenlou, a village where over 65 per cent of the population is HIV positive.

'Everybody in the village was selling blood. They [the local authorities] said it was a glorious and harmless thing to do,' she added.

Unfortunately for the impoverished donors, the blood collectors never tested the suitability of those donating blood, and used the same needles again and again with no disinfecting procedure. Blood from several people was mixed together and, after extracting plasma, pooled red blood cells were often re-injected into blood-sellers to prevent problems such as anaemia.

It wasn't until the mid-1990s when villagers were having their 'strange fever' diagnosed as HIV in droves that people realised there was a connection with the blood donations.

'I don't know how many times [I donated] but if you took all the blood I sold and put it into a barrel you wouldn't be able to lift it up,' said one villager, now HIV positive.

It is estimated that over half a million people in Henan have contracted HIV with some 10,000 in the area surrounding Wenlou. The trade in blood was covered up by provincial leaders and those detained by police for organising the donations secured release by paying bribes or fines.

'We don't have any hope; we don't have any money or medicine. We are just waiting to die,' said the woman. 'But we hope the person who is responsible for this tragedy, the blood collector, will be arrested,' she said.

Back at the factory things were progressing. A new, more transparent and effective sales system was put in place and some of the more corrupt sales staff had been fired. A young Hong Kong manager had been hired to direct marketing efforts and despite receiving a death threat from a disaffected former employee, had decided to make a go of it. But it was grindingly slow. I could see a lifetime of karaoke, inebriation, concrete and Coca-Cola stretching out before me. I was becoming disillusioned with the need for the continuous cultivation of relationships, the provincial arrogance, the endemic corruption and the constant references to a continuous civilisation stretching back 3,000 years (or was it 5,000?) while all around was the disorganised despotism that is provincial China.

The plane lands with a thump in Beijing. The taxiing to the terminal is accompanied by the click-clack of 200 seat buckles being undone. Tannoy pleas for people to remain in their seats until the plane comes to a halt are ignored and within seconds the plane is a mass of people leaping up, grabbing cases, swinging elbows and putting on coats. Phones ring and self-important businessmen shout ostentatiously to their chauffeurs that they have arrived ('*Gang gang dao!*'). People stand, fully coated and baggaged up for several minutes until the doors are opened. There is a slow wave of pushing and shoving that sweeps the queue. As the door opens and the noise of the engine fills the cabin, there is a pre-emptive push for a superior grid position, which is momentarily stayed by the three flight attendants. Once the stairs are connected however, there is no stopping the surge of people off the plane. I sit in my seat while fellow-passengers trudge past. One carries a newspaper with the headline 'ARMED GANGSTERS BESEIGE POLICE STATION IN HENAN.'

I was exhausted and tired of life amongst China's toughest provincials in the heart of China, and above all, the tedious insistence on drinking. I didn't want to drink anymore. I couldn't drink anymore. My growing concern as to the effects on my health of an almost daily combination of alcohol, cigarettes and fried food (albeit delicious) had begun to manifest itself in a nauseous reaction to any food whatsoever. Visiting a doctor in Beijing, I was informed that I had all the symptoms of 'banquet fever'. Apparently this is a new affliction peculiar to foreign businessmen who believe they can eat and drink on a large scale without suffering any side effects. It is the body saying enough is enough. I felt slightly embarrassed but relieved and somehow vindicated. Medical confirmation of my weary condition. I would be 'invalided out' of mercantile service and the Coke Mission.

My inability to take a more evangelical approach to sales was another deciding factor. Like a missionary without a strong faith, I had become prone to self-doubt and was becoming less and less effective. Did I feel guilty about promoting that icon of Western imperialist-capitalist domination in the heart of China? I don't think so. But it was hard to take the Mission seriously, and there perhaps lay my fatal weakness. Sales managers can't have doubts. They are meant to be focused, keen and energetic. They are the blitzkrieg gang of the operation. Shoot first, ask questions later. After all, if they don't believe, who will?

If I stayed I felt I would end up like some lonely Graham Greene character, occupying a formal position abroad, but in reality doomed to aimless drifting and alcoholism.

My time in Henan was beginning to affect my view of China. Would I end up as bitter about Chinese culture as someone else who spent too long in Henan, Guo Yidong? Born in Kaifeng in 1920, Guo Yidong wrote a famous book called *The Ugly Chinaman* under the pseudonym Bo Yang, in which he excoriated Chinese culture and society. It seemed more than a coincidence that the harshest critic of Chinese society should have spent his formative years in Henan. I liked China and its people, they were a constant, frustrating fascination. Yet I was tired of Henan and capitalism with Chinese characteristics. Perhaps I should be doing something else. Perhaps, after several years working in China, it was time for a break.

Darkness enveloped the airport and surrounding industrial countryside. In the back of the taxi I sank further into my padded greatcoat and shared a cigarette with the driver.

'Where have you come from? London?'

'No, Zhengzhou,' I replied.

'Aiya! What are you doing there?'

'I live there.'

'When are you returning?'

'I'm not sure.'

That weekend, while at a party in one of the foreign compounds where the Beijing government likes to corral foreign journalists and diplomats, a man walked into the room who would interrupt the unwilling rhythm of my life in Henan as low-flying corporate salesman. Amidst the chink of glass, cigarette smoke and waves of conversation, he cut a strange figure in a beige safari suit, with shorts that seemed just that little bit too tight. Small and wiry, he lacked the knee-length socks that could have identified him as either a scout master or a white African farmer. Either of these would still have required some explanation in Beijing.

Instead, from his knees to his ankles, there was a series of bloody scratches as if he had been attacked by a pair of vicious house cats. Round his neck, nestling in his blond chest hair, was a piece of leather with a large tooth hanging off it. He moved quickly and deftly around the room with a sort of controlled aggression. When he stopped, small knots of admirers would form. With excited eyes they listened to quiet understated stories, sometimes in Mandarin, sometimes in English, of his journeys outside the capital.

'Who's the boy scout?' I asked my neighbour.

'Harry. He works at the embassy. Not quite sure what he does.'

Later in the evening we were introduced and I asked him about his scratches. Staring down at his ankles, he explained that last week he had been sleeping rough on the Mongolian plain when he had been attacked by a wild dog. He had had to run through some thorny bush to find a piece of wood or a stone with which to defend himself and ultimately kill the beast. The tooth was from the dog.

We chatted on about travelling in China. I listened

attentively, ignoring the worrying shorts and feeling increasingly unable to engage in a conversation that didn't feature any of the lodestars of corporate life in the soft drinks sector. I realised that my points of reference would produce a polite blankness from this man. Karaoke, sales targets, monthly plans and distribution strategies would fail to provide a suitable basis for conversation. Moreover, I knew that his silence would confirm what I already knew to be the case. That the industrious struggle in Henan to sell someone else's soft drink was a surreal and ridiculous way to spend one's time in the Middle Kingdom.

Sensing my frustration, Harry spoke for me.

'This isn't the real China,' he said, looking round the room full of other people selling things. 'The real China is out there,' he raised his chin to an indeterminate horizon.

We stared at each other, then, hitching up his shorts and smoothing down his safari top, he shook my hand and was gone.

The next day in Beijing I bought a gleaming black and chrome Changjiang (Yangtze) 750, a locally made motorbike and sidecar. Squat, heavy and thoroughly unreliable, I kept it in a garage in Beijing and back in Henan I dreamt of a trip west across China's open spaces to the Pamirs. I was ready for one more adventure.

PART TWO

Chapter Nine

On the Road

Monday morning, but no sales meeting. I had resigned. Dolly Parton's 'Nine to Five' played on Beijing local radio. Laid out on the wooden floor was a map of China. Five of us sat around with tea and cigarettes staring at the different coloured markings, lines and shadings on the expanse of paper. The huge distances had me mesmerised and reminded me of the first time I had really looked at a map of China in a university corridor, next to advertisements for English teachers in Wuhan. Sitting on the floor were four others who had arrived in Beijing with the army of adventurers, sinologists and corporate pioneers. For different reasons we were all ready to leave and travel west across China to the border. On motorbikes and sidecars.

The idea of travelling together belonged to Tim, who was openly contemptuous of his job selling aeroplanes. I admired him in his role as Europe's aviation ambassador for carrying nothing in his expensive leather briefcase but a pair of socks, a pen and an old newspaper. The tools of the high-powered international businessman revealed. We hoped, in vain as it turned out, that having had a previous life in the army he would bring some robust practicality to our enterprise. Next to sign up was Fim, who had had enough of Han China thanks to too long spent in an ailing engineering joint venture in Shandong province. Then there was Ed, an English comprador whose knowledge of the political currents in Beijing was recognised by all. For five years he had followed the political and economic policy shifts of the government on behalf of Western business. There wasn't a minister he didn't have a file on, a restaurant he hadn't eaten at, or a commercial development he didn't know about. Now he was ready for a break. Finally, Dominic, whose desire for an adventure on motorbikes was stronger than the pull of a plush existence in advertising.

Despite having lived in China for some years, none of us had had the opportunity to visit the barren but enigmatic western provinces. We had been too busy selling things. Its mountains, deserts, unbelievable heat, poor roads, vast distances and random officialdom do not encourage a casual visit. Across an area the size of France a sparse population, including millions of China's ethnic minorities, huddle around a string of oases that stretch to the border. At the end is Kashgar, for hundreds of years a travellers' town and the only romantic city left in China. Beyond, the Pamirs meet the Karakoram, the other side of which lies the North-West Frontier province of northern Pakistan.

Not only were we going to cross China from east to west, and hopefully go even further, we were going to do it on the Changjiang 750. An unreliable but shapely local motorbike and sidecar named after the country's most powerful river. The same bike that still sat under a sheet in a garage, three months after I bought it in a moment of resolution on a weekend break from Zhengzhou. I had used it once, to go to a bar a few blocks away. We had one each.

We would be travelling along the ancient Silk Road, a collection of routes, which were the only link between East and West for centuries. Until the fourteenth century, merchants, scholars, soldiers, priests and diplomats all shuttled back and forth along this corridor in an exchange of goods and ideas that was to profoundly affect the history and culture of both Europe and Asia. More recently, in this century explorers and archaeologists have criss-crossed the region in search of the rich ancient sites that lie buried under the desert. It seemed a completely appropriate way to leave China.

'The yellow bit, that's desert right?' asked Dom. Hoots of laughter.

I was pleased Dom was coming on the trip because apart from being good company, it was quite obvious he was shaping up to be as impractical on the manly side of motorbiking as myself. Slightly cherubic in appearance, his refusal to travel without any of life's creature comforts was impressive. His purchase of a large tent complete with front awning for sitting under with deckchairs, and the most expensive sleeping bag available confirmed that he, like me, would need time to grow into the new role of hardened biker.

My finger followed the route we would take: Baotou, Yinchuan, Turfan, Urumqi, Kashgar, Tashkurgan, Pakistan. Afterwards we would take it one country at a time, hopefully all the way to London. The distances had us all grinning. As I looked at the map and tried to imagine the journey, it was clear that anything might happen and it might end anywhere.

In 1935 when Peter Fleming, *The Times'* correspondent, headed for the mountain ranges that mark the western end of China, he had employed three elderly Chinese to have lice-filled boxes clamped to their legs for two hours per day.

Each box contained 500 lice and after feeding on the legs, they supplied an anti-typhus serum for Fleming and his companions. Such organised pre-trip preparation. In contrast, our pre-leaving activity was limited. Vaguely productive meetings would lead to the preparation of long lists of action items. This was followed by individual shopping expeditions for the required materials and equipment. The cavernous sidecars imposed little discipline on what not to take. Mine overflowed with spare parts, books, camping equipment, pots, pans, cutlery and clothes. Not quite as minimalist as Chinese writer Ma Jian who walked around western China in 1984 and packed 'a change of clothes, a notebook, two bars of soap, a water bottle, torch, a compass, 200 yuan, a wad of rice coupons, my camera and Walt Whitman's *Leaves of Grass*.'

Fim, six-foot tall and with rugged good looks, came with the stature of a real biker. He had actually owned one back in the UK. He even had a photo. Not only was he comfortable with a tool kit, his bike had already been customised for speed and sound effects and had done some mileage. Mine had yet to do six miles. It was Fim who suggested we should all run ours around a bit before we left. After Dom tried to take his further afield on a trial run to the airport, I received a phone call.

'Simon?'

'Yes?'

'I've broken down.'

'Where are you?' I could hear the heavy rumble of traffic in the background.

'Somewhere near the airport.' Dom was shouting. 'What do I do?'

'How would I know? I know less than you. Maybe it's your regulator.'

'Which bit is that?'

'Behind the front wheel.'

'Where?' A traffic filled pause. 'Oh fuck! Do you have Fim's number?'

When Tim saw Dom the following day he scolded him in motherly tones.

'You should know better than to go out on your own.'

We left Beijing to the sound of bulldozers and jackhammers tearing the neighbourhood apart. Three weeks earlier red-painted characters had appeared on the doorways and walls of the warren of small wood and brick houses in the area. It was faintly medieval and reminded me of pictures in history books about the bubonic plague in London. Daubings on doors that signified life or death. The inhabitants of the condemned dwellings continued to live in their homes until the day of the appointed destruction. As the next-door neighbour's house was crushed, belongings were loaded up onto tricycles and then pedalled away.

Beijing was on a determined march into the Future. Nothing, not even neighbourhoods that had existed for hundreds of years, would stand in the way. In their place would be a block of expensive flats, a shopping mall or a wider road perhaps. The capital was hooked on Progress and Modernity. The scene was being repeated throughout the city. In the face of such powerful forces it seemed futile to protest or mourn the loss of traditional environments. In fact, it was an almost entirely foreign occupation to complain and express regret over the demolition of entire neighbourhoods of courtyard-style housing. Many locals, and especially younger Beijingers, had no such sentimental hang-ups. Apart from being dusty in summer and dark and damp in winter, it was like a small village; everyone knew everything about everyone else. What time you left in the morning, when you came back at night, what you had bought, whom you were seeing, whether you were happy or whether you were sad.

A friend explained: 'You don't know what it was like to live in these *hutongs*. People commented on everything. And those that didn't go out made more comments than those who lived a more normal life. For a teenage girl it was a very difficult and tortured existence. I much prefer the tower block where we live now. No one knows me.'

Anonymity is to be welcomed, even if this results in a grey, uniform, concrete and (reflective blue) glass city. Aside from a few large landmark monuments, the destruction of a previous Beijing is complete. Instead of pointed rooftops and wooden eaves, there are monstrous concrete constructions with mock pagodas on the top – an unconscious realisation of a heritage destroyed.

Our departure had an element of farce, which confirmed to those friends remaining in Beijing the unlikelihood of any of us making it to the next city, let alone the border with Pakistan 3,000 miles away. After a hastily arranged photo and drinks session with friends outside the huge rust-coloured walls of the Forbidden City, our leaving was delayed by the temporary loss of the key to one of the bikes. After much swearing, packing and unpacking, Ed found it in one of the many pockets on his new brightly coloured jacket. When we did finally depart, three of us rode off in one direction and two in the other. A frustrated news cameraman attempting to film our departure from the back window of a car screamed at us.

'You're going the wrong way!'

We hadn't even left Beijing.

We found each other on the third ring road and headed west as an enormous red sun slowly sank into the horizon ahead of us. I picked my way through the traffic atop a motorbike and sidecar that I did not fully understand, but which I had lovingly polished for the previous three weeks in heady anticipation. Cars hooted and people stared at our little convoy. The road emptied of other vehicles, and soon we were on a wide vista of tarmac with nothing on it but our five bikes; a dual carriageway of delight. I laughed and grinned from ear to ear. We were away.

Thirty miles north-west of Beijing is a cultivated green valley where the imperial dead of the Ming Dynasty rest in thirteen large tombs spread amongst pine trees and farmland. Known collectively as the Ming Tombs, one or two have been restored to pristine condition complete with coach parking, souvenir shops, ticket collectors and snack stalls. Several though remain untouched and hidden away from the casual visitor. Surrounded by dark cypress trees and high terracotta-coloured walls, smooth steps lead into weed-covered courtyards, crumbling archways and finally to the dilapidated tombs themselves. Single stone steles stand on the backs of giant stone tortoises, symbols of longevity. Overhead, birds nest in sloping roofs that threaten to disintegrate. It was in this still, regal graveyard that we spent our first night on the road.

I felt a quiet sense of satisfaction – 30 miles! Not bad. This was the farthest distance I had been on any motorbike, let alone the Changjiang 750. Maybe we would make it.

My naivety about the likely problems of riding such unreliable machines meant that I had left Beijing in a state of blissful ignorance. As an insurance policy though we had invited Xiao Li, a young Beijing mechanic, to come along. In truth, we had gone down on bended knee, begged and offered all sorts of inducements from the financial to a picture of nights under clear desert skies. This courtship went on for over two weeks and ended with Xiao Li agreeing to come as far as Urumqi, 2,000 miles to the west but over 1,000 miles short of the border. From Urumqi we would fly him back to Beijing. We hoped that by then we would know what we were doing with the bikes. We were buying large amounts of spare parts from his boss, a smooth ex-PLA man, and sometimes we wondered if he hadn't pressured Xiao Li into the trip in order to continue a lucrative selling opportunity. Initially reluctant at the prospect of bouncing around in a sidecar for a month, Xiao Li got into the spirit of things with his whole family turning out to see him off with the idiotic foreigners.

Tim asked him for his travelling kit to shove in one of the sidecars.

Xiao Li waved a toothbrush in reply.

'That's it?'

'That's it.'

'What about sleeping bag, extra clothes, goggles, maybe a tent?'

'Oh no, I haven't got any of that.'

Tim raised his eyes heavenwards. Ed assured him that this wasn't the placing of some macho marker in the sand before we had even started, but a signal that we would have to invest in some equipment for Xiao Li.

In the shade of one of the tombs we played at being adventurers and admired each other's bits of 'kit'. The interest we showed in these pieces of cloth, metal, plastic and canvas was probably a subconscious attempt to professionalise our amateur undertaking and make up for the lack of more thorough preparation. In a different age we might have made votive offerings, manufactured talismans or slaughtered a goat. Instead, we had bought large amounts of expedition equipment and convinced ourselves that such expensive gadgetry was crucial to the success of the journey. We 'ooohd' and 'aaahd' as each biker pulled forth yet another essential item: special fabric/metal/plastic containers, hats and helmets, expensive penknives, ingenious cookers, goggles and multicoloured ropes. My favourite was a small torch that could be attached to a stylish Velcro headband while Dom spent hours playing with a MiniDisc system that would ensure music in the evenings. He had taken on the responsibility for the first aid kit as he had known several Irish nurses in Beijing. A logic that worked as long as you didn't think about it for too long. None of us had asked him if actually knew what to do if there was an accident. To be fair, he had found a nurse to give us a fifteen-minute demonstration of the basics back in Beijing. But hungover and overexcited at our imminent departure, we had simply sniggered and giggled at this attempt to get serious.

Fim, the only one with any serious motorbike experience, was also the only one with a pair of tight black leather trousers. This set him apart from the rest of us who were clothed in a combination of reinforced Gore-Tex and wet-weather sailing jackets. I was convinced that Fim's biker trousers were completely impractical and the desert heat would make the leathers extremely uncomfortable. However, expressing doubt as to their practicality was not welcomed. I was therefore pleased when nearly four weeks later in the heat of the desert, Fim sped past me, trouserless, revealing white legs and a pair of skimpy pants (one of two pairs).

'Hot, yeah?' I shouted.

Fim scowled and pretended not to hear.

The acknowledged professional icon of the group was a handheld Global Positioning System loaned to us by a concerned friend. It was supposed to tell you exactly where you were. We all lovingly passed it around that first night – so professional looking. It was of course completely unnecessary, and proved useless in our clumsy hands. The one time we did use it, on the edge of the Gobi desert, the co-ordinates informed us that we were in the suburbs of Tokyo.

Awake under the childhood smell of new canvas, I found it difficult to sleep. Someone was snoring loudly. Was this going to happen every night? I lifted my head and looked out to see which tent it was coming from. Dom's 1970s family holiday-style canvas construct was illuminated from within, but silent. With a see-through porch extension I half expected it to have light fixtures and a folding shower. Looking out around the camp I located Xiao Li as the offender. I dropped my head back on the pillow. I had yet to tell my new biker colleagues that my fleeting visit to Britain to obtain a motorbike licence had ended in humiliating failure on a roundabout in south

London. As a foreigner in China a motorbike licence is not required; after China, it would be. I rolled over and adjusting the air in my brand new 'Wilderness' air-bed, decided that telling anyone now would lead to unnecessary worry and concern on my behalf. I resolved to wait for a more appropriate moment – perhaps the border itself?

Uncomfortable with my unspoken failure, I felt a need to make amends and prove myself now we that we were on the open road. The next morning, while waiting for the water to boil, I confidently perused the maps and announced that I was more than happy to be the map-reader. I had even bought, at some expense, a waterproof map-holder, the front of which was see-through, so theoretically one could strap it to the fuel tank or handlebars of the bike and take bearings as one went along.

At the beginning I did just that, but as our top speed was 50 miles per hour, punctuated by numerous breakdowns, our progress along the thin red line that marked the road west seemed painfully slow. After a few days, the map staring up at me only served to highlight how far we had to go. 'Only two thousand eight hundred and seventy-eight miles to the border!' It doesn't matter how heartily one says it, it is still a long way. The map was shoved into the sidecar boot. As it is, there are only two roads across China to Kashgar; one that skirts the north of the vast Taklamakan Desert, and one that edges round the south. It would take quite an effort to get lost.

We headed north-west through Hebei, the province that surrounds Beijing. Out past the Great Wall and beyond the tourist coaches and tacky commercialism of Badaling. To accommodate the thousands of visitors that come to this small section of China's most prized cultural relic, the government has built a smart motorway that cuts through the sandy rock of Hebei. We drove with the Wall high up on our left, festooned with pastel flags and advertising hoardings. (Kentucky Fried Chicken's Colonel Sanders occupies a prominent position here.) We rounded a bend and entered a tunnel dug underneath it. Emerging out of the reverberating darkness and into the sunshine on the other side, the road narrowed and straightened out. The traffic lessened and it seemed as if we had crossed some unmarked boundary. Behind, the watchtowers of the Great Wall stood sentinel along a mountain ridge, receding with each mile into the distance. This extraordinary monument to Han insecurity would appear again and again on our journey west until it stopped dead at Jiayuguan, a thousand miles away.

We drove through a green hilly land edged with bare brown mountains. Ploughed fields bumped up to the nearest hills. For the first few days there was the joyous air of an unexpected holiday as the scenery rolled past. An unreality to the whole undertaking, a growing realisation that *this was it*, the culmination of more than five years in China, a road trip across the Middle Kingdom.

There was little traffic apart from the odd minibus so stuffed with people that any movement inside seemed impossible. Peasant children ran to the side of the road and waved as we swept past. The sun shone. We passed enormous white characters carved into the hillside: 'Population control is everybody's responsibility.' We engaged in biker-like activities, riding in pairs, lots of eye contact and thumbs up signalling, helmetless of course. Every couple of hours we stopped for a cigarette break and discussed bike performance, comfort levels and checked spokes and oil. We were still holding our breath and savouring each moment; surely crossing the Middle Kingdom couldn't be this pleasant? At the same time I was conscious of having no idea how the bike worked. I could not picture how all the bits connected up in my head. While I realised that the regulator played a crucial part in ensuring the bike moved forward, I was lost as to its relationship with the other bits of the engine or why it sometimes refused to function. Three thousand miles later I would still be none the wiser.

The first man to travel through western China on two wheels was a German-American on a bicycle just after the turn of the century. He caused great excitement wherever he went and despite anti-foreign riots at the time, he returned unharmed. He attributed his successful journey to persistent smiles, great patience and playing a mouth organ whenever he felt slightly threatened. It wasn't until 1935 that the first person crossed China by vehicle. Sir Eric Teichmann, an English diplomat, drove from Beijing to Kashgar in a Ford truck.

We had only heard of two people who had driven across China by motorbike and specifically on Changjiang 750s. One biker was a German who had supposedly got as far as Munich. Despite a stunning lack of detail about his trip, we were all believers. This unnamed German became an inspiration to us all and his (apparent) success was proof that it could be done. The other was an Englishman called Will Brent who had got as far as Urumqi, the capital of China's furthermost western province, before heading back. Will had apparently broken all the rules in his three-wheeled bid for the border. He drove (a) someone else's bike (b) without papers (c) without helmet, sleeping bag or stove and (d) at night. But what impressed us most was that he had done it alone. While never openly acknowledged, the extra mental support provided by being in a group was a constant source of strength when elements or people conspired against us. To have crossed China without a shared moment with a fellow-conspirator seemed to us to propel Willie into another, almost Victorian, league of adventurers. True heroes, we knew, were solitary figures.

There was one story about Will's trip that we never tired of hearing. Having camped at night, he woke up one morning to find several villagers standing around him chuckling and clucking to themselves. Looking around, he saw that he had spent the night in what was the village latrine. We told this story with relish until, about three weeks later, we did the same. The temperature at night had been low enough to block out all the smell, but with the morning sun came the unmistakable stench of human shit, and just next to our sleeping bags were little mounds of excrement.

Chapter Ten

A Scarred Land

We camped in rustic splendour in the hills far above Hohot. The browns and greens of Inner Mongolia lay spread out before us in hazy hues as we slurped instant noodles from the local village store and sipped whisky. The previous night had seen us crouched in a ditch by the side of a cornfield as khaki-clad figures walked about and martial exhortations were tannoyed out across the countryside. We had inadvertently chosen to camp on military farmland. Outside Beijing, in Hebei, a vast swathe of countryside is farmed by and for the military. It is a major source of food for the million-strong PLA. While realising we had to drive through the area, we had had no idea of the sheer scale of the agriculture. By nightfall, we were still not out of this sensitive region and we had no choice but to turn down a track and remain as unobtrusive as possible. We didn't dare light a fire in case this attracted attention.

We retained a fear of being sent back to Beijing by some official. While not technically illegal, our trip was out of the ordinary enough to attract official interest and interference. Proof of official displeasure in seeing foreigners ride around on motorbikes was apparent when several weeks before we left it became almost impossible to buy Beijing license plates for the very motorbike and sidecars that we had. As it was, unknown to us, our departure from the Forbidden City had already been reported by Xinhua, the state news agency. We were in several Chinese newspapers the day after we left under the headline: 'FIVE ENGLISHMEN TO DRIVE TO LONDON ON CHANGJIAN 750s.' I'm not sure what was more newsworthy, the five foreigners driving to London bit or the 'on Changjiang 750s'; did the Chinese have even less faith in our trusty machines than we did?

We only found out we had made the papers weeks later while stopping for petrol. The cashier told us that he had read about us in the local paper. I felt guilty at having deceived the security guards on my tower block back in Beijing. I had told them we were off to Mongolia for the weekend.

It was strange to be sleeping in countryside where tannoyed instructions echoed amongst trees and across fields. I felt as if I was a fugitive in a cheap science fiction film. The disembodied compère of camp life broadcasted in fits and starts. Just when we were dozing off a guttural bark would jolt us awake. For a second we would freeze, wide-eyed, convinced a puttee-clad guard was standing over us, bayonet aloft, demanding we give ourselves up.

Until recently every aspect of 'public space' was a legitimate canvas for political chit-chat. Railway carriages used to have a tannoy that would blast out martial tunes, Beijing opera, instructions and 'news' (propaganda) at a decibel level just loud enough to prevent you from falling asleep or listening to your own music with headphones. In 'soft sleeper' these broadcasts could be avoided by simply flicking a switch in one's compartment. In 'hard seat' class (peasant and worker), no such luxury was available. On regular journeys this meant not only sitting in an upright position for over twelve hours, but also listening to politically correct operas (*Peasant Girls of Mount Wu Defeat Japanese Tank Division*) and endless economic reports with vast amounts of positive statistics. Personally, I found it unbearable. As students, during the night, we used to stand on each other's shoulders and physically dismantle the state's mouthpiece. I never saw a Chinese person do this and I always felt a bit guilty afterwards. Had someone actually been enjoying one of the broadcasts?

While these relics of a more political time can still be found on minor rail routes, on the big inter-city showcase runs, the programme of educating the masses continues in a different form. On televisions mounted at each end of the carriage, *The Capitalist Way* is now showing. Poor quality Hong Kong kung fu films are interspersed with dozens of adverts, karaoke hits, more adverts, news about celebrities (top leaders) and finally more of the same adverts. The volume is as loud and distorted as before. Perhaps learning from earlier incidents, the authorities have made it impossible for the travelling public to switch the television off.

In some villages the tannoy tradition lives on, broadcasting at set times while villagers carry on with their daily routines. Maybe the background of phantom official-like voices is vaguely comforting, like the shipping forecast in the UK. Certainly many of the urban Chinese we knew hated the countryside with a vengeance and the one damning epithet they would use was that it was 'too quiet'.

Inner Mongolia stretches in a 1,800-mile arc from the north-east of China towards the south-east. In contrast to its far larger, independent and more romantic sibling across the border, there has been large-scale Han immigration over several decades. Mongolians in Inner Mongolia are in a minority and account for less than 17 per cent of the total population. Traces of a former nomadic existence exist, but Beijing has never warmed to the idea of people just drifting around. Agricultural settlement and industrial development have been actively encouraged with a consequent sharp increase in population. With increased demands on water and the environment, the traditional grasslands of the region are suffering. According to official figures, of the 88 million hectares of grassland in Inner Mongolia, an estimated 44 per cent has turned or is turning into desert. It is no coincidence that along with neighbouring Ningxia and Gansu provinces, the region suffers the worst dust storms in China. These are increasing in their frequency and severity.

It was therefore perhaps not surprising that we had failed to see the traditional nomadic *ger*, a round tent made out of felt. In fact, the only one I had seen had been in Beijing during a bizarre evening at the Mongolian Embassy.

The new Mongolian trade minister was visiting the capital and there was a banquet at the Mongolian ambassador's residence, a large grey building in a leafy diplomatic area. I was invited as part of the small expatriate British business community. I was greeted at the enormous mahogany front door by an elderly Mongolian in white high-necked jacket, who spoke with a polished French accent.

'*Suivez-moi!*'

Following the stiff back of the embassy's major-domo along a high-ceilinged corridor, we turned left into a large room full of light. Here, grouped in small bunches, was a collection of European businessmen. Introduced to the extremely young

and affable trade minister, we were seated at round tables of
ten with our hosts and munched on peanuts and Mongolian
stew washed back with Genghis Khan vodka. The trade
minister and his entourage were young, keen and charming.
In short, totally unlike the average Chinese official one
encountered. Carried away by the vodka, I was soon drawing
plans on the tablecloth for large-scale beverage investment
in Ulan Bator and discussing joint venture law with the
nearest Mongolian official who looked about 16 years old.

'Mr Ma, I hope you can find time to come up to Ulan
Bator and look at the investment potential for your company.
We need hi-tech investment such as you can provide.'
Elevated from marketing fonctionnaire to industrial saviour,
I beamed with pride and launched enthusiastically into my
new role. Before I began to make truly outlandish promises,
the doors swung open and the grey-headed retainer appeared
again.

'*Son excellence l'ambassadeur vous attend!*' he boomed.

I had completely forgotten; there was still the ambassador
to meet. We exchanged excited glances. We were being
summoned in imperial style. Just as is should be, I thought.
I knocked back my chair in my haste, and an English voice
mocked, 'You must be patient to unlock the mysteries of the
East.'

I blushed but didn't care. After the logical, puritanical,
calculating and bureaucratic Chinese, at last here was a slice
of true Oriental despotism. Haughty, spontaneous, disdainful
and imperious. I hoped we would we be asked to kneel.

We followed the retainer down another long corridor and
stopped abruptly at large double doors. The doors were
pushed open and suddenly we were transported into a

different world. The walls of the room had ceased to exist and in their place was a warm woollen womb. Sitting cross-legged on the floor of a Mongolian *ger* was His Excellency, the Mongolian ambassador to the Communist court of Beijing. Embroidered rugs and cushions covered the floor while the walls of the tent were of dyed wool embroidered with traditional Mongolian patterns.

The odd polished gold plate lay across low tables and by the entrance was a massive tome, a visitor's book for us to sign. With a gentle wave of the hand we were beckoned in by the ambassador who wore a buttoned-up collarless shirt, and encouraged us to make polite conversation. Taking off our shoes, we sat down cross-legged and chatted.

'You must come to my country, it is a wonderful place.'

We all nodded. Could it be more magical than this?

The separation of Inner Mongolia (a province of China, albeit 'autonomous') and Mongolia proper (an independent country) is relatively recent. While there have always been divisions amongst the Mongols, Sino-Russian rivalry from the seventeenth century on ensured that these divisions were encouraged and exploited. After the fall of the Manchu Empire, the Russians supported first (outer) Mongolia's autonomy, and later its independence, which China eventually accepted. The Gobi desert, over 3,000 miles of stony sterility, straddles both of them like an ill-fitting quilt.

After ten minutes of conversation, the retainer and second commercial secretary appeared and asked us to leave. The ambassador needed to rest as he was to have another dinner that night – with the Chinese president. Suitably impressed, we withdrew. The large mahogany doors closed and we were back on the cold, dark Beijing streets.

Three Mao-jacketed old farmers with caps and cigarettes rolled with newspaper squatted together in a row to watch us deal with our first breakdown. One of the wheels on Dom's bike had buckled. In a field by the side of the road Fim and Tim had stripped off their shirts and had their forearms covered in black oil and grease. Xiao Li directed and handed over various tools while Fim shouted out requests for spanners as if in an operating theatre.

'Number ten. Number twelve. Number nine.'

Knowing little of mechanics at this stage, Dom and I made a pot of tea.

Villagers stared at the sight of two semi-naked foreigners huffing and puffing over an upturned bike. The three old men discussed the scene amongst themselves.

'Why did the wheel break?'

'Dunno.'

'I do. That foreigner is too fat.'

The bikes, the bikes. They dominated our lives. They dictated the pace of the journey as well as where and when we would stop. They were as capricious as any mule and reduced us to incoherent rages and tears on several occasions.

The Changjiang 750 is a beautiful but lumbering motorbike and sidecar that has a top speed of 50 miles per hour. Originally a 1938 BMW design, the Soviet army took the factory back to Russia after the war. In a fit of short-lived Sino-Soviet solidarity, they donated the design to the Chinese in the 1960s. The Nanchang aircraft factory still churns them off the production line, but the technology has hardly changed in the intervening years. With a dry weight of 350 kilos, they broke down constantly as poorly made parts simply expired.

They drank gallons of oil and due to the air-cooled engines, were also prone to overheating. Each wheel had around thirty spokes and at the end of every day we would compare how many had been broken, then sit down with two spanners and replace the broken ones. I had to learn a whole new language: regulator, alternator, solenoid, piston, steering bearings, drive-shaft bearings, valve seals. As much as I tried I could never really get to grips with the relationship of each constituent part with another. Just what did they do to each other? The mechanical intestines of the bike baffled me.

While the Changjiang was not reliable, it was sturdy. It is almost impossible to fall off one – although I did – and their bulky size meant that luggage and spares could be accommodated easily. A combination of simple technology and ease of access to the bike's mechanical bits meant that mending the bike didn't require huge amounts of specialist equipment. I once walked past Fim whacking his engine with a large metal mallet in one hand and an instruction manual in the other. Sensing my surprise, he remarked that he was 'fine tuning'.

For all its faults, the Changjiang 750 is a locally made bike which ensured the availability of spare parts across the length of China and perhaps more importantly, a minimum of paperwork. Those who have ever inquired into making such a journey by motorbike will know that bringing any foreign-made vehicle into the country is prohibitively expensive. In the long-distance adventure-biker bible, the *Adventure Motorcycling Handbook*, China barely rates three sentences as the country's obstructive bureaucracy puts it effectively off-limits for non-residents.

A SCARRED LAND

Baotou is not a Westernised city like Beijing or Shanghai, so it is a great place to have a 'real' China experience.

– Advertisement for teaching post at Baotou Iron and Steel Corporation.

After Hohot, the green hills faded and we gradually entered a semi-industrial landscape of redundant factories, rubbish-strewn linear developments, hazy skies and blackened buildings. The surrounding land was neither quite desert nor fertile, but an arid scrubland. Chalkpits and coalfields lined the road. Coal dust hung everywhere and the sun reflected off the broken black landscape. Trucks lumbered to and fro delivering black briquettes. Soon we were all covered in thick black coal dust. From the side of the road, blackened faces with matted hair stared blankly at us as we rode past.

At the epicentre of this scarred environment is the largest city in Inner Mongolia. Baotou, which actually means 'land with deer' in Mongolian, is 15 miles of terrifying urban sprawl. The days of any wildlife have long gone. Formerly a bleak frontier town of traders and immigrant farmers, Baotou has become one of the largest steel-producing cities in China. It is a truly monstrous urban development. Enormous factories pump noxious gases into the air or stand idle with holes in their walls like the hulls of rotting ships, their rusting innards revealed. A grim film hangs over the functional concrete buildings that line the road and the coal-laden air mixes with the diesel fumes of hundreds of lorries to make one choke. The noise of grinding machinery and snorting vehicles is everywhere.

At one end of the town a sort of purple cloud hangs low

over the city. This marks the city's main employer, the Baotou Iron and Steel Corporation. The 'pearl on the prairie' as it used to be called, like any other large state enterprise, effectively used to run the town. Education, housing, health, university and teacher-training facilities, and even a newspaper were run by the state enterprise. A complete community of hundreds of thousands of people organised around production at all costs. While undermined by a new market economy, it still dominates the city.

Just past a large roundabout we have to pull over as one of the bikes has lost power. A traffic policeman in a scuffed white jacket comes up and salutes. He asks if there is anything he can do to help. We thank him for his offer of assistance but tell him we just need a few minutes to make some repairs. We are excessively polite. The thought of spending a minute longer than is necessary in the city fills us with horror. He marches back to his position in the centre of the roundabout directing traffic – the lights do not seem to be functioning. But there are no collisions, everyone magically negotiates around each other – something uniquely Chinese.

While reaching for the toolbox, a taxi screeches to a halt next to us and a high female voice shouts out in plummy English.

'Yoohoo! I said yoohoo! I love foreigners! I *love* foreigners.'

Spanners hang in mid-air in confusion.

We turned round to see a short Chinese women skip out of the taxi towards us. There was a slightly frantic air about her that was disturbing. With her impressive English and non-stop chat, this was no ordinary Baotou citizen. As we conversed (in English as she refused to speak Chinese) it became evident that while she was indeed local, she was not at ease in her environment. Her eyes flickered across our little group. She had an insatiable appetite for our words and devoured everything we said. We were the first foreigners she had conversed with in twenty years. Maybe it was her desperate situation as permanent resident of Baotou that led her to start saying, 'I am single woman,' every ten seconds accompanied by a short high-pitched staccato laugh. We were not sure whether this was supposed to be an enticement or a simple statement of fact. Whichever, it became apparent that her first opportunity in two decades to communicate with foreign friends was to be seized with both hands and at full voice. Her words tumbled over each other in their haste to get out.

'I used to be a teacher. I learn English at university in Baotou. I love foreigners. I hate Chinese. They are ugly in their hearts. I am single woman. Where are you from? Do you like my English? I hate Chinese people. Are you from London?'

On and on. A never-ending monologue of rhetorical questions, bald statements and heart-felt self-pity. Our questions were jumped on and thrown into the verbal torrent. Her loneliness was awful to behold. She talked until we had finished repairing the bike, then lapsed into silence. I turned to say goodbye but she had already hailed another taxi in anticipation of our departure. She drove alongside us shouting encouragement and hurling abuse at other Chinese who dared to look at the bizarre convoy. At one point her taxi was so close that my handlebars scraped a metal scar right along the side of the car. The taxi driver immediately slowed and this was the opportunity we needed to escape. As we dodged and weaved through the heavy traffic to leave the city centre, she slowly gave up the chase and I looked back to see her waving and shouting in our direction.

I felt I had crossed the path of someone completely desperate, the sort of person who would lay explosives next to the local police station over some perceived slight, or spray a crowd with an automatic weapon. It was an extraordinary performance for its very 'un-Chineseness'. The mainland Chinese are a tight-lipped nation; what previous Western generations used to describe as inscrutable. Emotions are bottled up. People do not talk openly about their feelings or problems, and they most certainly do not attract attention to themselves. While children are outrageously indulged to a certain age, once past puberty they are expected to behave like an adult and proceed with care and caution. Extrovert adults are rare.

I once overheard someone whisper of a lively, pleasant female colleague, 'She has too much spirit,' as if this was something worrying, something that could lead to trouble. Spontaneous behaviour is frowned upon. Who knows where it could lead, what repercussions your remarks or behaviour could have? One is taught to think and think again before speaking or acting. Frankness and speaking one's mind are not encouraged and are viewed as selfish or irresponsible. Caution and calculation are encouraged. Such a mental attitude inevitably encourages mediocrity; don't rock the boat, don't do anything out of the ordinary, keep your head down. If history was not enough, there are numerous Chinese idioms that highlight the wisdom of such behaviour. 'The first duck in the flock is the one that is shot', 'The tallest blade of grass is the first to be cut down' and so on. Several thousand years of suffering have made people shrewd at survival; the greatest goal is, in the words of The Bee Gees, 'Staying Alive'.

Slightly unsettled from our encounter with the mad and lonely woman, we were determined to get well past Baotou before making camp. Unfortunately, Baotou stretched on and on. Spread out and run-down, the western suburbs were if anything more depressing than the city itself. Rain had turned the roads to thick mud that covered people, vehicles and houses. The nondescript nature of the buildings meant that one couldn't tell where a house ended or a shop began. Was that a warehouse? School? Metal workshop? Butcher's? Yards of nothingness separated one set of low-rise brick buildings from another. Trucks lumbered past on their way west, people thronged the edges of the street, occasionally crossing with no regard for their safety. A man with a face like a punctured football shambled out from behind a parked truck. On his arm, another man with head bandages and a lacerated face. An industrial accident? A sulphurous odour hung in the air. There was the constant grind of mechanised machinery, if not a truck then a train or a lathe. We crossed several small bridges underneath which sat foul liquids. One such stagnant stream was a bright fluorescent green.

It was with relief we stopped under a sign that advertised the end of the city. A swarm of children surrounded us and we were subjected to our heaviest staring session yet. They let out a peal of manic laughter as Ed read aloud the sign in Chinese: 'The world understands Baotou.'

Soon after we left the city limits, the sky darkened from battleship-grey to black. As the rain fell, we stopped outside a half-built house by the side of the road and ran inside. Three sheltering labourers sat down with us to share a cigarette. Exhausted, we slumped back against the rough brick walls and gazed out onto the bleak landscape. A row of low-rise buildings lined one side of the road for about 200 yards, then there was a muddy flatness of poor quality, overused agricultural land. We were on the edge of a semi-arid area that would stretch for hundreds of miles. Within minutes the road had disappeared under a greasy film of water.

The terrifying traverse of environmental degradation that is southern Inner Mongolia is an appropriate place to mention the environmental catastrophe that is modern China. Of the top ten most polluted cities in the world, nine are in China. Two-thirds of China's cities have severely polluted air quality with the result that millions of urban children have excessive amounts of lead in their blood. Over 90 per cent of urban water resources are polluted and more than 300 million urban residents face severe water pollution problems. A recent inspection of 62,000 miles of 700 of the largest rivers in China revealed that over half were severely polluted.

This is perhaps not surprising given that in 1999, 40 billion tons of untreated industrial and human waste were discharged into rivers and waters. Around 20 per cent of China's farmland, about 186,000 square miles of agricultural land, has been severely polluted by industrial waste or by agricultural chemicals. (Chemical fertiliser and pesticide usage per hectare is twice the world average in China.) The continued dependence on coal, serious soil erosion, increased water shortages, a rise in industrial and household pollution, along with increases in population, will create an unpleasant scenario for Chinese society. Acid rain, lack of water, soil erosion, polluted rivers and air pollution will be China's modern apocalyptic horsemen. Evidence that the pollution problems are reaching a level in China where they are beginning to severely affect the health of the general public is everywhere. The State Family Planning Commission has blamed an increase in air and water pollution for causing a 10 per cent drop in sperm counts between 1981 and 1996.

While since the twelfth century China has been one of the most urbanised nations on earth, the sheer scale of modern environmental degradation silences even the most sceptical. A cocktail of Stalinist economics, Maoist exhortations to dominate nature for the benefit of man, and now a capitalism 'with Chinese characteristics' (more rapacious) has produced some of the most depressing square miles of human habitat on the planet. What we had witnessed in Baotou was a particularly bad case of something that afflicts every major city in China. In Nanjing, reckoned to be one of the greener of the large cities, the prestigious Zijingshan Observatory had to move out of the city because air and light pollution have made it increasingly difficult to see the planets.

In the north, water in particular is a source of concern and will undoubtedly become a bottleneck constraining industrial, agricultural and urban development. From 2010, China will enter a permanent period of water shortage that will gradually get worse, according to the Ministry of Water Resource. In 2000, over 100 cities in northern China were forced to limit water usage, and for the first time in many years Beijing has introduced water rationing. The city authorities have had to repeatedly assure nervous residents that the water shortage is not a permanent feature of life and no water crisis could happen. The deputy mayor of Beijing has appeared on TV urging residents to take action to save water. Newspapers have highlighted the low level of water efficiency by producing fantastic statistics that showed that in Beijing 600,000 water taps and 200,000 toilets were leaking, and that together more than 100 million tons of water is wasted each year.

Paradoxically, it is China's industry that threatens the country's development. The water shortage is exacerbated by rising water pollution, much of it caused by industrial activity. Relatively backward, it makes inefficient use of resources and largely ignores the human costs of environmental degradation.

Dust storms have been increasing in their frequency and severity in the dry north of the country. Sandstorms are worrying for the city authorities. They remind everyone of just how fragile the current status quo is, a tangible sign that the environment is changing for the worse. They spread fear and panic, threaten law and order and they also kill. The desert belt across China is 2,800 miles long and 370 miles wide and already makes up about 18 per cent of China's total land. It is estimated that this barren strip grows by over 1,530 square miles per year. Only 45 miles from Tiananmen Square lie the deserts of Huailai county. Local scientists have announced the sands have moved over one yard to the south in the last year. 'Without taking firm action to control the desertification process, Beijing itself will eventually be threatened' warned the *China Youth Daily*. As long as the desert nibbles away at the fringes of Han China, the response will probably be muted. But perhaps the threat of a sandier future for the capital will prompt a greater response from the authorities. Maybe the capital will return to the dusty pictures of turn-of-the-century Beijing with camels a feature of life as much as trucks are today.

Increasingly, news stories are environmental. Thousands of tons of dead fish washed up on shorelines; mudslides; protesting villagers battling with factories that pollute the surrounding land, and increasing desertification. The Ministry of National Land Resources has admitted that over half of the geological disasters in China are now man-made.

The government response, hamstrung by an official ideology of 'growth at any cost' has largely been ineffectual. While it has drafted hundreds of new laws relating to the environment, enforcement is weak and in some areas non-existent. The problems are not unknown, but a lack of political will and coordination means that the vast majority of plans and laws are not implemented.

While official newspapers often carry stories of the number of factories forced to close because of failure to meet environmental standards, a healthy scepticism should be maintained. An alliance of local entrepreneurs, underfunded state companies and local officials see that legislation at the ground level remains ineffective and unenforceable. Impotent ministers are left with platitudes.

'Xie Zhenhua, director of state bureau of environmental protection said that China would try to reduce pollution, slow the trend of ecology deterioration . . .' or more pathetically, a headline in the *Beijing Morning Post*: 'BEIJING ACHIEVED PROGRESS IN ENVIRONMENTAL PROTECTION: THE SKY IS BLUER FOR A MONTH.'

Despite the good intentions of several government departments and increasingly, several community organisations, it will be hard to turn around such powerful trends. A survivalist mentality has ensured that the countryside is seen as being there to be exploited. Only in China could the concerned city elders of one large city, Lanzhou, which lies in a valley, seriously plan to blow up a mountain so as to let in a breeze and thereby lessen the city's chronic air pollution. It would be unfair to solely blame officialdom. It is unkind but nevertheless striking that the majority of people have lost any sense of natural beauty.

In Beijing I delivered a film to a department store to be developed. They were mediocre holiday snaps of south-western China, an area with miles of still-stunning landscape. On picking them up, I opened the paper envelope and briefly looked through the photographs. There seemed to be quite a few absent. I counted the photographs and checked against the negatives. I was missing about ten photos. What was strange was that all the ones that had disappeared were of scenery.

'Er, excuse me, there are some pictures missing.'

The white-coated assistant picked up the negatives, gave them a quick look and then tossed them back onto the glass counter.

'None missing.'

'No, but there are. Look!'

I highlighted the negatives that had not been developed.

'These ones. These are the ones missing.'

'What? But why do you want to have pictures with nothing in them? There are no people. It's just background!'

'It's just background' is as good a summary of Chinese attitudes to the environment as any. The family, food and children are at centre of most people's lives. The landscape is not something to be held in awe or to be protected and conserved. It is a resource. It is likely that the environment in China will continue to decline until, through its sheer exhaustion, nature will exact her revenge. Only then, when the degraded environment poses such a risk to economic and social stability, will firm action be taken. By then of course, it will be too late.

'Fish all the fish, burn the forests, eat all the animals, build on the land, overuse the earth until it is a desert.' Bo Yang's morose summary of Chinese attitudes to the environment is slowly becoming a reality.

Chapter Eleven

Biker Brotherhood

We needed shelter from the storm and trudged, heads bent against the wind and rain, to a building with a flapping red lantern outside, the village restaurant. Next door was a house that had been boarded up since the death of the family matriarch, but the owner offered it as shelter from the brewing storm. Inside there was a six-inch coating of sand on the floor. Tired and wet, we half-heartedly shovelled out what we could in the dark. We slept in a line as if in a dormitory, with the rain drumming on the windows. I woke up six hours later and it was still raining. Xiao Li's snoring was louder than usual thanks to the concrete acoustics. There seemed to be more sand in the room than when we had gone to bed. I shifted in my sleeping bag, pulling it up around my neck to keep out the cold and the sand and went back to sleep as dawn struggled to arrive. There was no way we were going to play at being bikers in this sort of weather.

When we finally ventured out we drove through the nondescript town of Xishanzui and across an arid flat featureless landscape with the now ubiquitous dilapidated factory blocks dotted around randomly.

For several hours there was a brief respite from the appallingly bleak landscape as we entered a strip of lush irrigated agricultural land. Green fields hug the banks of the Yellow River (Huang He), the second largest river in China after the Yangtze, over 3,000 miles from source to the sea. There is a strange, ambiguous relationship with this massive river. Here, it was treated with the all the respect and warmth of a giver of life. I had last seen it in Henan as a broad channel enclosed by raised dikes where its propensity to flood has earned it the name 'China's Sorrow'. The dikes were built over a period of centuries to control the river and prevent floods, but they have actually had the opposite effect. The large amount of sediment carried downstream has silted up the bottom of the riverbed and the level of the river has risen, so the dikes have had to be built higher and higher. As a result, many parts of the river are as much as 70 feet above the surrounding plain, and when the river level rises, disastrous floods occur.

Probably the worst flood in modern times occurred in 1931. About one million people died in the flood itself and in the following famines and epidemics, while about 80 million were made homeless.

We followed the Yellow River from east to west on our way from Baotou to Yinchuan. The road stayed close to the river as it meandered west across China. Strips of green cultivated land and trees gripped the sides, but further away from the river the land was dead. Occasionally the road veered too far away from the life-giving waters and the desert imposed itself. For brief stretches a thin layer of sand granules, blown on and off the tarmac by a shifting wind, obscured the road: a warning of what lay ahead. I felt a quiet thrill.

On the edge of a city called Wuyuan we had our first brush with authority. It was a trivial incident that highlighted the different worlds foreigners and locals inhabited in the same country. A national long-distance road official wearing a large peaked cap slowly held up his hand, palm facing outwards. He wore the familiar uniform of the junior Chinese official: scuffed shoes, see-through socks, baggy jacket and trousers, fake designer sunglasses with a constantly lit cigarette in his hand.

Not until we rolled to a stop did the palm drop in a theatrical manner, and from behind the large sunglasses came a command to hand over driving licences.

I had, unusually, been wearing a helmet because of the rain. Riding a Chinese motorbike the official had assumed I was Chinese, and therefore like the vast majority of the population, at the mercy of petty officialdom. He peered through my visor; his breath smelt of *baijiu*.

'Licence or fine?'

'Hello,' I replied in English, and the sunglasses leapt back.

There was a startled, *'Waiguoren!'* ('foreigner!') and with a curt movement of his arm he waved us on.

Foreigners are treated differently from the locals in China. There is a greater leeway, an unspoken official understanding that they are more trouble than they are worth. Their general conspicuousness and the transient nature of their presence undermines any possible threat. Not subject to the same social pressures as the rest of the population, they are harder to push around. They can check out.

We camped near an irrigation canal lined with poplar trees. A child raced along the towpath, another waved from across a field. There were several rudimentary mosques in the area. Many of the people were Hui or Chinese Muslims and some wore the white cotton cap. The Hui are the descendants of centuries-old intermarriage between Han Chinese and the Arab and Iranian traders who first came to China in the seventh century. 'Hui' in Chinese means 'returnee'. Some Chinese used to say that it is because they had originally arrived in the land unwanted and promised to leave, but never did so.

While they are not supposed to eat pork, smoke or drink, many have been assimilated into mainstream Chinese life. They look the same and dress the same, but despite being hard to tell apart, both sides agree they are a distinct ethnic group. For most Han Chinese the defining characteristic is of course culinary: 'They don't eat pork.'

The high-pitched whine of a small motorbike grew louder as its driver energetically wrestled with the muddy path in front of our camp. A man in a flared grey nylon suit and long hair appeared and stopped in the middle of our tents. He sat perched on the edge of his bike seat, legs astride, with his arms dangling over the front. His shirt was open to the waist and he sat there slowly taking everything in with a large smile and small nods. The engine continued to hum. The only thing that this man lacked to complete the picture of the village Lothario was a large amount of gold jewellery. Presently a swarm of children in pastel colours appeared, stood next to the agricultural dude and stared. Occasionally they would whisper amongst themselves and burst into frenzied whispers or laughter.

'Where are you from?' was asked with the confidence of someone supremely sure of being on his own patch.

'Beijing.'

A frown appeared. This obviously wasn't the right answer.

'What is your nationality?'

'*Yingguo.*' ('British') Now a smile and a couple of nods.

'*Yingguo! Yingguo!*' The children whispered loudly behind hands pressed against each other's ears. I felt as if we were in a light opera with the under tens as the chorus. The muted hissing subsided and they waited for the next question from their older cousin.

The bike coughed to a standstill. The farmer ignored the interruption and swept his arm in an arc.

'I work here.'

'Very beautiful countryside,' we all offered at once.

'Very beautiful,' hissed the juvenile chorus.

He beamed. A pause. 'I know.'

Despite the pretty countryside we were soon hearing about the difficulties of making a decent living. He hinted at recent village riots expressing local discontent with the county officials who demanded a cut of all sorts of economic activity. Unjustified tax increases on various areas of life had provoked similar peasant demonstrations elsewhere in China.

He wasn't optimistic, however, that there would be much change.

'We are just the common people. Nothing we can do. *Mei you banfa.*' No way. A deadening phrase that is heard again and again in China amongst those not part of the coastal prosperity. A phrase that reflects the resignation of people who are used to having little control over their own lives.

In the following days, the familiar depressing landscape of decaying factories reasserted itself and continued into Ningxia, the smallest and one of the poorest provinces in China. We passed assorted monstrous constructions standing alone on the plains. Chemical factories, steel works, mines, black and filthy petrol stations, a prison, half-built and empty constructions.

In between were one-tractor towns where dishevelled people stared out from behind rubbish piles and blackened doorways in bovine wonder. In the distance, regiments of trucks moved earth or coal with no apparent purpose. In the cold half-light of the evening, the landscape filled us with a certain dread.

A bike ahead suddenly jerks out into the middle of the road and glides to a halt. A broken clutch cable. It is our second breakdown of the day. We pull over to fix it. The withered grass and trees by the edge of the road are smudged black with coal dust from the passing trucks. We are tired and fed up and want to leave this desperate area behind us. To our left an exhausted-looking woman crouches amongst the bushes and directs several small children dressed in rags to scoop up small rocks of coal that have fallen off the passing trucks. People appear as if from nowhere, and before long a large gathering hovers around the broken bike.

'Where are you going?' asks one man with a thick accent.
'Yinchuan.'
'Where are you from?'
'Beijing.'
'Which country are you from?'
'England.'
'Can you speak Chinese?'
Even though we had been conversing in Mandarin, the fourth question still has to be asked, a ritual completed.

Seemingly satisfied with our responses, the crowd turns to the repairs in hand. There are many suggestions as to how the two foreign friends mending the clutch cable could do a lot better.

'He should pull it like that, then twist it around like that.'

'Yes, he is rushing too much.'

'What's that?'

'He should screw that.'

'Foreigners, they don't understand Chinese mechanics.'

All this is accompanied by lots of finger pointing, touching of bike parts and earnest looks. A quick poll revealed that none of them had been near a motorbike in their lives, but this was quite rightly not going to hold them back. Meanwhile, the truck traffic in coal was immense. Every few minutes a large Liberation truck would screech to a halt and the driver and his two mates would shout questions at the assembled crowd. I expect another truck to come screaming up behind and smash into the stationary one, which sits in the middle of the road. One driver looks on in disbelief when the reply comes back that we are tourists on our way to Yinchuan.

'Why don't they take the plane?' he asked in genuine confusion.

'Why don't you fuck off?' said Fim in English.

Given the scenic delights of the last two days, it was, however, quite a reasonable question. Obviously, no one goes on holiday to southern Inner Mongolia.

We were headed for Yinchuan, the provincial capital of Ningxia and a former base of Hui Muslim political power. Since the 1950s this arid part of China's north-west has seen a large influx of Han Chinese seeking to better their lot, and the Hui now account for only about 15 per cent of the region's population. The smallest province in China, it is also one of the poorest with a per capita GDP one-sixth that of Shanghai.

We stopped for lunch at a trucker's roadside café. It stood alone by the side of the road, a concrete box with a door at the front and one at the back. Sitting down, one could see straight through the kitchen, out the back, across miles of stony scrubland. On the wall hung a glossy poster of a tulip park in full bloom and a graphic close-up of a continental breakfast. The waiter wore pink nail varnish while the waitress had huge hands. I couldn't take my eyes off them. They were enormous – hands that could lift up a camel. Had there been some terrible kitchen accident that had led to them swapping hands by mistake during an operation? There was an overpowering smell of pure alcohol. The basic Mandarin and heavy accent of the waitress with enormous hands made communication difficult. She replied to our questions with a slight lilt at the end of the sentence. We felt we were nearing the edge of Han China and entering something different, more fluid and unfamiliar.

Three truck drivers at the next table stared at us throughout our meal. We ate with bowed heads, not daring to make eye contact in case we were invited to drink their half-open bottle of *baijiu* that stood on the table.

I lay in my first bath in nearly two weeks. Such pleasure. A mixture of coal dust and sand had found its way into every pore and crevice of my body. The water was an impressive black. Had I ever been this filthy? The dark corridors of the Yinchuan International Hotel echoed to our scrubbing and splashing.

There was a banging on the door, and Xiao Li appeared to

announce that there was someone to see me in the lobby. I couldn't think who it might be; Yinchuan was not a city we had any connection with. In the hotel, apart from a Cantonese tour group in matching baseball caps, we seemed to be the only guests.

I went down to the cavernous lobby and there, reclining on a plastic burgundy sofa, was a short roly-poly man with large round glasses. He stood up as we walked towards him.

'Mr Ma, I am Mr Zhang, chairman of the Yinchuan Bikers' Association. We heard you were in town. We would like to entertain you during your stay in Yinchuan.'

'Er . . . um . . . great. Thank you.'

Any hesitancy at taking up the offer on my part was as a result of wondering just what 'entertainment' in (a) Yinchuan and (b) with the head of the local bike chapter would involve. Would we be spectators as young Yinchuan blades raced past on custom-built bikes pulling live chickens along in their wake? Would there be stunts? Would we be forced into speed competitions, with the loser having to drink large amounts of Golden Phoenix liquor? I was also curious as to how they had found us. Chairman Zhang enlightened me.

'One of our club members heard the Changjiang 750 engines; they make quite a distinct noise you know. We are always on the look out for new bikes in town. When he saw a foreigner on top, well that was just too much!'

Zhang whipped out his mobile phone and in short, terse conversations summoned what I guessed to be other bike club members to the hotel. With an anxious expression, we both waited and sipped tea. Mr Zhang's portly shape and almost cherubic face, coupled with the glasses and an intense frown was not really what one would expect from the leader of a bike gang. Leathers would have looked ridiculous.

The bike gang drifted in one by one. After some initial stilted conversation, we were soon engaged in swapping bike stories and road tips. One tall man with a Frank Zappa moustache showed me photographs of their own bike club excursions across various parts of China. Picture after picture was casually dropped on the table: 'Me and my bike in front of the Potala Palace, Lhasa', 'Me doing wheelie on Great Wall' and 'Little Wang's circling of Tiananmen Square.' (At 16, Little Wang was the most junior member of the chapter.)

Their enthusiasm for all things motorbike was wonderful to behold, and our own bike excursion seemed not nearly as impressive as we had begun to believe. They insisted on being our hosts and giving us a tour of the city the following day. My polite protestations were drowned out by sincere exclamations of biker brotherhood. I went to my room strangely elated.

I woke to the sound of engines being revved. The bike club appointment, of course. Walking quickly out of the hotel lobby, I was almost knocked down by a bike flying past on one wheel. Under a bright sun, the Yinchuan Bikers' Association was out in force. In the forecourt was a collection of motorbikes, photographers, a traffic cop in a smart white jacket and Raybans, and two-dozen biking aficionados. Not a leather jacket or tattoo in sight. Tim, Ed, Fim and Dom were already amongst the excited throng answering questions, swapping cigarettes and then, as is customary, good-naturedly arguing over the privilege of lighting them. Fim pulled out a dog-eared shot of his motorbike back in the UK, signed it and handed it over to a Yinchuan biker who promptly handed over a large glossy photo of him jumping across the Yellow River on his Yamaha 125. There was much firm handshaking and clasping of arms. I was grabbed by Mr Zhao, the *jiatong jingcha* (traffic cop), for a photo opportunity with the reporter from the *Ningxia Times*. We all grinned and held hands. For such a reserved people, when it comes to having their photo taken, the Chinese can be amazingly tactile.

One man was pointed out with respect as having traded in his Lexus (the ultimate status symbol in China) for custom-built motorbikes for all his family, including his seven-year-old son. Laughter and respectful nods.

I watched as a local biker drove a motorbike and sidecar around the hotel forecourt on two wheels at a 45-degree angle. The sidecar tilted up and off the ground, its wheel spinning uselessly in the air above the driver's head. There was by now more than one Chinese Eddie Kid on the hotel forecourt, and I feared that sooner or later we would be asked to do something equally foolhardy.

After a couple of wobbles, the stunt motorbike and sidecar came to a halt in front of Fim and the driver motioned to him to climb into the sidecar. Having only just been accepted into the biking community, failure to respond and the subsequent loss of face would have been unthinkable. Along with the rest of the crowd we urged Fim on: *'Jia you! Jia you!'* ('Go on! Go on!')

Fim gingerly sat down in the sidecar and asked Yinchuan's Evil Kenivel to *'man yidianr'* ('go slowly'). This nervous request elicited guffaws from the assembled crowd who, of course, would have liked nothing better than to see the foreigner tipped out onto his head.

Along with the other spectators, who now included several hotel *fuwuyuan*, the receptionists and the waist-coated concierge team, we watched wide-eyed as Fim and sidecar were hoisted into the air and driven round in a circle. We cheered wildly at Fim's insane bravery and all felt a guilty sense of relief that we had not been picked.

Despite Mr Zhang and biker club's friendliness, it was extremely hard to elicit any information about the road ahead. While not expecting landslides, flooding or marauding bandits, we did know that the ride would not be comfortable. I asked how long it would take to Urumqi, 500 miles away, on our bikes.

'That depends on you,' came back the reply.

'Have you ever taken the road to Urumqi?' someone else asked me, staring meaningfully.

'No,' I replied. (Is it really the sort of thing people do more than once?)

'I have done it. It's very hard.'

We had been reluctant to let on as to our intended final destination. This was partly due to our own doubts as to how far we would get, but also as a precaution to avoid unwanted official attention. Yet in the face of so much conspicuous biker celebration, including official traffic authority participation, caution was thrown to the wind. Completely swept up in the cordial atmosphere of biker bonding, I let slip our ultimate goal to several people close by, including Mr Zhang. There was a momentary silence, then he whispered, '*Yingguo,*' part question, part statement, which others in the crowd took up.

As news of our 10,000-mile destination spread, there were incredulous shouts of 'Yingguo! Yingguo!' and finally wild applause. We all beamed with pride apart from Tim, who in best English tradition looked embarrassed at all the fuss. Dom punched the air with both fists and turned slowly, as if on an Olympic podium.

Maybe the scale of our intended journey tipped the scales from warm greetings to outright celebration. We were led, at a presidential pace, on a motorbike procession through the town. Zhao, the traffic cop, was at the front, complete with revolving red light and gun, our five motorbikes and sidecars were behind him and we were followed by a flotilla of bikes of all shapes and sizes.

As we entered the town's main square, I stared in amazement. Bordering the north of the square was a large traditional gate and tiered rows of seats for high-ranking officials. There was a large portrait of Mao Zedong and above it characters shouted: 'Long Live the People's Republic!' It was a mini replica of Tiananmen Square in Beijing.

Which particularly zealous official in this small and impoverished community had overseen such a project? It was a strange site. The icons of the Communist era are disturbingly impressive seen in remote parts of China; they seem to have a larger effect, uncluttered by the big buildings and exhortations of the modern megalopolis. While many cities still have a large statue of the Great Helmsman looking moodily into the distance with arm outstretched, this 'son of Tiananmen' is, I believe, a unique structure in China.

We halted for a team photo and a crowd of several hundred quickly formed around us. Soon we were hemmed in from all sides by curious locals. Dark faces, lined from years of toiling under the sun, stared on; farmers in patched blue cotton jackets, unkempt with wild hair, women in shapeless clothes, and snotty-nosed kids. We were told that there were five million people in Yinchuan, and half of them seemed to be with us.

We moved off at the command of an increasingly anxious Mr Zhang, who straddled a tiny Yamaha 125, and headed for a small compact temple complex. An 11-storey pagoda pointed to the sky and a large reclining Buddha relaxed inside a darkened room. The Chengtian Monastery dates from AD 1000. There are no monks, but like all religious sites in China it provided an oasis of calm. (Monastery life never really caught on in China, perhaps because it interfered with the family too much. The monk or nun in literature is always a slightly suspicious character.) From its elevated position we had a view out across this sleepy city to the Yellow River.

As we lit incense sticks and asked for a blessing for our trip, chairman Zhang and I engaged in earnest conversation. He explained how the Yinchuan Bikers' Association had come into existence and why it had become a part of his life.

'The bikers' club has been going for some years now. We are all motorbike enthusiasts. Motorbiking gives us a special feeling,' said Mr Zhang.

We stood looking at the Buddha with his pendulous earlobes for a few more minutes until Zhang indicated it was time to leave.

'All Buddhas look the same. Let's get out of here.'

Zhang's curt dismissal of Yinchuan's local Buddhist heritage hinted at the hidden discomfort many Chinese feel when faced with religious or spiritual intangibles. A Confucian heritage which is all about getting on in life, *this* life, is the nearest China has come to an organised belief system.

It is strange that in the West, for many people, China has

managed to acquire a timeless image full of monks doing tai-chi and mystical old men imparting elliptical words of wisdom, when in reality the Chinese are the most relentlessly practical people on the planet.

The Han Chinese incomprehension of anything approaching a degree of spirituality is most evident when they are in contact with their neighbours, the Tibetans, Hui, Mongolians and Uighurs. Religions are central to these non-Han civilisations, and it is this more than anything else that divides them from China's ethnic majority. There is mutual incomprehension at each other's belief systems. Rather like an urban yuppie visiting his country cousins, many Han find such habits and customs bizarre and slightly distasteful. Refuge is sought in light-hearted but nervous banter or mimicry. While not expecting an understanding of every nuance or even the main tenets of someone else's religion, the absence of any empathy is unsettling. There is no innate softening of the heart, desire to understand, or curiosity about the obvious importance of faith in these people's lives. Instead an embarrassed laugh or nervous joke; religion, 'so backward and so unmodern.' Such attitudes are officially encouraged by a state that sees salvation in placing the pursuit of materialism above all else.

After a noisy and cheerful feast of steaming *jiaozi* (dumplings stuffed with pork and chives) and cold beer, we were all formally presented with a certificate, bound in red velour and adorned with gold characters. Inside it simply read, 'Ma Shi Min is a member of the Yinchuan Bikers' Association' with a large red official-looking stamp.

'With this,' said Mr Zhang solemnly to a hushed room, 'you should meet no problems.' Applause.

We were thrilled and touched. After only three weeks as tentative bikers, we had been accepted into the biking fraternity of China, a subculture that, according to Zhang, stretched from Tianjin to Tashkurgan. Zhang explained that by producing this certificate we could get help and special prices for spare parts along the way. In return we handed over a team T-shirt and a bottle of gin, and I gave a clumsy speech.

Milling around after lunch amongst the bikes, I asked one teenager if he was a club member. Oh yes. When I asked which bike was his, he lowered his head and pawed the ground with his right foot.

'I don't have one – yet.'

Was this the only bikers' club in the world where you could join without two wheels? What a generous outlook to not only accept passing foreigners, but also people with no bike, but 'bike enthusiasm'. What other motorbike club has a traffic cop as the secretary?

We were escorted out of Yinchuan, still with the uniformed Zhao erect at the front, but now slightly wobbly after a large lunch.

Our little convoy headed west on a straight flat road, trees, houses and irrigated land gradually falling away until we stopped on a dusty plain edged by the Helan Shan mountains.

Here the area was dotted with mounds and mud fortifications of various sizes, including substantial pyramid-shaped tombs. Whether by wind erosion or design, these odd-looking structures, the largest of which is about 40 feet high, contain the remains of the emperors of the long forgotten Xi Xia (Western Xia) Dynasty. The plain shimmered as millions of fragments of broken tiles reflected the rays of the sun.

This is all that remains of a rich and sophisticated

civilisation that became wealthy and powerful as a result of dominating this part of the Silk Road. In the eleventh and twelfth centuries the Tanguts, related to Tibetans, controlled oases along the Silk Road and extracted heavy taxes from passing caravans. They had their own written language, produced fine silk scrolls and carried on as the middlemen on a then-thriving trade route. Too much of a good thing, perhaps, made the rulers cocksure, and after failing to pay annual taxes to the Mongol overlords, their relatively short but glittering time came to a horrific halt. From his deathbed, Genghis Khan ordered the wholesale destruction of the Tangut capital and the slaughter of its inhabitants while the 'lucky' ones were taken away as slaves. So complete was the obliteration that for hundreds of years the dynasty was literally 'forgotten' by historians.

The tombs are an impressive sight for two reasons. Their tapered shape is unusual in China. The violence of Chinese history plus the absolute domination of the Confucian heritage which stresses conformity as a virtue, make it very difficult for the modern traveller to find any building out of the ordinary or just a bit different. It was a delight to see something unexpected. Secondly, their relative remoteness lends an air of mystery. They stand alone in a landscape that hasn't changed since they were built. There has been no obvious attempt at restoration. The lucky geographical position of the Xi Xia Dynasty, which first brought it wealth and prosperity, is also the reason for the continued peace of its tombs. It is too isolated here for the industry of shops, cafés, stall holders, car parks and children's playgrounds that have overcome many other ancient sites.

All plans by the local authorities to bill these ruins as 'the pyramids of Asia' and earn large amounts of money from coach-loads of tourists are unlikely to succeed. There is a fierce wind that whistles across the plain. One can easily imagine that in fifty years the tombs will simply have been blown away. This seems quite appropriate for a dynasty that, after lasting for only 190 years, was wiped out by Genghis Khan's hordes.

Amidst wishes for a safe journey and long goodbyes with Mr Zhang and the Yinchuan Bikers' Association, we drove away into the emptiness. Soon we were alone again, crossing a drier, stonier landscape. Clumps of grass held themselves low to the grey gravel, either side of a road that stretched to the horizon. Not one tree, bush or dwelling as far as we could see. We measured our progress against a range of low mountains to our right. We were on the edge of the Tengger desert, part of the infamous Gobi, which runs from Manchuria to the Pamirs. Entranced by such an unbroken wide open space, we stopped and turned off the engines. There was nothing but the sound of the wind.

The midday heat is uncomfortable for the first time. A loud crack. One of the bikes ahead starts to wobble and heads into the verge. A puncture. We slip off the road on to sandy ground and begin the laborious process of replacing the inner tube. This involves prising off the tyre with two iron bars. While pulling and pushing, a shiny landcruiser appeared out of the haze. It stopped, cornered and charged towards us, tearing up a parachute of dust.

We all stood up. Police?

The gold-coloured vehicle pulled up alongside us and the

blackened windows came down. Cantonese pop music broke the still desert air.

An inquisitive local playboy (driving) and his two women (in the back) stared out. While the girls giggled, the driver exchanged pleasantries with us. It turned out they were just driving around for fun. It seemed quite strange that anyone would voluntarily just race around on the hot, arid and featureless plain. But then he pointed to the horizon to where they lived; a concrete mirage complete with giant water coolers and spewing chimneys hovering in the haze.

'We're from Electricity City.'

After they had left I was reminded of the story of a friend in Beijing who had lent his car to a Chinese colleague while he was away for two months. He had come back to find the windows had been blacked out.

'There is nowhere else where we can be alone.'

His colleague had been using the car as his love-making venue of choice.

Chapter Twelve

Shangri-La

'Do many get lost in the desert?' I enquired.
'Very many,' he said. 'Some miss their way and die of thirst and others are frozen to death in winter blizzards. You don't yet know, Lady, the terrors of that journey. Must you go out into the Gobi?'
— Cable and French, *The Gobi Desert*

We have rejoined the Great Wall for the first time since leaving Beijing. For the last few days the Wall has followed us, weaving across our path, disappearing from view only to appear several hours down the road. Sometimes on the left of us, sometimes on our right, sometimes so close we could stop and touch it, other times a distant smudge. It rises to twice the height of a man, but in some places sinks completely into the ground. It is like the broken spine of some massive ancient dinosaur; its vertebrae scattered across sand-blown plains. At one point the road actually cut through the Wall.

This far west, the Wall is not the solid, seemingly impregnable barrier one finds around Beijing. Unlike the manufactured strength near the capital and the theatrical air of Badaling, here the wall seems to be of a different age and quality. Here it is all mud; baked hard under the sun, in some places low enough to skip over it. An ancient and fragile construction, we started to become attached to it. Whenever we caught a glimpse as we rose on the crest of some hill, we would slow to admire it. There are gaps miles wide where the wall has simply vanished. I imagined the holes were where the Mongols had smashed through on their way to sack another city of terrified people. Wild-eyed and cruel men on short fast ponies wielding death and destruction. Yet the truth is more prosaic; as the wall fell into disrepair whole sections simply collapsed. This process was aided and abetted by local peasants who took any stones that were left to build their own houses.

We were on the back roads of Gansu, a thin slip of desert and mountain territory, with a large Tibetan, Kazakh and Mongolian population. After Yinchuan, I had pulled out my expensive see-through map holder, confident that at last it would see some action. But in fact the road we were driving on was not on our map. We had been advised by chairman Zhang of this short cut just before leaving Yinchuan. All other major traffic had by now headed south for Lanzhou or south-east to Xian.

As we entered Gansu province the landscape became wilder and harsher and the Tengger desert became a constant companion. This southern-most part of the Gobi juts down into Gansu province from Inner Mongolia. The only traffic on the road is the odd antique truck or a mule driven at a leisurely pace. We passed through stunning fragile farmland where farmers are involved in a never-ending struggle with the yellow desert to the north. Villages here are isolated and far apart with the road rising and falling in between. We were pointed at, stared at and, on some occasions, chased after by locals who were not quite sure what their reaction should be. In each village we passed through, our progress was slowed to walking pace as a throng of tractors, people and livestock choked the narrow road. Canvas-covered wooden stalls at the side sold parched vegetables, plastic bowls and sweets with shiny wrappers. Scales were the old imperial 'stick and weights' measurement, now illegal. Old men with elaborate dark glasses crouched low over games of Chinese chess. Peasants in dusty cotton jackets strolled around with no particular destination in mind. In one village, a man with a tufty white goatee, long blue gown and tasselled skullcap stared hard at us as we pushed through the crowds; an image of a much earlier China.

We camped under the lee of the Wall, close to one of these tough isolated communities. Here the Wall seemed to act as a dividing line between two very different environments and two very different worlds. Behind us lay the small back-breaking plots of the village, while on our side of the Wall, covered in tussocks of scrawny grass, stretched the rocky beginnings of the desert. In the distance, a figure with a large animal approached. An old man appeared, leading a camel on a piece of rope. It was not immediately obvious where he had come from. He walked right up to our camp as if we were his destination, and after a good look round started a conversation.

His accent was so thick that it was difficult for us to make out what he was saying. This was complicated by a set of broken teeth. We asked him what he did with his apparently domesticated camel. I had the idea that maybe he climbed on it when it all got a bit much back at home, and wandered across the Tengger for days for some spiritual recharging. A Chinese Obi-Wan Kenobi whose desert wanderings had taught him a wisdom beyond that of the ignorant villagers who never ventured from their fields.

It turned out that this beast worked for him on the land, pulling the plough. In this part of Gansu many farmers used several camels to plough the land, he said. Apparently, running a set of camels was much cheaper and more reliable than a Chinese tractor. He assured us that in the morning we would be able to see this agricultural phenomenon. Behind him the camel stared at us with the aloofness of the supreme desert wanderer. We couldn't quite believe that this forced indenture was anything more than a temporary existence for such a proud animal. Perhaps it was a bit like a summer job, transient in nature, and before long he would be back in the open desert.

Later that night I awoke to the stumbling and mutterings of the village headman who was tripping through our tent pegs and guy ropes. He was quite obviously drunk. I did not poke my head out of the tent for fear of being dragged into a drunken embrace and forced to sit down and drink hideous amounts of local *baijiu*. I screwed my eyes tighter and forced myself to sleep. I think I even managed a few fake snores when he passed my tent. It was only when I heard him engaged in conversation with Xiao Li that I was able to drift off to sleep.

The party chief was still there when we woke in the morning, smoking. He had been hanging around the tents in a grey baggy suit and tie since six a.m. He had come to invite us for breakfast. I looked at my watch; it was just after eight. He had probably only had a few hours' sleep. Chinese hospitality never ceases to amaze; it is nothing if not insistent. There could be no refusal of this invitation. As we packed up the camp and loaded the bikes, a funereal air descended.

Breakfast is the only part of Chinese cuisine that has most definitely not caught on amongst foreigners. *Mantou* (doughy buns), rice gruel, dried spicy fish, dry biscuits and sometimes, if one is lucky, a really hard boiled egg. While we had all eaten Chinese food for lunch and dinner almost every day for the last four years, Chinese breakfast was strictly a no-go area. In Beijing many young people, on other occasions a patriotic lot, have given up on their own country's attempts at breakfast, and have started to have toast, bacon, scrambled eggs and fruit juice.

One could only imagine what culinary delight awaited us in this Gansu village. There would almost certainly be some sort of meat as we were honoured guests. We hadn't seen many animals in the village on our way through apart from scrawny chickens and several dogs. Braised dog's paw, perhaps.

We rode to the village with the party boss taking a ride on the back of one of the bikes. Despite being sober, he swayed violently as we bumped and jolted over the fields to his settlement. As we approached his house, he began to beam with pride and attempted to sit just a little higher, straight-backed. Lined up outside was surely the whole village and several knee-high children. He raised his arm in an imperial salute. The elder members of the crowd waved back while the children jumped up and down with excitement.

Ushered through the courtyard of the house, we sat on a large *kang* (a stone bed heated from underneath by coal). As with all peasant houses I had visited in China, it was spotless and spartan. There were a couple of interesting photographs of the village chief (Mr Wang) in his younger days. In fact one was taken in 1970 in the midst of the Cultural Revolution, a decade of incredible chaos and upheaval in Chinese history. I wondered what had happened out here in the back of beyond. What was his story? Struggled against as a member of the party hierarchy? Or did he organise the humiliation of others from his position of authority? It was certain that in the village there would be no secrets, but asking Mr Wang himself was out of the question.

We moved off the *kang* and, at Mr Wang's insistence, sat down on the sort of chairs that normally come with a doll's set. Facing each other around a table that reached to just above our ankles, we sat uncomfortably on the massively undersized plastic furniture and made polite conversation with Mr Wang while we waited for breakfast. Cigarettes were distributed and before long other villagers were introduced. Soon we were all puffing away, the room a blue fog in the early morning light. We were not introduced to Mrs Wang who, we were told, was busy preparing the meal. ('Skinning the camel – one hump or two?' was Tim's whispered jest.) The conversation was somewhat stilted as the knowledge of certain discomfort made our polite enquiries somewhat forced.

Mrs Wang came in carrying the most enormous white bowl, which was placed smartly in the middle of the table. As we peered closer, Mr Wang encouraged us all to start eating away. It was hardly a racing start. I picked up my chopsticks and gingerly delved into the steaming dark brown sauce that surrounded a mound of chicken bones. I was lucky, my chopsticks emerged with a leg. By a stroke of misfortune, Fim landed himself with a chicken's head. He held it between the chopsticks for some time while smiling at Mrs Wang, who beamed back with culinary pride. Everyone knew what he had to do next, but we still couldn't quite believe it when he actually took a bite. He crunched away very slowly, and raised his chopsticks to Mrs Wang.

'*Hao chi!*' ('very good!') he managed after a rather long silence.

The bowl consisted of every bit of the chicken that you normally avoid eating. Feet, innards, head – everything is actually savoured by the Chinese. It was unthinkable that we would refuse and anyhow, Fim had now set the standard. Under the friendly but stern gaze of the Wangs and assorted villagers we ploughed on through the contents of the bowl. Shapeless lumps were surreptitiously eased out of the dark waters and if not immediately recognisable, were allowed to slip back in. I took to chewing a small bone for a ridiculously large amount of time while making a lot of appreciative noises, delaying for as long as possible any encounter with other parts of the dead chicken. Occasionally there was an outburst of group hysterics as one of us grappled with some particularly inedible part. When Mr Wang personally offered me the floppy red bit on top of the cockerel's head from his own bowl, I felt the time to end the charade was at hand. He was grinning from ear to ear which was the excuse the other bikers needed to laugh uncontrollably and say helpful things like, 'Go on, it's the best bit!'

I looked at Mr Wang and then back to the chicken head held out between his chopsticks. Mr Wang moved the head about, just as one would with a bone before a dog, causing the red floppy bit to quiver. I could feel my throat tightening; I just couldn't do it.

'I'm really sorry Mr Wang, but I've already eaten a lot.'

I knew that in China this excuse doesn't always work as no one is convinced you have enjoyed your meal until you are fit to burst, so there was some wrangling over just exactly how much I had eaten before I was allowed to escape this particular culinary honour. Relief brought on a cold sweat. Mr Wang looked at the head and offered it round the table, sending everyone straining back in their seats as if he was waving a loaded gun. He then popped it in his mouth and chewed away.

We pushed our bowls away as soon as was politely possible. All except Xiao Li who signalled he was happy to polish off the bowl. He was unfazed by our feeble eating habits by now, and had long since given up scolding me for not finishing at least one bowl of rice. Canned coconut drink was offered to wash the chicken bones down. We slurped away before slipping outside for several formal group photographs and more cigarette offering. As we shook hands with the party chief and thanked him for his generosity, Mrs Wang shuffled out of the courtyard and placed a small paper bag in my hand.

'In case you are hungry,' she beamed. I didn't need to ask what was inside.

Several miles outside the village, we saw the ploughing camels that Obi-Wan Kenobi had mentioned the night before. There were four hitched up to a plough, behind which walked a man wearing patched cottons. The earth behind their stately progress was a streak of dark brown. It seemed quite fitting that in this landscape, where the desert is a constant threat to the local livelihood, the camel should have been pressed into service for the villagers' endless struggle with nature.

We emerged from our cross-country route close to a town called Wuwei, coated with various layers of sand and saddle-sore from the bumpy surfaces. Fifty miles of road repairs meant driving on sand and stones in competition with large buses and trucks. Over such terrain it was inevitable that the bikes would suffer. We stopped in a patch of shade under a row of small trees to wrestle with spokes and change tyres.

Tim offered the leftover chicken around, but only Xiao Li showed any interest.

'It's so poor here,' he said in between mouthfuls.

We were now back on the main Lanzhou to Urumqi road, and the traffic was heavier with many more trucks thundering past. We followed the road onto a smoothly tarmacked new highway. After the slow and uncomfortable progress of the last day, we relished this polished surface and room to manoeuvre. We played at being in *CHiPs*, driving side by side as if we were Baker and Poncherello under the Californian sun. I must have continued this particular diversion for too long as my biker comrades were soon failing to respond to the cheesy grins, high fives and thumbs aloft.

At the other end of the road we were stopped by three officials, all in different uniforms, who were seething with indignation that we were on their pristine new highway. They were, I suppose, a sort of Chinese Highway Patrol, and while the three men in front of us lacked the glamour, height and bikes of the Californian TV stars, they made up for it with their aggressive demeanour. We stopped.

Ed and Fim went over to negotiate. They made an unlikely pair; Ed in full British-diplomat mode, striding forward, big smile and with hand outstretched, and Fim, sauntering alongside, head in the air, chewing gum, his boots scraping the ground in a sort of biker's roll.

One of the cops kept pointing at a large picture of a motorbike with a red line through it. This picture was to the left of a cow, a tractor and trailer, and a bicycle, all similarly marked with a red line. The sign actually faced away from the direction we had come, but this feeble excuse was not accepted.

'You are breaking the law!'

A pair of oversized sunglasses threatened to slip off the nose of the one shouting. Truck drivers passed and smiled at our predicament, some offering a surreptitious thumbs up – an acknowledgement that we were in trouble, they were not and wasn't the situation hilarious. I felt as if we had been caught smoking behind the bike sheds.

Ed and Fim stood arguing near the tollbooth for some time. They were polite but insistent that the large fine being discussed was wholly inappropriate. The three officials eventually gave in and dismissed us with strict warnings never to repeat the offence. The uniformed ticket-seller inside the tollbooth waved us through with no charge and giggled behind her hand, while several trucks tooted their horns. A small victory to be celebrated over an arbitrary authority. Fim raised his fist in a sort of power salute, acknowledging the support.

A spokesman for the police recently admitted to the *China Youth Daily* that while one-third of the 1.5 million police officers in China did the work, the rest either watched or 'created trouble'. He confirmed that two-thirds of the police force in China were 'useless'. It is perhaps no surprise that most people do their utmost to avoid anyone in a uniform.

As a team we were proud of Ed's negotiating skills and Fim's attitude, honed over several years of business encounters and bureaucratic wrestling with stubborn officials. While we could all argue in Mandarin to a greater or lesser extent, none of us had the formidable patience that enabled Ed to overcome seemingly immovable objections, or Fim's controversial balance of lackadaisical disdain of authority and studied interest.

Negotiating with the Chinese has become a whole separate discipline in itself. Much has been written on this subject, and the Chinese have come to be viewed as wily and clever negotiators that one has to be on permanent guard against. Despite the hyperbole, there is an element of truth in this. The official Chinese way of arguing is clever in its simplicity. An agreement must first be reached on 'principles'. In fact these are not principles, but a stated position. Once you have agreed to a position, it becomes apparent that your room for manoeuvre is limited. The position becomes a verbal anchor that limits one more and more. It is impossible to renegotiate. The other side, knowing this, press home their advantage and demand concession after concession. This Maoist-style of argument, based as it is on unquestionable premises, has nothing to do with resolving differences, reaching an agreement or compromise. It is about achieving an objective through remorseless logic, grinding down your opponent's will. This could be because the ones negotiating are not the ones with the power, but are there with strict instructions. Therefore they have no room to manoeuvre.

An example is a discussion on Tibet. I admit that this is not a very fair example as an emotional layer of nationalism is ever present. But the discussion would go something like this:

Foreigner: 'Isn't it terrible what's happening in Tibet? They seem a different people, why can't they be left alone?'

Chinese: 'We are helping them. Providing electricity, work, we are bringing progress.'

Foreigner: 'But why the destruction of the monastic way of life? Why don't you give them some autonomy, real autonomy?'

Chinese: 'Look, Tibet is part of China.'

Foreigner: 'I know but . . .'

Chinese: 'Do you agree that Tibet is part of China?'

Foreigner: 'Yes, but . . .'

Chinese: 'Good, Tibet is part of China.'

A pause.

Foreigner: 'Er, but what about the religious life of Tibetans?'

Chinese: 'Tibet is part of China. They should respect the laws and customs of China.'

Every answer will now be prefaced with, 'Tibet is part of China . . .' rendering any objection redundant. Such a tactic guarantees a frustrated and exhausted opponent.

The man who knows more than anyone else about arguing with the Chinese is Mr Alan Paul. He led the British diplomatic team that negotiated the return of Hong Kong to the motherland in 1997. Meeting almost on a weekly basis for nearly four years with mainland officials, he was involved in a tortuous and protracted process that tested the limits of patience on both sides. He would emerge blinking from a small air-conditioned office where another round of interminable negotiations had broken up with microscopic progress. Afterwards, each side would repeat their stated position to a bank of microphones. Alan Paul always looked steadfast, but completely drained.

Your golden hair and blues eyes or your black complexion and curved hair might make the local people feel curious. Even in Beijing where there is the most foreign population, you might be surrounded or observed by some people from other provinces. Some naughty youngsters might tease you about your characteristics . . .

– *Study in China: A Guide for Foreign Students*

We camped 25 miles west of Wuwei on hills close to a village. There were wonderful views of the valley floor and the Gobi desert in the distance. About fifteen villagers surrounded me as I scribbled into my diary. The capacity of the Chinese for staring has been noted by many travellers (Peter Fleming, who rode a horse from Xian to northern India in the 1930s, called it 'magpie-like'). It is an overpowering experience. Everything one does is a source of silent curiosity. Putting up a tent takes on a ritualistic, religious aspect with an audience of twenty-eight. One's every movement is followed by dozens of pairs of eyes and is often accompanied by a running commentary, punctuated by laughter. The fascination of someone changing a wheel, reading a book or washing seems to hold an appeal out of all proportion to the actual act. Surely there are some things that are more interesting than others to watch? Two people having an argument or making supper on an open fire are two things one would think are more interesting than someone reading a book or cutting their toenails. Yet this is never reflected in the amount of staring time people are prepared to spend. If you stood on your head and took all your clothes off you would get no more intense stares than another foreigner who made a cup of tea. What does this say about the Chinese masses and their attitude to foreigners? That foreigners are weird, full stop. Therefore everything they do is odd without exception. It is this all-encompassing curiosity that can sap a traveller's fortitude.

Just occasionally one's strangeness is actually commented upon. Soon after arriving in Changchun for the first time, I was on a crowded bus when I noticed a young woman staring at me. Despite looking back, she refused to take her eyes off me. Initially embarrassed, I then felt flattered. Maybe she found me attractive? Maybe she fancied me? Maybe I was already in the throes of some early courtship? This seemed to be confirmed when she reached out her hand and started stroking my forearm. This brazen piece of affection was done with a casual arrogance that left me breathless.

She beckoned me a little closer.

'You are very hairy. In China, we call you monkey!' With that she collapsed into giggles, hiding her mouth behind her hand. A large number of the people on the bus joined in laughing and soon there was general hilarity. Red-faced, I fled at the next stop.

In a life of excoriating routine, foreigners make good entertainment. Getting upset not only betrays a lack of appreciation of your own inherent entertainment value, but guarantees that your unwitting tormentors are unlikely to leave you alone. One of the many complaints of Western travellers in China is that there is no privacy. This is because there is no privacy in China. There is not even an accurate word for privacy in Chinese. The character used (*si*) has pejorative overtones, hinting as it does at selfishness, or something illicit and illegal. It doesn't help that it sounds very similar to the character for death (also a *si*) either. A twentieth-century Maoist heritage has further enforced the notion that individual privacy is somehow bourgeois and illegitimate. The lack of personal space in China, physically and socially, means that you won't be left alone very often. As a foreigner one is more noticeable than others, so one can't melt into anonymity and your every action, look or raised eyebrow is studied and followed with an absurd degree of interest. Trying to outstare a group of Chinese is a futile task, like trying to outstare yourself in the mirror.

We were the first Europeans to stay in the village. Dom stooped and put his blond head close to a tiny boy in a gesture of friendship. The boy promptly burst into tears and called for his mother.

'We don't get many tourists around here,' explained the tallest farmer, whose land we were camping on. He had a hangdog expression, reflecting the life of unremitting dawn-to-dusk work of the peasant farmer. A child with split pants hugged his ankles and stared.

'Beautiful agricultural land,' Ed offered.

'It's shit,' came the reply.

Polite small talk out of the way, we got onto the price of land, county corruption, crop rotation and the surrounding geographical highlights. There was much clucking and shaking of heads at the state of our motorbikes that had had to traverse a narrow muddy track to get to open camping ground. One bike had suffered a broken gear lever.

'Your bikes are Chinese, aren't they?'

A reply in the affirmative led to several creased brows amongst the men in the group. Pride at a foreigner buying a Chinese bike and riding it across China was mixed with confusion that any foreigner (who all have huge amounts of money) should spend it on a locally made Changjiang 750. Seeing the damage to the gear lever, one man blurted out, 'You should have bought a foreign bike. These Chinese bikes are extremely poor quality.'

There was silence as our reaction was assessed. I noticed the old crone who had actually pointed us in this direction as somewhere to camp, which had resulted in our getting stuck in a narrow mud track with no option but to continue forward. It seemed churlish to mention that the breakage had occurred due to her less than helpful directions. When we smiled and agreed that the bikes were, well, shit, there were hoots of laughter and slapping of backs. When Tim told them how much we had paid for them, several villagers doubled up in delight and the old woman nearly fell over. There is nothing so certain to elicit gales of gleeful laughter from Chinese as a foreigner being ripped off. There is a strongly held belief that foreigners are pretty stupid about money, having as they do far too much of it. Tourists, of course, do nothing to alleviate this belief. While I did not feel that our particular motorbike purchase in any way fell into the 'dumb foreigner' category, in their eyes it obviously did.

Clouds gathered overhead and the first light drops of rain began to fall. This was the cue for all the villagers to wander back to their houses and leave us on the exposed hill. We spent the night under flapping canvas. We had to tie various parts of the tent to the spokes of the bike wheels as the ground was too hard for tent pegs. A villager came to visit us in the morning and invited us for breakfast; we politely declined.

Stopped by driving wind and rain west of Yongchang, we took shelter in an isolated and dilapidated restaurant while waiting for the storm to abate. A concrete box construction, barely warmer inside than out, a single light bulb hung from the ceiling. We were cold in our wet clothes and we sat huddled together on plastic stools around one of the two tables. Unwashed windows kept out the worst of the wind, while the room itself was dark with grime. The main road passed right in front of the door, and every now and then a large truck thundered past with a loud swoosh. Hanging over a dresser full of chipped crockery and dirty glasses was that poster again, the one of the tulip park that seemed to be everywhere.

An unsmiling exhausted woman appeared with boiling water. After several enquiries as to what dishes were available, it emerged that despite the 'Restaurant' sign outside, there was no food.

'Why do you have no food?'

'We don't get many guests.'

We sipped our jasmine tea in silence and listened to the falling rain.

Large primary-coloured tulips in the foreground with manicured parkland behind and trees that reached up to an impossibly blue sky. A glossy vision of earthly paradise. This picture of natural perfection appears in countless small restaurants the length and breadth of China. It has become so much a part of the cheap restaurant environment that I wondered if there was a 'starter kit' for small eateries in China, which included the plastic or tin thermos, blue and white chipped bowls, plastic tablecloth, jars for chopsticks . . . and the picture of the tulips in the park.

But this would not be enough to explain its popularity or durability. I liked to think that it had become a sort of talisman, a vision of an easier and softer world. An inspirational oasis of bright colour and calm amidst the grey reality that is modern China. An environment in which not only flowers actually grew and there was real grass, but there was an ordered peace and tranquillity. Presented in glorious technicolor, the picture serves to highlight the essentially man-made aspect of this superior and controllable natural order. This vision of nature 'as it should be' seemed to me the response of people living harsh, predictable but precarious lives. Here was a desire for a softer, brighter, prettier environment where dust, dirt, pollution and noticeably, other people, were banished.

Two years later, after I had left China, I discovered where this mystical place, this 'natural' idyll actually was. Taken on a visit to the Dutch tulip fields outside Lisse, I entered the Keukenhof Gardens with hundreds of other people and stopped dead in my tracks. People bumped into me from behind and cursed. I stared at the man-made horticultural celebration with a slack jaw. This was it! This was the icon that adorned thousands of small white-washed restaurant walls from Anyang to Anxi. I felt vaguely religious, as if I had arrived at the end of a long and arduous pilgrimage. And looking around, I saw that I was not alone. There were hundreds of mainland Chinese tourists wandering the gardens. Strolling, taking pictures, they had arrived at their Shangri-La. I followed a party of young urbane Sichuanese around, hoping to find out the reasons for this place's popularity in the Chinese psyche. They were not interested in the flowers particularly, but rather the sense of ordered calmness, the manufactured stability that had been achieved. Unlike the uncertainties of Chinese life with its millions of people, unpredictable nature and random officialdom, here was an environment that could be predicted. No soaring mountains, swirling rivers or unbroken horizons, but rows of synthetic-looking flowers (all the same) next to acres of manicured lawns. An environment that I had never seen in China and never expect to.

Strong winds and poor roads made for extremely slow progress. Our bikes seemed heavier and slower than usual. The terrain lifted and dropped in slow waves for hundreds of miles. It seemed ages between each crest of a hill and the next. As you came over the top of one ridge, another would appear in the distance and as you breached that, another and another. I felt listless, hypnotised by the endless road and hills, hardly acknowledging the surrounding landscape.

Zhangye, a city that had prospered and declined with the Silk Road, had a slightly wealthier air than previous towns and it heralded the start of softer countryside, more grass, and even trees. The two twentieth-century heroes of the Silk Road and its buried treasures, Auriel Stein and Sven Hedin, passed through Zhangye themselves. Hedin was here as late as 1934 surveying the feasibility of building a proper road along the old Silk Road. We stopped in a village just past Zhangye to buy vegetables and rice. Rounding one corner we came across a donkey sliced in half, its pink innards spilling across the road. Further along a truck driver crouched next to his cab, smoking a cigarette, while a policeman asked him questions. A group of villagers stood on the verge and like us, looked from the pink bubblegum goo that had been the donkey's stomach to the truck and back again. We gingerly edged our bikes past the dead animal and rolled past the traffic cop.

We had been reminded that this was the main road between two of China's largest cities, Xian and Urumqi. Trucks driving at high speed shared the road with old men on donkey carts, horses, children herding sheep, and babies on the back of bicycles. The accident rate is horrendous.

We nearly contributed to the high death toll on this stretch of road. A farmer, in his amazement at seeing *laowai*, turned his head so violently that his tractor swerved sharply to the left and the tiny child that had been on his lap was thrown into the middle of the road. The farmer was off his machine in seconds and had the child scooped up in his arms, whereupon he was immediately surrounded by several of his neighbours assessing the damage. I was sure that the child had landed on his head but he was crying, which we took as a positive sign. We were reluctant to hang around for too long in case we ended up being blamed for the accident; calculated behaviour that left an unpleasant taste in our mouths.

That night we rationalised our swift exit by telling each other stories of foreigners caught up in accidents where they had had to part with everything they owned in order to keep the baying crowd away or to stop the local authorities from locking them up. There is one apocryphal story of someone taking an unconscious crash victim to hospital as everyone else was just standing around staring. On waking up, the crash victim promptly announced his intention to sue his rescuer for the cost of the hospital care, medicines and mental trauma.

Xiao Li, now fully relaxed in his role as travelling mechanic, expressed amazement at our pangs of liberal guilt. He dismissed the idea of the Good Samaritan as not applicable in China.

'Chinese are different. You shouldn't look for trouble.'

Xiao Li's comments reflected the psychological status quo in China; getting involved in anything where the end result could be unclear is asking for trouble. Why take the risk? Such an attitude is endemic in modern China and is closely related to a traumatic past where individual initiative can be a dangerous thing.

In *Please Don't Call Me Human*, the Beijing novelist Wang Shuo has a character, an anti-hero, Yuanbao, who neatly sums up this civic cynicism:

> 'Tell me this,' Zhao smiled and said with the patience of a teacher. 'If you saw someone being bullied, would you just stand by and watch?'
>
> 'Why not?' Yuanbao said. 'I'm no cop.'
>
> 'What if it were a relative?'
>
> 'I'd have to know why. Did he deserve it? Stick your nose in where it doesn't belong, and you're just asking for trouble.'
>
> 'I'm surprised you have such a keen sense of right and wrong.' Zhao's smile now seemed a bit forced, but there it remained. 'So no matter who's getting beat up, as long as it isn't you, it's none of your business. Is that right?'
>
> 'Why not? That's what the government and the police are for. Who am I to take matters into my own hands?'

Two days later we had our first crash.

Dom was in a head-on collision with an elderly cyclist. A

man had gently cycled out from between a row of poplars lining the road, straight into the path of Dom. The amount of lead-time he needed to stop was greater than everyone else's, though this had never been explicitly spelt out for fear of causing offence. The sidecar hit the front wheel of the bicycle, and the old man was thrown completely clear. Screeching to a halt, we ran over. One of us pulled the old man up, another dusted him down and apologised profusely, while a third handed over a folded 100 yuan note in compensation. Accepting the money with a shaky smile, the man stood up and took a few tentative steps. Nothing seemed broken.

'*Zou ba! Zou ba!*' ('let's go!') shouted Xiao Li.

We left the accident spot before the whole village descended. I turned to look back and saw our traffic victim's white head in a sea of black hair, re-enacting his momentary involuntary flight path with his hands.

Chapter Thirteen

Beyond the Wall

No other state in human history has ever put as much effort into walling itself off physically from the outside world as did a number of Chinese dynasties. Nobody knows how much frontier wall was built in north China between the 6th century BC and the 16th century AD, estimates range up to 50,000 km . . .

— W. J. F. Jenner, *The Tyranny of History*

The Great Wall eventually comes to a halt at the great fort of Jiayuguan, 1,400 miles from its other end, Shanhaiguan on the coast. With 30-foot-high walls, pavillioned watchtowers and a desert and mountain backdrop, Jiayuguan represented the western tip of the Han Empire and has become one of the most famous parts of the wall.

Until recently, the empty expanse around the large brooding fort provided a vivid illustration of why most Chinese considered this the end of civilisation. Out of the gates to the west lay nothing but savages, bandits and the deadly emptiness of the desert. In imperial times it was here that disgraced politicians, out of favour courtiers and convicted felons were sent into exile. They were ejected dramatically from the 'mouth' of China, the Gate of Sighs. Beyond the Wall and the fort, imperial rule was cosmetic. It is this picture of 'civilised' Han China suddenly coming to an abrupt halt, and the wild, the unpredictable beyond, that has so captivated travellers for decades.

While the fort has managed to retain a mournful elegance with its empty windswept courtyards and sand-coloured walls, semi-industrial buildings have gobbled up the land between the town and the garrison so that a visitor searching for a desert fortress almost drives past it. There is a car park to the east and from the battlements a terrifying vista of a range of factories marching up to the fort's walls. However, the view out to the west has not changed, just a grey limitless emptiness. When we visited, it was as if we were walking around a film set with a desert backdrop, devoid of people and activity.

Since the fourth century the Great Wall has been the inland border of China. To the north are the nomadic societies of Central Asia; to the south, Chinese agriculture. Inside the Wall, despite different dialects, everyone speaks Mandarin; outside the Wall are Manchu, Mongolian and other Central Asian languages. To the south the water that flows is alive, that is to say, it is going somewhere. To the north there are no rivers with outlets; water here does not reach the sea. Around the Wall the rains begin to slacken off. To the west and north oases are isolated from each other by deserts and vast reaches of arid and semi-arid steppe. For thousands of miles men neglect agriculture altogether and carry on a nomadic existence.

From time immemorial until only about four hundred years ago, the major movements and influences that shaped the Chinese nation, history and culture came from beyond this inland border. The Manchu conquest of China in the seventeenth century was the last of these Central Asian tidal movements. However, it is ironic that when the real challenge came, it came not from across the Wall, but from the sea. Europeans arrived with all their maritime might and it was they who humiliated China on the battlefield and at the negotiating table, and laid the foundations for the eventual destruction of imperial China.

The Great Wall was 'built' by Emperor Qin in the third century BC by linking up several different sections of wall that had been built by Chinese border states over the years, making one system. Thousands died building it in appalling conditions. The Wall was not only about defence, it was also about control. No one could pass through either way without a permit, thereby affording effective control over trade and travel.

Walls have been a feature of the Chinese world for centuries, and still are. It was with the walled compound that China first hoped to enclose and contain strange foreigners.

One often sees enclosed land in China, sometimes in the city, but more often in the countryside. A featureless plain and then suddenly, a brick-walled compound. What makes it so striking when repeated on a large scale is that there is often nothing inside the walls. They seem to take on an almost religious air, an unusual statement from an otherwise practical people. Did the owner run out of money? What was going to go inside? Goats? Farm machinery? A house?

Somehow these enclosures, ranging from several square yards to several acres, do not seem fundamentally optimistic attempts to grab the future, but rather attempts at blocking out the surrounding awfulness.

Most country dwellings are still enclosed. One effect of

the courtyard is that within the enclosure the resulting intimacy means that there is little room for privacy. The distinction between the inside world of the home and the outside world of the town, village or city is absolute. This clear delineation has disappeared in the city with the arrival of tower blocks and the wholesale destruction of courtyard housing. But it survives in the walled-off work unit. Offices, factories, hospitals, schools and housing projects are bricked and fenced off, and gatekeepers are put in place to monitor the movements of all who come and go. These gatekeepers range from the feeble and ineffectual to the zealous, who thrive on denial. To be fair, the recent rise in crime in the larger cities has provided some justification for this defensive posture.

One side effect of the national obsession with building walls has been to encourage a vast brick industry. The total production of bricks in China is 700 billion per year, which as the *China Economic Times* points out, 'is enough to circle the equator 1,600 times.'

Anxious to continue the Great Wall theme, we stayed at the Great Wall Hotel, a squat grey building with mock towers and crenellated roofing. Inside it was dark, damp and gloomy, but we had our first running water since Yinchuan. We ate supper in a huge banqueting room that could seat two hundred people, next to a waterless rocky fountain. We were the only guests and the waitresses outnumbered us by three to one as the Titanic theme song (instrumental version) wafted around the room.

We passed the fort early next morning and were suddenly beyond the Wall. Within minutes we were crossing true desert with nothing to see in a 360-degree radius except sand and stone. Driving on a thin strip of tarmac in the early morning light, the surrounding desolate landscape took on an unearthly beauty. When we stopped to rest by the side of the road none of us spoke for fear of breaking the spell. The sun had returned after days of cold rain and strong winds that had hindered our progress. The landscape had been passing so slowly that I had begun to feel slightly ridiculous in the face of such distances, rather like someone riding a tricycle on a motorway, or choosing to hop from Ipswich to Istanbul.

Driving a motorbike over hundreds of miles revealed subtle differences in our various riding styles. Fim tended to be in the lead. Head jutting out from shoulders hunched over customised handlebars, he leant much further forward than the rest of us. Whether this decreased wind resistance, adding to his speed I don't know, but it certainly looked more 'biker-ish' (tougher and harder). Ed came next, sitting upright and tall as if he was an Oxford vicar or a policeman, and then Tim, who rode in a relaxed manner, all elbows and forearms. This was partly a reflection of his laid-back nature, but also a reminder that for the first part of the trip Tim had had to drive with an inflatable rubber ring to cushion his bottom after a recent piles operation – doctor's orders. This had resulted in much hilarity as he was forced to drive with his arse stuck in the air like Donald Duck. Dom sat on his saddle as if ensconced on a throne. He rode with the supreme assurance of the wealthy part-time biker. He reminded me of a Californian lawyer taking his Harley Davidson for a Sunday afternoon spin. When it was cold he wore a large bright red wool headband in the shape of a fez which completed his magisterial look.

Dom and myself, for some unknown reason, always seemed to bring up the rear of our mini convoy. In the absence of traffic, we often rode side by side, which I was later informed by Fim was 'poncey' (i.e. not what real bikers do).

At a petrol station, a smiling petrol attendant in oil-stained trousers politely informed us that we were not alone.

'We saw one of you lot go through here two days ago on a bicycle.'

'Do you know which country he was from?'

'*Deguo*.' ('Germany.')

This was the second time we had been told there were other foreign travellers on the Silk Road. The first had been back in Inner Mongolia when, to much excitement, we had been told of a lone foreign female biker a few days ahead of us.

'Attractive?' Ed had enquired.

'Beautiful,' came back the reply.

She immediately took on semi-mythical attributes and kept several of us awake at night with the tantalising thought of what might lie around the next corner. This frustrated fantasising came to abrupt halt when we discovered at a spares shop that she had headed south to Xian after Yinchuan.

As for the German on the bicycle, we all expressed our admiration. The distances involved were colossal, not to mention the increasing temperatures – and he was travelling alone.

As I screwed my petrol cap back on, the attendant said, 'While you foreigners all look a bit strange and scary, you are actually very friendly.' I looked at myself in the side mirror and then at the others. It was true, we looked a fright. Hairy and filthy with large reflective goggles and padded jackets, we looked as though we were from another planet. I wondered what the German looked like.

We camped that night by a large turquoise lake edged by bulrushes. In the middle was a small fishing boat with two men casting nets. The sun was high in the evening sky. We made a fire. Tim shuffled around making supper. Someone spotted a heron amongst the grasses at the water's edge. This was the only wildlife we spotted the entire length of the trip (yaks not included). Given the population pressures and poverty of many areas, it is perhaps not surprising that there is little wildlife left in China. In a country that continues to destroy its natural habitats and where eating is a religion, the outlook for wild animals is bleak. While there are over nine hundred nature reserves in China, many exist in name only, while others are expected to fully exploit the natural resources from the reserve area itself.

A friend who worked for the World Wildlife Fund in Hong Kong visited a forestry reserve in the north-east of the country, and was invited to dinner with the head ranger and various other officials. The first course arrived in a large bowl, and the foreigner was encouraged to serve himself. Lifting up the ladle, a familiar shape appeared. Flustered, he asked, 'Is this bear's paw?'

'Yes,' replied the headman beaming.

'Where did you get it from?'

The headman jerked his thumb backwards, 'From the reserve, of course!'

When the authorities do try to protect the animals, they are not very successful. Corruption and a lack of natural empathy combine to produce few positive results. An example of this can be found at Guangdong Zoo where, since 1997, over four hundred 'incidents' have occurred. These include tigers killing each other, dead pandas, the deaths of ten deer, nine parrots and one boa, and the theft of six giant salamander. Some put their faith in greater tourism as an incentive to protect and promote China's natural habitats, yet these hopes seem fragile. Tens of thousands of fish were killed after toxic discharges from a nearby factory into Baiyangdian, the largest lake system in north China. The local party secretary, Gao Jianpo, was interviewed. His comments highlight just how far the official psychology needs to change.

'There is no problem with the water quality. There is no industrial pollution.' When specifically asked about the appearance of thousands of dead fish, the official paused to sip tea.

'We are promoting tourism here. We should talk less about this.'

'Lords of the Road! You guys are the new Silk Road warriors!' screeched Maggie, a New York photographer we had bumped into the night before in the only bar between Xian and Urumqi. We blushed and grimaced, yet carried on posing.

'That's great! That's great! Keep those wheels turning!'

We manoeuvred our bikes into a V-formation on the outskirts of Dunhuang, a large oasis town in the middle of the desert. Maggie was the glamorous and experienced photojournalist incarnate. Tall, attractive, with lots of hair and a flowing scarf, she was the first foreigner we had seen or talked to since leaving Beijing. Pouncing on the sophisticated alcohol available in the Manhattan Café, we had competed for her attention in a haze of cigarette smoke over cocktail after cocktail. She paid polite smiling attention to our stories and told us that she was on an assignment, covering the Silk Road as it was today.

Now we were part of her shoot.

'Hold it! Hold it! Come closer! Great.'

Maggie climbed into Fim's sidecar and, scarf flying, yelled detailed instructions at us as we picked up speed and crossed the desert on the way to the reason why we were all in Dunhuang. Just outside town are the Buddhist Mogao Caves, *the* buried treasure of the Silk Road and one of the wonders of the world. This is despite the ravages of time, squatters, treasure hunters, botched restoration techniques and the wholesale removal of frescoes and literary treasures. Here, buried for centuries under the shifting desert sands, are 490 caves displaying priceless Buddhist murals and statues in varying degrees of workmanship and condition. There are many different styles as the caves were decorated over hundreds of years between the fifth and the eleventh centuries. They were created by an army of monks and artisans, and were paid for by wealthy merchants seeking heavenly blessings on their journeys west along the Silk Road.

The caves were 'discovered' by a British archaeologist, Auriel Stein, in 1907. He stumbled across the honeycomb of caves in this desert hillside after tracing an ancient wall in the desert. Several years earlier, a local Taoist priest, Wang Yuanlu, had come across a walled cave that had been blocked up some nine hundred years before. Inside was a library containing thousands of silk paintings, manuscripts, Buddhist texts and legal documents. Wang, who had taken on a caretaker function, was coaxed (with offers of a large donation to his religious practice) to hand over large tracts of ancient written material to Stein who, working with a Chinese assistant, selected items to take back to Britain as fast as he could. The items were a confusing mixture of Chinese, Tibetan, Tangut, Khotanese, Songdian and Uighur.

Despite finding the buried Buddhist treasures, Wang, who started the great sell-off at the turn of the century, remained ignorant of their importance and value. They included the oldest printed book in the world, the Diamond Sutra, now in the British Museum. Printed on fine yellow paper several centuries before paper was known in the West, it is the earliest example of block printing with a date, 11 May AD 868 (or more enigmatically in the Chinese classical calendar, thirteenth of the fourth moon of the ninth year of Xiantong). Much of the later work, which Abbot Wang himself supervised, jars with earlier statues and murals from a different age. These bizarre cross-century clashes stand as a permanent testament to the amateur caretaker.

After Stein's discovery, word got around the international archaeological adventure scene and there were several more visitors to the site, including Pelliot, a Frenchman, Tachibana of Japan, a Russian called Oldenburg, and even Beijing government employees.

The last treasure hunter to get here and remove large amounts of material was an American called Langdon Warner. He arrived in 1924 after the caves had been used to house nearly four hundred Cossacks fleeing from the Russian revolution.

Visiting one of the caves where the Russians had camped, one can still see the blackened walls caused by cooking fires and the graffiti that has destroyed parts of the murals. Face to face with such casual destruction one can understand

Warner's horrified reaction and his desire to remove many of the murals to somewhere less exposed. He recorded his reaction in *The Long Old Road in China*: 'But it was with a shock that I traced, on the oval faces and calm mouths, the foul scratches of Slavic obscenity and the regimental numbers which Ivan and his folk had left there.'

Unfortunately, Warner added to the destruction himself by attempting to remove some murals with a flawed technique. Where he was successful, there are now great gaps in the tableaux where a head or torso is missing. Mrs Ma, our local guide, seemed remarkably even-handed about these imperialist looters who had acted with such impunity and complete disregard for China's sovereignty. While mentioning with regret that a lot of statues, written Buddhist texts and murals were now overseas (primarily in London, Bombay and Berlin), Mrs Ma spoke of the many murals and other items lost for ever as a result of local ignorance. Some of the caves were until recently regularly used by farmers to put their goats in at night. The unwillingness or the inability of the Beijing government, thousands of miles away, to look after the site had not helped. After the Communist victory in 1949 steps were taken to preserve what was left of the painted caves. There is now a large research centre nearby.

In an ironic twist to the Dunhuang story, foreign treasure hunters may have inadvertently saved the caves from total destruction. During the early 1970s, Cultural Revolution-fever in China was at its height and the whole country was exhorted to destroy their feudal heritage. Young Chinese went on an orgy of destruction that saw vast numbers of irreplaceable works of art smashed to bits. When a group of zealous Red Guards turned up in Dunhuang intent on trashing the caves, there seemed to be no authority strong enough to stop them. When they arrived at the caves they found the local mayor standing guard. Asked what he was doing guarding such feudal relics of China's hated past, he replied that he had been personally asked to stand guard by one of Beijing's top leaders, Zhou Enlai (second in the pantheon of Communist heroes to Mao Zedong) in case any more foreigners walked off with Chinese property.

The Red Guards, moved by his patriotism, instead of destroying the caves stood guard with the mayor as well. The official's quick-witted appeal to the ever-present nationalism of his countrymen saved the caves and the murals from certain destruction.

Despite the ravages of time and humans, many of the caves remain breathtaking in their beauty. Not only do they represent the pinnacle of Chinese religious art, but they act as an ancient Tardis, transporting one back to a different age.

> The desert that lies between Anxi and Hami is a howling wilderness, and the first thing which strikes the wayfarer is the dismalness of its uniform, black, pebble-strewn surface.
>
> – Cable and French, *The Gobi Desert*

Real rocky desert now encompassed us and the temperature rose. To our left were a series of low mountains. A herd of camels crossed the road in front of us, untended and with seemingly muffled hooves. We passed several decrepit mud and stone structures of ill-defined shape, the sun-blasted remains of temples where travellers made their offerings for a safe journey. We stopped by a one-domed stone structure, which rose about 20 feet out of the desert. There was no window, doorway or ledge and we scratched our heads as to its original shape and purpose. Perhaps it was a marker to stop people from losing their bearings. It is difficult to gauge distance in the desert, like when one stares out of an aeroplane at blue sky.

We camped under a vast pink desert sky, at its edges every shade of blue. Despite the sometimes monotonous grey grit and heat of the landscape, there was a calmness that affected us all. Our talk was subdued and unhurried. Worries, concerns, plans and anxieties had been left behind. On the bikes the long distances and wide horizons encouraged daydreams, whole realms of thought and internal conversation. The trivial, the serious, the life affirming, the idiotic and the fanciful. Gradually, over hundreds of miles, we realised we were all at it. When we stopped to rest the bikes and our arms, spinning fragments of thought were shared. The waitress you should have asked out, food you missed, politics, a bath, the distance to the Russian border, the distance we had travelled, what others were doing at that precise moment, history, what you would eat tonight, how you ended up in China. Nothing and everything.

On a couple of occasions when we stopped, I noticed that Tim was a bit stiff getting off his bike. Worried at a possible piles-related situation, I asked him if he was all right.

'Yup. Fine. Just a case of Convoy Cock,' he said as he gripped his groin and made a face.

'Convoy Cock?'

'A stiffy. It's a medically recognised condition in the army brought on by the vibrations of a long journey.'

Tim remained straight-faced as we collapsed in laughter.

Tim's vocabulary had by now degenerated into a military slang that appeared in short staccato bursts of energy. Every new phrase was greeted with bemused grins from the rest of us. As the trip progressed, more and more words and phrases emerged and a subculture of slang piled up. Much to our hilarity and Tim's annoyance, we spent several evenings concocting an A-Z of Tim-speak.

A is for Arse. C is for Clickety-Clicks (kilometres) or Crack On (Let's get moving!) or of course Convoy Cock. D is for Dosh. F is for Fucking Wanker (usually reserved for anyone else not in our little convoy). K is for Khazi (toilet). R is for Recce (as in recconaisance). S is for Sparrow's Fart (dawn). T is for Tea (large amounts drunk at every available opportunity). W is for Wallah (local person of any nationality, their profession to be inserted before wallah, e.g. petrol-wallah, peasant-wallah, truck-wallah).

Further evidence, if it was needed, of Tim's retreat into a previous military persona came with the sighting of a kukri, the curved regimental blade of the Gurkhas, underneath his sleeping bag. Strategically placed within an arm's reach of action, its nightly presence became strangely comforting. Despite Tim's hope that it would be flashed in anger at some stumbling intruder, it remained quiet and sheathed the whole journey.

Chapter Fourteen

Uighurland

The people are all idolaters and have a peculiar language. They live by the fruits of the earth, which they have in plenty, and dispose of to travellers. They are a people who take things very easily for they mind nothing but playing, singing, dancing and enjoying themselves.

– Marco Polo

'We are in China, but not amongst Chinese,' I wrote in my diary. We were in Hami, a town of 300,000 in Xinjiang, the westernmost province of China that borders Kazakhstan, Kirgyzstan, Tajikistan, Pakistan and Tibet. The city is a mixture of Chinese, Hui and Uighur peoples. We sat in the Uighur part of town feasting on kebabs, mini-pasties stuffed with lamb fat, and home-made noodles. The Uighurs are of Turkish origin and their first language is not Chinese, but a Turkish-related dialect. They do not look Chinese; many are darker, have blue eyes, lighter hair and are Muslim. Their more extrovert behaviour marks them out from their reserved Han neighbours. Our arrival in this part of town set off a flurry of activity amongst the owners of the restaurants that spilled onto the street.

Loud whoops and shrieks of excitement, banging of pots and pans, barking dogs and thickly accented shouts of 'welcome' in Mandarin greeted us. A crowd swarmed around the bikes and several fired up waiters tried to manhandle us to a table outside their particular restaurant.

The Uighur part of Hami is a collection of winding streets, markets and mosques with a charm totally lacking in the rest of the city. It is filthy and noisy, but has retained some essential quality and is full of atmosphere and life. Many of the Uighurs looked almost Mediterranean in appearance and could pass as Sicilian or Albanian. Two attractive young women in summer dresses and loose scarves walked slowly past our table, turned their heads and smiled. They put on a flirtatious act before collapsing into giggles further down the road. Their frivolity was a breath of fresh air after the unrelenting practicality of their Han cousins. We realised we were now in a different country.

Xiao Li felt for the first time the peculiar sensation of being in China, but outnumbered by different-looking people. He was uncomfortable and was unusually agitated.

'Where are these people from? They don't look like us.'

He ate his noodles with grumpy jerks of his chopsticks and watched the street with lowered eyes.

While there are many Uighurs in Beijing, we all felt a fresh excitement at finally meeting them on their own turf. They are the great underdogs of Chinese history. They make up about 7 million of Xinjiang's 16 million people, and it is fair to say that they are looked down upon by the majority of Han and Hui. The government lectures them endlessly about the perils of separatism. It is on their land that the government also chooses to carry out nuclear bomb tests. 'A patient, contented and submissive people, made to be ruled by others,' was how Eric Teichmann, who drove along this route in the 1930s in the aftermath of a failed uprising against Han rule, described them. While patronising, there is an element of truth in his comments. The Uighurs have none of the glamour or mysticism of their Tibetan cousins to the south, and their little-known sporadic struggle for independence from their Han overlords has absolutely no chance of succeeding.

Uighurs complain of religious restrictions and job discrimination in favour of newly arrived Han immigrants to the region. Many Chinese see them as spoilt, convinced that the region receives outrageous amounts of state subsidy in the form of development aid. Exemption from China's one-child policy, like other minorities in China, fuels an image, in Han eyes, of an ungrateful people.

If you say 'Hami' to most Chinese, they will immediately respond with, 'Hami *gua*, Hami *gua*.' One should nod vigorously in agreement at this point for this is not the beginning of some ritual chant which will end in injury, but an affirmation of the tastiness of Hami's most famous product. Hami is known throughout China for its melons, the 'Hami *gua*.' There are over thirty different varieties, and the humble Hami melon achieved its fame through being on the table of the imperial court in Beijing. After several emperors had extolled the delights of melons from Hami, no other melon would do.

Today, Chinese still insist that Hami melons are the best in China, and indeed the world. Any attempt to suggest that you might have eaten one once a long time ago that tasted better than a Hami melon is met with disbelief. This is impossible. The Hami melon is one of the bricks in the mental construct that supports the superiority of Chinese civilisation over all others. To deny the Hami melon its exalted position is to start playing footloose and fancy-free with the building blocks of the Chinese cultural makeup. They are extremely good.

While Marco Polo almost certainly did not visit the town himself (if he even made it to China) there is a passage in *The Travels of Marco Polo* where he describes a delightful Hami custom and one that we would have been happy to have experienced:

> 'And it is the truth that if a foreigner comes to the house of one of these people to lodge, the host is delighted, and desires his wife to put herself entirely at the guest's disposal, whilst he himself gets out of the way, and comes back no more until the stranger shall have taken his departure. The guest may stay and enjoy the wife's society as long as he likes, while the husband has no shame in the matter, but indeed considers it an honour.'

While we were several centuries too late to enjoy the hospitable Uighur tradition of letting a complete stranger sleep with your wife, we did manage to visit the medieval tombs of the Hami kings and queens. Tucked away on the edge of the Muslim quarter, an old mosque and the remains of the Royal Mausoleum stand behind a large green iron gate shrouded by yew trees. One of the two tombs (the rest were destroyed by Red Guards during the Cultural Revolution) is a strange hexagonal shape made of packed mud, with latticed wooden windows below a domed top. The other, squat and square, has brilliant turquoise tiling peeling from its outer walls. There is a calmness and serenity to the place. Even the obligatory guide seemed softer and more sympathetic than the usual official guardians of historical sites.

A serious young man, he asked us what we were doing, and we explained that we were driving back to London, having lived in China for a while.

'How romantic,' he sighed, brushing a long fringe away. We were unused to such a positive view of our journey. The usual reply was, 'You're mad!', 'You're what?', 'Why?' and the group favourite, 'Why don't you fly?' His response reconfirmed that we had left China proper and were amidst people that did not accept the unremitting obsession with practicalities that so characterises the Han Chinese.

Here rest the Muslim Hami kings and queens, a reminder that Xinjiang has a more lively and complex history than many Chinese want to know. Hami had its own Muslim king until the 1930s. Their writ ran only to the edge of town and one is tempted to dismiss them as a Ruritanian joke. Yet outside the town lie thousands of square miles of desert and the only shelter from the inhospitable terrain is Hami, the 'eastern gateway' to Chinese Turkistan. The oasis town occupied a strategic position through which every traveller and merchant would have to pass through for supplies on their way east or west through the Gobi. It was a prosperous and pleasant place, something that can still be felt today.

The khans of Hami were tolerated by the Chinese as they were supposed to keep control of the locals. They managed to continue their laid-back rule into the 1930s when three remarkable Scottish missionaries, Mildred Cable, and Eva and Francesca French, 'staunch, stout, with thin wispy buns', visited Hami and recorded their experiences in the book, *The Gobi Desert*.

When they visited Hami, the Khan, Maksud Shah, 'King of the Gobi' was already a very old man. From his luxurious palace, which is described at length, he claimed to rule a territory 'as far as you could see and more.' He had three palaces, the largest of which was in Hami. Another at Lukchun, close to Turfan, contained his harem. These three upright ladies visited the harem and paint an extraordinary picture of harem life, complete with gardens, peacocks, bitter jealousy and insecurities. They went to stay at his summer residence, north of Hami, with its *Alice in Wonderland* gardens planted with every imaginable tree and plant.

While in the region the missionaries were witness to scenes that would spark upheaval and turmoil for years to come, and resulted in the destruction of this small imperial world. The khan died and his son, the heir to the throne, was seized by the Chinese, taken to Urumqi and jailed. As a result of this and other heavy-handed actions by the Chinese, there were several armed uprisings across the north-west. Several years and thousands of deaths later, the Chinese finally gained control of the area with Russian military help. The glorious gardens and palaces of the khan, as well as most of Hami, were destroyed.

The town sits between the two great deserts of China, the Gobi to the north and the Taklamakan to the south. Mildred Cable and the French sisters, unlike our own fleeting embrace, crossed and re-crossed these deserts of western China for an incredible fifteen years. This required a physical and mental stamina beyond anything we could muster. It can only be explained by their strong religious beliefs. Years later, in an attempt to explain the attractions of this uncompromising part of the earth they modestly wrote: 'The desert had its terrors, but it also had its compensating pleasures . . . solitude provoked reflection, wide space a sense of proportion and silences forbade triviality.'

We sat in the shade of a large boulder in the most inhospitable natural environment I have ever seen. In wonder we looked out on a completely still and unbelievably hot vista of rocks, stone and gravel. Apart from the rock behind us, there seemed to be no shade in a 40-mile radius. The temperature had pushed up towards 40 °C and we had had to stop riding and find somewhere to hide from the sun. Worried about the motorbike engines overheating, we had rolled them into a low concrete storm tunnel under the road. It was impossible to stand up or sit down in this scrap of shadow as, apart from the motorbikes and the lack of height, there was human shit everywhere.

The large stone offered just enough shade for all of us to huddle under. The road behind us shimmered in the heat and brown desert rock was everywhere. There was no noise, no trees, no grass, no houses and no wildlife – only the occasional passing truck. The desert had become, for the first time, a truly forbidding place. Our long search for shade had made me slightly nervous. An element of danger had crept in, as if we were novice sailors at sea and the wind had picked up, becoming stronger than we had realised or planned for. We had entered the Turfan Depression, a 2,500 square mile area of desert whose lowest point, Aydingkol ('Moonlight') Lake, at 505 feet below sea level, is the second lowest spot on the planet after the Dead Sea.

We watched in silence as a man on a camel moved across our range of view from left to right. They walked across the stony ground, the camel's hooves making a faint noise as they touched the road, and then man and camel floated off across more scorched rocks. We remained hidden from view in the dark shade of the rock, immobile like lizards. Where was he going? How could he move about in this heat? I pressed myself back into the rock as I tried to keep my limbs out of the sun.

When we felt that the heat had spent some of its force, we dragged ourselves out from under the boulder's shade. Retrieving the bikes, we rode on west and almost immediately headed steeply down into the bowels of the earth. The road ran down and down while in the distance the other side of the valley rode up like a giant tidal wave of rock to meet us. The hot air felt as if it came straight out of a convection oven. I imagined we were well below sea level. We sped along the bottom of the basin floor that was covered in fine golden sand.

The road climbed again and I revved the engine for the steep climb up. The tarmac seemed like greased paper and I seemed to struggle to gain any distance between myself and the bottom of the basin floor. The engine lacked power. The unremitting sun and the thought of breaking down in this cauldron of trapped heat made me nauseous. Anxious to be out of this sinister depression, I began willing the bike on, even whispering encouragement as if it were a horse. The other bikers were above me on the road, hunched low and black over their machines. Such slow progress; I feared to turn round in case I felt dizzy from the steep climb.

As we inched out of the cauldron of scorched earth, we

passed two huge and bloated dead pigs lying by the side of the road. They must have fallen off an overloaded truck, an unconscious sacrifice for a successful crossing. Their presence reinforced a feeling of unease.

I hid from the afternoon sun under the heavy trellised vines of an empty hotel. Outside the darkened cool corner of sanity it was blinding white. Turfan is one of the hottest places on earth, reaching 54 °C in the summer. I was amazed at the stamina of my fellow-bikers who had all gone sightseeing.

The town is a splash of luxuriant fertile green in a gravel wasteland. It is to grapes what Hami is to melons, producing over 100 varieties. They are dried on trellises throughout the city and its suburbs to produce sweet seedless raisins that are famous throughout China. In the older parts of town the streets between the houses are dark as covered heavy trellises cross the streets blocking out the sunlight. Water is provided for irrigation by means of ingenious subterranean canals of glacial water that flow down from the Tian Shan ('Heavenly Mountains') to the north. Known as *karez*, these underground watercourses hold the key to Turfan's survival and prosperity in a land of virtually no rain and scorching temperatures. This extended system has been built over the centuries and the total length is said to equal the length of the Great Wall.

All along this part of the Silk Road are the ghosts of ancient cities buried under the sand, destroyed by Mongols or inter-oasis battles. The area is criss-crossed with archaeological remains from previous centuries, BC and AD; grottoes, forts, temples, whole cities and tombs. Thanks to the dry and hot climate, thousands of unearthed cultural relics are preserved. Twenty-five miles south-east of Turfan is a series of tombs that hold more than 500 people whose dried-up bodies have been preserved by the sand.

We were pleased to be here. After the valley of heat we had continued towards Turfan across a blackened burnt-out desert. Waves of dark pebbles had been formed by the wind into large mounds and ridges and lay to our right like black mountains. This was a prehistoric landscape, it looked as if it had been consumed by fire. It now lay completely barren and inert. One expected an enormous Komodo lizard to emerge and slither across the road. As the Tian Shan appeared on our right, the snow-capped peaks and sloping glaciers seemed to have a cooling effect. Their melted waters softened the hard brutal landscape as we edged towards Turfan, allowing the occasional sign of life and a variation on the colour black.

In the last hours before the city, the road ceased to exist and we were forced to scrabble over sandy tracks with huge bumps and dips. We arrived, as always, filthy and exhausted.

I drifted off into the half-sleep that is the afternoon siesta. In the heaviness of the mid-afternoon I could hear the scrape of metal against tarmac in the courtyard. Xiao Li, organising more spare parts for the bikes to get to us to Urumqi. Unlike the others whose wanderings in the sun I could not fathom, I was not surprised by Xiao Li's activity. He had become more and more restless the further we left Han China proper behind. This made me think that it was not so much the discomfort of the journey, but rather his unease at being in such foreign parts and amongst such strange and different peoples. His greatest unspoken wish now was to cross the desert as fast as possible and get to Urumqi where, as agreed, he would fly back to Beijing.

I made one feeble sortie to buy some cigarettes. I entered a black hole in a wall ringed by empty cigarette and fizzy drink packaging. Inside it was cool and dark. The earth smelt deliciously damp. My eyes took time to adjust to the sudden change in light and I stumbled, hitting my head on something hard. There was shuffling and noises off stage. I had the feeling of being watched.

'Hot, eh?' said a voice. Gradually I made out an old man standing stock-still behind a glass counter to my left. I wasn't sure if this was a question or a statement.

'We Turfan residents stay inside during this heat.'

'That must be almost every day,' I quipped.

'Yes, it is.'

We drove straight into the sun as we headed west out of Turfan for Urumqi. We had left in the evening thinking it would be cooler, but we still encountered a heat of biblical proportions. Aitchen Wu, a former Chinese official, wrote of it: 'The hot wind is worse than anything that can be imagined, shrivelling the skin, scorching the eyes; and the direct rays of the sun carry death.'

We drove hunched over the handlebars. Despite goggles we could only lift our heads so that we had a view of the road immediately ahead of the front tyre. Lifting one's head any further brought a blast of white light that threatened disorientation and temporary blindness. The sun's heat was still ridiculously strong. I checked my watch; it was 8 p.m. I realised we must still be on Beijing time. A hot wind picked up, gusting down from the mountains to our right and blowing so hard that our progress was reduced to a crawl. Trying to keep the bike going in a straight line was exhausting as the wind threatened to push us into the path of an oncoming truck or off the road altogether.

To our left lay what looked like a long range of small mountains that ran parallel to the road. They were actually gigantic mounds of small black stones that the northerly wind (down from Mongolia) had deposited in its sweep across the vast open spaces. We stopped at an isolated petrol station where the pumps were in a hollow in the ground. Vehicles had to drive into a sort of concrete pit to get refuelled because of the wind. We watched the sky turn dark and looked across at the mountains of shingle with apprehension. If the wind picked up and changed direction, these walls of pebbles would be flying towards us.

We rode on for hours across the hostile landscape with the skies darkening and the bikes being pushed around by the wind. Only two of the five headlights were functioning. We stopped to put the only bikes with lights at the back and front of our convoy. At a junction where the road split for Urumqi and Korla, there were several thatched brick shacks serving beer and instant noodles for the truck drivers that thundered past in clouds of dust. We huddled in the porch of one, out of the reach of gusts of sand. My arms ached.

We discussed the wind with the owner, a fat unshaven man in a filthy vest.

'This is nothing. When the wind really blows whole trucks are overturned and pushed across the road.'

With that he looked at our motorbikes and sidecars and shook his head. He advised us to keep going towards Urumqi, saying that the wind should drop considerably in a nearby mountain range. I was not inclined to hang about and find out whether this café owner was just jesting with the foreigners or whether his stories of eight-ton trucks being picked up on a regular basis by the desert wind were genuine. It was dark now and I was tired of fighting the elements. As we left the crossroads there was a sudden gust of wind that knocked over the café's outside pool table with a loud crash. The owner seemed not to care, as if this was a regular occurrence and he let the balls lie as they fell. His casual acceptance of the destruction of the only entertainment in an eighty-mile vicinity seemed to confirm that he had been telling the truth about the wind. We hurried on.

The wind died down as we entered a mountain range south of Urumqi. The roads though became more dangerous as we competed with drugged up night-time truck drivers in their huge Liberation trucks. Bend after bend with no end in sight. Every corner was a terrifying experience as we would see the headlights before a convoy of wild lorries screamed round the corner. I felt as if I was in some cartoon that would soon have us smashed over the side of the road. We must have all felt the same uncomfortable loss of control; as soon as the narrow valley would allow, Tim and Fim pulled off the road and we all followed. We laid out our sleeping bags on a dry riverbed in the dark, and went to sleep to the noise of passing trucks.

We woke up to find that we had slept on what was obviously the local dumping ground for truck drivers caught short. Emerging gingerly from my sleeping bag, I tried to pack up without stepping on any of the human waste that littered the ground. There was a thatched dwelling nearby made of rubber tyres, scraps of wood and plastic bags. The wild-eyed owner emerged like Stig of the Dump with his toothless wife.

Just outside Urumqi the road came to a halt and we drove

across churned up sand tracks with hundreds of other vehicles. I caught sight of Xiao Li in Ed's sidecar, adjusting his cotton mask to keep out the sand. The dust made it difficult to see what lay ahead and as there was more than one route, there was constant interweaving of traffic. This was further complicated by the fact that we were driving through a landscape dominated by hundreds of wind turbines. This wind farm was not on the scale one might find in Europe, a few acres set aside for experimentation, but a vast tableau of whirling white blades that stretched across the valley floor. We were amazed that the company that bought such expensive equipment would let Chinese truck drivers into such close proximity.

Urumqi is the heart of Chinese administrative control over Xinjiang. Despite its importance, it does not get favourable reviews: 'The town has no beauty, style, no dignity and no architectural interest. The climate is violent, exaggerated and at no season pleasant.' The comments of Cable and French in *The Gobi Desert* are typical of the impression Urumqi leaves on the foreign traveller. Sven Hedin wrote on a visit in 1930 that 'No one leaves the town with regret, and it is full of people who are only there because they cannot get permission to leave and may not leave without permission.'

This visceral reaction to what is now an enormous sprawling urban conurbation is understandable. We had driven on highways of mud with hundreds of other vehicles into the suburbs of the city. Shacks of wood and corrugated iron lined the unpaved road underneath a chaotic canopy of wires and there was the stench of raw sewage everywhere. Large puddles of filthy liquid lay around and watermelon skins, flimsy striped plastic bags and hundreds of empty plastic yogurt pots lined the road in shallow ditches. A massive underground coal fire has been burning for over twenty years. Driven by poverty, local farmers have dug thousands of small mineshafts down into the coal seams. It is thought an accident inside one of these amateur and illegal mines is to blame for the fire. The subsequent sulphurous gas, along with other toxic factories, has contributed to serious air pollution in a city that is amongst the top ten worst-polluted cities in the world.

However, in the centre, tall modern buildings dominate, neon signs proliferate and there is a bustle and an activity that is lacking in many cites. For all its peripheral wretchedness, there is an edge to the city, a sense of a town on the cusp of the known world. Foreigners are welcomed with a warm normality. Relaxed conversations are laced with ironic smiles and pauses, as if the vast surrounding wilderness set its own particular pace. In a bar we struck up an easy rapport with people, all stranded on the wrong side of the desert. A stylish woman drank with Ed, glass for glass, at the bar. She parried his ABC of Chinese chat-up lines with a lazy smile.

'What do you do?'

'I am a student.'

'Where are you studying?'

'I am going to Beijing.'

'Will you come back?'

'That depends on what I find there.'

'What are you going to study?'

'Astrophysics.'

Ed hesitated. Dom and I smirked into our glasses.

The evening was spent in the company of one of Urumqi's largest private wholesalers, the formidable Mrs Shan (translation: Mrs Mountain). In her mid-forties, with a booming voice and shrewd business acumen, she was now one of the recently successful. The boss of a medium-sized company, one that actually made money, her hospitality and largesse were on a grand scale: dinner in the top Uighur restaurant, introductions to all and sundry, and a tour of the bars with her staff as guides. Her enthusiasm and spontaneity were refreshing after the traditional Henan wholesaler experience.

'Mr Ma, did you ever meet the late Princess Diana? She was a role model for me,' she sighed as another plate of grilled mutton and onions arrived. It was more likely that her role model was another Uighur woman, Rebiya Kadeer, at the time the richest businessperson in Xinjiang. A folk hero to many, she would be sentenced to eight years in jail less than two years later on charges of engaging in separatist behaviour. She had collected newspaper clippings on riots and demonstrations in the province and sent them to her husband in the US.

As we left the third bar after dinner, a large car appeared from around a corner and she climbed into the back.

'I have to go home as I am getting too old for such entertainment,' she giggled.

She issued orders for her staff to continue without her. I stumbled back to the hotel at four in the morning, delightfully drunk.

Briefly independent from China in the 1940s as 'East Turkistan', Xinjiang has for some time been billed as an autonomous area by the Beijing government. In the past it definitely was, its remote location ensuring that semi-independent warlords rather than central government ran the place. Yet Beijing now keeps a tight grip on this land with its rich oil and mineral deposits and its sensitive borders. Despite an influx of Han settlers and prominent army personnel, discontent simmers and sometimes boils over. There have been reports of rioting and arrests, a string of bomb blasts (some in Beijing) and executions. Military personnel and vehicles proliferate. The excuse is often religion as the Chinese are atheists and the Uighurs are Muslim. Yet racial animosity also plays a part. The Chinese look down on the Uighurs and see them as unstable, uncouth, illiterate and plain dirty. For the Uighurs, their relationship with their Han neighbours is more complex. They do not have the same certainties about their own history and they have been ruled over for thousands of years with only one very brief moment of self-rule. Their towns are far apart and they need the Chinese for business and investment as much as the Chinese need their land.

For the most part there is an uneasy compromise. It is from Urumqi that the government co-ordinates efforts to develop Xinjiang economically. While much has been done in the last thirty years to 'attract the phoenix' (investment) there nevertheless seems a feeling of frustration in Beijing that more has not been achieved. Officials in the capital look at all that space on the map and can't quite believe greater efforts cannot be made.

'West China makes half of China's total territory, has 27 per cent of the farmland and 46 per cent of water resources,' complains the official *Science and Technology Daily*. 'All this plus rich sunlight, provide the region with advantageous natural conditions for cotton, tobacco, fruit and flower production. However, the area is much less developed compared to the eastern coastal area.'

'Unexploited opportunities for economic growth' loom large. The west of China is like the slow boy at the back of the class, forever receiving end of term reports that hint at untapped potential and urge him to 'try harder.' Vague figures regarding massive investment and bombastic statements are thrown about, but in the absence of transparency it is difficult to know what is accurate.

The bold claims of the early 1990s have given way to a more realistic assessment. Many are aware that greater 'exploitation' would further undermine the already extremely fragile ecological situation. Some officials feel confident enough to argue that in an area with 2.6 million square miles of bleak desert, development should come secondary to environmental protection and restoring damaged grasslands.

Still, old habits die hard, and the Xinjiang provincial authorities cannot resist coming up with 'blueprints for the future' that will 'accelerate the pace of development.' 'Do you not see that the spirit of opening to the world that once created the Silk Road is being forcefully promoted in the vast land of Xinjiang once more?' commented the *People's Daily* after yet another plan was outlined.

We left Urumqi without Xiao Li. I can't have been the only member of the team to have felt nervous and uneasy about his departure. He had been an easygoing member of the team and the friendliest mechanic I had ever met. I had, however, failed to gain the elementary understanding of the Changjiang 750's engine required for the journey ahead, despite more than three weeks on the road. Whilst I now had a good understanding of the bike's topography and could point out the regulator, alternator, solenoid and other highlights, I was still in the dark as to how it all worked. Check the oil, change the spokes, test the spark plugs, change a wheel, yes. I had done so already on numerous occasions. When one writes it out on paper it actually sounds like an impressive list. But actually fix a mechanical fault – no. I had tried. In Xiao Li's last days with us I had spent several hours going through a repair manual in Chinese, while he pointed out the relevant parts of the bike. It felt as if the next day there was going to be an almighty exam, one that you couldn't bluff. After one particularly perplexing session I closed the book with its diagrams and strange terminology and asked Xiao Li what he thought our chances were of reaching Pakistan, 1,300 miles of desert and mountain away.

'*Hai keyi ba.*'

This is a polite phrase often used in Chinese when one does not want to offend. The nearest translation is 'maybe' or 'possibly'. Whilst not technically negative, the equivocal tone gives the game away. In a country where flattery and positive comments are the norm, the lack of a ringing endorsement is highly noticeable. The person replying is less than enthusiastic. As an example, if I bought a pair of trousers and asked someone what they thought of them and the reply was '*hai keyi ba*', I would know that while he or she was being polite, what they really thought was that the trousers were a disastrously unfashionable and inappropriate purchase. The clever thing about this phrase is that without actually saying anything negative, thereby causing offence, the other person knows exactly what you really think. After Xiao Li's less than ringing endorsement, we headed off again into the desert with a certain apprehension.

Less than 48 hours later, I lay underneath my bike in the hot and dangerous bends that are the Toksun Gorge, traditionally one of the most unpleasant and difficult parts of the journey. I attempted to find the cause of the lack of power. I decided the best course of action was to let the overheated engine cool off. The others joined me and we sat by the side of the gorge and lobbed stones into the void to a dry riverbed hundreds of feet below. There was a satisfying click-clack as they bounced off the yellow rock face. It was some compensation that our forced halt would have been understood by the many previous travellers, including Sir Francis Younghusband, Sven Hedin and Erich Teichmann, who had all been held up in the Toksun Gorge. The last British consular official based in Kashgar, Eric Shipton, cracked the cylinder of his Ford truck and had to abandon the vehicle in the desert in the early 1940s.

That night we searched for a flat piece of ground away from the road to camp. Trying tracks that left the main road, we were forced to scrabble higher and higher over stones to find shelter. A vicious wind howled through the small empty canyons. We ended up camping in a disused quarry. Climbing up black scree, one could see the lights of the next town, Korla, in the distance. In the night, under billowing canvas, there was the occasional crash of stone as the wind dislodged loose rocks. I couldn't sleep with all the rustling rocks and spent the next day in a foul mood.

Chapter Fifteen

Heat and Dust (and Mud)

A tough, burly woman with curly hair argued over the bill with me. She smoked a haystack of a hand-rolled cigarette as she cooked. Her face was covered in several layers of make-up. She was the monstrous owner of a 'café' we had optimistically stopped at. In her huge blue nylon dress, thick black stockings and fluffy slippers she could have been a brothel Madam. While we haggled over the price of one modest, fatty lunch, she turned her head to shout at her hapless husband to hurry up and write the bill.

All smiles at the beginning, she was now furious with us for daring to challenge, in her eyes, the quite legitimate mark-up of around 4,000 per cent for foreigners. Despite being warned in Urumqi that Korla was a desperate place ('evil and windy'), we had not bothered to check the prices before wiping the dust from our stools and sitting down to eat. Overcharging is a problem for travellers everywhere, but in China the situation can usually be resolved with a minimum of fuss; it was quite rare to encounter such vehement opposition to a compromise on the part of the restaurant owner.

I was more indignant than cross. How could she possibly have mistaken us for her proper target, a coach-load of tourists? We were hardy independent travellers who all spoke the same language. We were still residents of China, for goodness sake. How could she bracket us with other foreigners? Didn't she see that trying to rip us off was plain wrong?

Her aggressive demeanour in the kitchen reminded me of that other culinary battleaxe, Fanny Cradock. For those too young to remember this British culinary doyenne, she lectured millions of aspiring housewives in the seventies through her books and TV series on how to prepare a decent meal. She always remained a slightly terrifying figure and seemed to enjoy ordering her husband around both on and off stage as if he were hired help. She once stayed with my grandparents on the island of Alderney where between giving cooking demonstrations and shouting at her husband, she fell asleep on the lavatory and burnt a hole in the wooden loo seat with her cigarette.

While Tim and Ed mended a broken gasket in the muddy forecourt of the café, I struggled on with Fanny Wong in an attempt to bring down the price of our lunch of mutton fat, stale bread, boiled-to-death cabbage and chemical beer from its current stratospheric sphere. I felt obliged to haggle on behalf of the group, as it was I who had chosen the 'restaurant' out of about twenty that ran parallel to the main road. They all had the same open ceramic coal-fired ovens, seats outside under plastic grapes and all were covered in a layer of coal dust. Dotted amongst them were one-man repair shops, with screeching lathes spitting fiery sparks. The one I had chosen had potted plants in a row along the top of the low outside wall that separated the foul mud where customers parked from the restaurant itself. Seduced by this attempt to soften the surroundings and hinting as it did at a sensitive soul, we had sat down at her café. She now scraped her chair closer to mine and lectured me on the current cost of food in Korla.

'Nothing grows around here,' she said with a massive shake of her flabby arms. 'Everything is imported from other parts of China.'

'Even cabbage?'

'Even cabbage! Everything around here is rotten and polluted. There is not enough water to farm properly. This is a horrible place!' she said.

Her argument had now subtly shifted from the high cost of obtaining food in the area to the more general and emotive argument that Korla is one of the foulest places that anyone could ever end up. While I did not believe her on the first count, her rail against the truck-stop of Korla attracted my sympathy. Korla was a desolate spot.

Outside, dogs played in litter and shit while trucks thundered past on their way somewhere else. The city was a drab concrete affair, its ancient glories having either been destroyed, stolen or hidden so far in and under the desert that they remained elusive to all but the most intrepid and specialist experts. The harridan ranted away, occasionally stopping to dab an eye with a soiled cloth for dramatic effect. This was undermined by her intermittent yelling at her out-of-sight husband to fetch her tea or check on the stove.

The couple were not from the area and had come from China's overpopulated and poor central provinces. They opened the restaurant to make a better living for themselves, but found it very difficult. When Teichmann went through Korla, Kulcha, Aksu and other towns of the desert in the 1930s, there was hardly a Han Chinese in sight. In the 1950s, millions were encouraged to settle in this semi-arid fragile environment. Immigrants from the overpopulated Chinese interior, like our formidable hostess, had gradually changed these Uighur communities into predominantly Han settlements.

To come and live in Korla her previous town must have been of unimaginable dreariness. While sympathising with her plight, I refused to give up on making some sort of dent in the overblown price. My refusal to compromise led to an explosion.

'You don't have to live in this fucking town!' she screamed. 'You can leeeeave!'

With that she clutched my arm in an iron grip, looked straight into my eyes and waited for my submission on the price. Next door there was a truck driver whacking at huge back tyres with a steel hammer. Uighur guitar music played out of some backroom, a plaintive wailing that added the final desperate edge to her words.

I gave way and she leapt up triumphant, thumping the table for good measure. She had hit a raw nerve. The whole area was amongst the most wretched I had seen in China. It was not just the poverty or the fact that it was surrounded by some of the most sterile and hostile desert in the world, but because of the semi-urban mess inhabited by these displaced people. No one seemed to care about their immediate surroundings; the whole town was one big rubbish dump. Small sand tornadoes containing plastic bags and other debris hurtled between miserable buildings. Memories of Inner Mongolia two weeks earlier came flooding back.

Having handed over a princely amount, Madam insisted on a team photo to show there were no hard feelings. Her husband gingerly stepped forward for the peace ceremony but was firmly told to clear up the tables. He shrank before her words and stood near the tables, pretending to wipe something while surreptitiously watching our frozen grins.

These recent migrants along the most ancient trade routes are on the wrong side of history. Many formerly prosperous stops on the Silk Road have been declining for centuries. The invention of the modern aeroplane and the internal combustion engine sped up this process and sounded the death knell of many small isolated communities. Journeys that used to take months or weeks now took days. Before Teichmann drove the first vehicle overland from Beijing, travellers spent months on the road. Gradually, people stopped at fewer and fewer places because they didn't need to stop. Powerful trucks meant that people could bypass whole communities. With the dwindling of the transient travelling population came a much-reduced income. As we left, I pointed out that if she directed her energetic performance towards a coach full of tourists, she would make some real money.

'What tourists?' came the mocking reply as she theatrically scanned the horizon.

We had stocked up with supplies and a large box was strapped on to one of the bikes. As we drove through the outskirts of Korla, the box fell off the bike and spilled its contents across the road. Tins, packages and vegetables bounced in front of my bike. Swerving, I stopped in time to see a crowd of people sprinting towards the scattered food. Dom turned his bike around and drove back shouting, 'It's ours! It's ours!'

Several people had scooped up armfuls of potatoes and

one was clutching a cauliflower. They looked at us, and then sensing we were serious, dropped what they had picked up. One man with a glum face dropped a couple of bottles of oil and vinegar with a loud smash before stepping back to let us pick up the remains. A precious can of beans lay unharmed in the middle of the road but as I walked towards it, a bus ran over it and the contents sprayed over the road.

The speed of the crowd's reactions to the falling food provisions had come as a surprise and reinforced the sense of desperation lurking just underneath the surface of the town. Yet upon being confronted by us, there was an immediate volte-face and potatoes, cabbage and teabags were handed back without a murmur. People trudged back to their former positions and hung around as if nothing had taken place. The ease with which, when challenged, people capitulated was disturbing. Perhaps it is part of what academics have referred to as a peer group morality: everything is legitimate until someone tells you otherwise: a group-orientated rather than an individual morality. The focus is not on the issue at stake, but rather on the group response. There is an unconscious desire to side with the majority and avoid open conflict. The group can be friends, colleagues or strangers on the street. This is in contrast to Westerners who are more likely to put the issue before the integrity of the group as a whole, and are more prepared for confrontation and disunity.

In Beijing I hailed a taxi which did a U-turn in the middle of the road in order to pick me up. He was spotted by a policeman and duly fined about 100 yuan. The driver continued on to deliver me to my destination, but on arrival produced a figure for payment that included his fine. I argued with the man, standing on the road outside his taxi. He got out and before long a crowd had formed. We shouted at each other until blue in the face – I failed to see why I should pay for his fine. He refused to give me change and there was a stand-off. He appealed to the crowd now hemming us in to support his position. At this point a bespectacled suited man said that the foreigner should not have to pay as he had not broken the traffic laws but the taxi driver had. A second man supported this view and suddenly the taxi driver caved in. He handed over my change and got back in his car, mumbling abuse about his fellow-Chinese to himself. He had not been suddenly persuaded that my argument was better than his, but peer pressure had forced him to alter his behaviour. The focus is on defusing any disagreement, not on evaluating the issue.

The drive from Korla towards Kuqa was gruelling. Strong overnight rains had turned the road to sludge and the traffic had became heavier. Our bikes slithered in a concoction of oil, mud and water. We stopped in pouring rain at another Uighur outside café and warmed our hands and feet over the huge coal-fired clay oven. It was cold and my feet were wrinkled and white, the skin peeling away with the water. The recently purchased 'All Weather' bike boots did not seem to include Xinjiang weather. A crash ahead had led to a complete blockage; trucks, jeeps and buses sitting in a long line. We waited, trying to get warm while eating mutton and warm bread and then rode on, weaving in and out of the huge trucks and coughing buses.

The road was terrible and the ride was made harder by knowing that if my battery gave out and I stopped, I would not be able to start again. We were all spread out amongst the traffic and in the heavy rain it was hard to know who was ahead and who was behind. Either side of the treacherous raised road were fields of mud. To the left and right lay overturned trucks that had slipped off on earlier crossings. One crash was so recent that the drivers were still standing around. Panic at the thought of getting stuck, being marooned in this ocean of sludge and snorting diesel meant that I held on grimly to the handlebars and trundled on. For some of the way I had to drive with my legs raised in the air, like an excited 12-year-old with a new Chopper bicycle. Eventually, sliding to a halt outside the only petrol station we had seen all day, I fell into the sidecar and waited for the others.

Wet and hungry, I succumbed to the temptation of eating the last of the baked beans. Acutely aware that I was finishing the group's last delicacy by myself, I guiltily spooned them into my mouth. Satisfied but uneasy about my selfish behaviour, I felt the need to dispose of the evidence as quickly as possible. I carefully placed the tin in a tiny wicker bin in front of the muddy café next door. When Ed and Tim arrived I was toying with a mutton kebab.

As the others arrived, the owner of the café picked up the bin and tossed the contents into the middle of the road and out clanged one Heinz baked bean tin. The group looked at the tin, to the owner, to me and back to the tin. I looked from the tin to the owner. I had completely forgotten the local rubbish-disposal system.

I pleaded guilty to the bean-eating while the café owner looked on with arms crossed across an enormous chest. The Uighur family who ran the restaurant followed the heated conversation with interest. The women talked behind their hands about us while the alcoholic male with several missing teeth muttered comments such as 'not good' in between swigs from a beer bottle.

Looking out for and after each other was something that everyone tried to do. Some of us were better than others, but on the whole there was healthy give and take. If there was any irritation it was always with the trivial, the unimportant. The greatest restraint needed was with food. This is surely the test of the true travelling companion. Wilfred Thesinger, the legendary explorer and unwitting authority on traveller etiquette, judged a person by whether they offered food or water to others before themselves even if they were half-dead from heat, hunger or exhaustion.

At several of our stops west we had heard references to a group of 'foreigners on bicycles'. They had proved elusive, but at each stop we learnt we were edging closer until we expected to round a corner and nudge their back wheels. We finally spotted them, a smudge of bright colour in tight Lycra by the side of the road.

We drove past waving and continued on without stopping. Further up the road we pulled in and had a lengthy discussion on correct traveller behaviour. Should we go back and introduce ourselves? Was it rude to continue without stopping? We turned back. They were the first Western travellers we had seen on the road since we had left Beijing and we all felt there was some unspoken bond.

We found them sitting down to bowls of steaming noodles in a roadside café. They were a group of twenty extremely fit-looking middle-aged Dutch cyclists. Lean, tanned and direct, they were quite unimpressed with our adventure which Dom and I found quite annoying. While we exchanged pleasantries, Tim wandered round the side of the building and was greeted by the sight of one of the cyclists, standing legs astride, having a shit. He waved a cheery hello and held out a hand.

'Er . . . hello.'

'Strong thighs from the cycling,' said the moustached biker, slapping his exposed skin.

After shaking hands with Tim, he wiped his behind with a scrap of newspaper, hitched up his cycling shorts and strode off to join his colleagues.

We camped on a level mud-packed threshing area in a part of Xinjiang that was almost exclusively Uighur. Dishevelled and debilitated after the third hard day on the road, we found it difficult to make progress towards Aksu. Breakdowns, dust, poor roads and heavy traffic slowed our journey. We had passed countless Uighur villages of mud and wood, horse-drawn carts full of men in embroidered caps and women in coloured headscarves. The women wore cotton long johns or heavy nylon stockings under their sparkling polyester shifts; dresses with ruffles, shiny plastic beads and lace trimmings.

We were not the first travellers to note that it was the women who were in charge and do all the work. In the little restaurants, they take the orders, cook the food, control the cash, clear up and do the shopping. In the fields they are the ones bending over, planting crops, grinding corn. The men just hang out.

A group of Uighur villagers appeared silently and discussed amongst themselves all our equipment that was strewn about. A farmer and his three grubby pint-sized sons stood over me, seemingly mesmerised by the shapes of ink that flowed from my pen. Dom invited them to kick a football around and they tore off. In truth, the Uighurs were a lot less curious than Han Chinese and tend to give foreigners more space. They do not smile as readily as their Han neighbours, but are undoubtedly an easier people to travel through. They appear wilder but are without an ounce of aggression, despite the daggers that are tucked into every male waistband. Whenever we asked for assistance they were kind and generous. When we complained of the dust to our new audience, they told us that three weeks ago a massive sandstorm swept through the area killing 32 people.

The white-topped Tian Shan mountains still followed us west. Fim was underneath my bike while Tim was recovering from having had his sidecar dragged 50 yards down the road by a truck. Fim, more mechanically minded than the rest of us, had blossomed into the saviour of the bikes. The unacknowledged hard man of the group, he would sit for hours cleaning pieces of bike in petrol while smoking a cigarette. Sometimes he would take an engine to bed with him and from his bivvy bag could be heard the sounds of the furious scrubbing of toothbrush on metal. His patience with the more practically challenged of the group was admirable.

The traffic had been frighteningly heavy with everyone forced off-road and onto sandy tracks. The vehicles threw up a choking dust which became all enveloping, and visibility became non-existent. A truck had clipped Tim's handlebars while he was bending over his bike at the side of the road and had begun to pull the motorbike and sidecar along the road. Tim had fallen back onto the verge before picking himself up and running after the truck. He had attracted the driver's attention by hurling rocks at the cab. Just when it seemed that his bike would disappear off into the distance and would never be seen again, one particularly well-aimed shot hit the side mirror and ricocheted into the cab, hitting the driver in the side of the face. Brakes screeched and the truck came to a lumbering halt.

While Tim was disentangling his bike, he received a tap on the shoulder. Turning round, he came face to face with a peaked cap. Looking out from underneath was a traffic cop. Scanning the horizon, it was not clear where he could have come from.

Discussion followed between the traffic cop, the driver, who was dramatically clutching his face, and Tim. After listening to both sides of the story, the official pronounced in imperial fashion that the driver was at fault for driving dangerously. The driver started shouting and the official gladly joined in.

Tim shook the official's hand while hurling obscenities at the truck driver, and then disentangled his bike and drove off. We all felt that this was a small victory in the recent daily war of attrition with the Liberation lorries that threatened instant death and mutilation. For most of the journey we had been plagued by these lumbering workhorses, symbols of economic development. (Further east, on the prosperous coast, it is the minivan that has become the distributor of choice.) They rattle across provinces delivering the staples of everyday life: coal, vegetables, beer and rice. They would overtake on blind corners, pull alongside to get a closer look at us, head straight towards us and then swerve at the last minute. Driving at crazy speeds, they would crescendo up behind the bike and then stay within inches of the back tyre. A sudden halt would have been fatal.

A few days earlier Fim had suddenly braked in front of a truck whose constant proximity to his rear wheels had become too much to bear. The truck came screeching to a halt. Fim grabbed a thick bamboo pole tied to his sidecar and stood up on his bike with the pole held aloft. The stick was the same height as the truck's windscreen.

Swearing in Chinese, he dared the driver to continue. There was a several-second stand-off in which neither side moved. A local road café crowd stood by, watching the unlikely encounter. Eventually the driver apologised, after much prodding from his terrified colleague in the cab. Fim sat down, turned round and we continued on.

Although relieved, I was a bit disappointed. We had all had several scrapes with death with these beasts of the road, and the thought of smashing in one of their windscreens seemed quite appropriate and justified. Fim had apparently got the idea from riding in a local minibus on the new Guangzhou-Shenzhen highway. After some reckless driving from a following lorry, the minibus driver swerved in front of the truck and slammed on the brakes. When the lorry stopped, the minibus driver calmly stepped down and picked up a long wooden stave that was attached to the chassis of the vehicle. He walked up to the lorry and proceeded to smash in the windscreen, mirrors and side windows. The truck drivers cowered behind their seats. When there was no more to smash, the minibus driver walked back to his vehicle, stowed the stave, climbed aboard and slowly drove off. His actions were greeted with wild applause from his passengers.

We stop for warm bread and mutton kebabs. Dom, who is sporting a cowboy-style hat as a precaution against the sun, is receiving a great deal of attention from two of the other customers. Two hirsute Uighurs nudge each other and mutter under their breath. We exchange glances with Dom, who feigns an air of indifference at the attention. As a foreigner in China, it is true we had become immune. But I was intrigued as to why Dom in particular was held up for special attention. His blonde curls were hidden away under the hat. Had his presence aroused a dormant sexual consciousness in that large fellow who was wiping grease from the side of his mouth? I was annoyed that I had not undertaken more research into Uighur attitudes towards sexuality, and wondered if their Turkic cultural heritage did not encourage a laissez-faire attitude to one's sleeping partner.

As the two men stumbled out, one of them, the biggest, thrust his face close to Dom's and let out a loud exclamation, '*Zollo! Shenti bangbang de!*' which translates as, 'Zorro! Strapping giant of a man!'

The caped wonder had fans even out here. His face black from the dirt and the dust, white patches remained around Dom's eyes where his goggles had been. Coupled with his hat it is true that he did bear a striking resemblance to the TV hero. Fatty stuck out his hand, grinning from ear to ear. Dom smiled weakly and shook it. A massive slap on the back that had Dom doubled up indicated he was leaving. As he did so, he did a delicate pirouette and made a lunging movement with his right hand – obviously the sword hand. With another cry of 'Zollo!' his mate ushered him out of the café.

We camped that night in a picture-postcard agricultural setting. Neatly planted fields, low hedges, irrigation ditches and cherry trees. Tall poplars shaded us from view. The farmer came out to see us and we smoked cigarettes while crouching over the stove in the moonlight. We discussed agricultural politics. He was Han Chinese, an immigrant, and the difference between his approach to the land and that of the indigenous Uighurs was obvious from the ordered rows of vegetables. He farmed intensively, they didn't. His land was neat and tidy, theirs was wilder. From a mere 300,000 people fifty years ago, the Han Chinese population in Xinjiang is now more than six million, about 38 per cent of the province's total. Yet the two main ethnic groups have very little to do with each other.

After he retired to bed we listened to opera and talked in low voices over the fire. We had our sleeping/eating/washing outdoors down to a humming domesticity by now. Our good humour and mellow feelings were disrupted the next morning by the theft of one of the fuel cans during the night.

'Must have been an Uighur,' said the farmer who appeared silently by our side.

The driving terrain deteriorated still further. It had become hotter. The land on either side of the road had reverted to a shimmering desert grey and was without features. In the afternoon we were forced to seek refuge on the forecourt of a huge petrol station, partly because of heat and exhaustion, but also because of a litany of broken and ailing bike parts: spark plugs, alternators, wiring and spokes. With great arches that crossed over each other, the fuel stop seemed incongruously large and sophisticated for the surrounding area. The canopied roof though provided a welcome respite from the sun. We lay there on the cool concrete, like dogs escaping the heat, while outside all was white. My hands were a greasy black from rummaging around the engine. There was no movement apart from the odd lumbering Liberation truck. We were on the edge of the Taklamakan – 'the desert you go in but don't come out of' – 105,000 square miles of barren nothingness.

In the distance a matt-green mechanised centipede crawled towards us. A convoy of green army trucks on the desert road. We counted them as they swept past. One, two, three, four. Eighty-three in total.

Petrol stations are the temples of the new China. They are huge, new, shiny (for a while) and promise rest and repose for the traveller. They were the only large constructions we had consistently come across on our journey. Here they seemed a sign of the Beijing government's success in controlling and 'civilising' this dusty far-off region. They went hand in hand with the straight new roads. Now police, official and state security land cruisers could range further afield without fear of being stuck amongst a hostile populace. The persistency with which Beijing has attempted to control this part of the world through the centuries is impressive.

Chapter Sixteen

Close to the Edge

A city of over 200,000, Kashgar has been the major trading oasis on the old Silk Road for centuries. Despite losing its pre-eminence in trade, it remains a magnet for local merchants, farmers and travellers. At the junction of routes which cross the Taklamakan, Tibet, Pakistan, Afghanistan and the former Soviet Union, it is one of the few large towns in China to have retained a distinct and romantic appeal. The old city is a warren of mud brick and tile work with Russian and Islamic influences. It remains over 90 per cent Uighur; Chinese here are few and far between. Kashgar's political significance has waned since the days of Russian and British diplomatic presence, now over 50 years ago. Fearful of the other's local influence, they spied on each other's activities from consulates in the town centre. The only foreign visitors now are travellers coming to the still-spectacular Sunday market on the edge of town. Here one is transported back to a different time, the age of the town market, an agricultural fair, medieval in flavour and on a scale that leaves one reeling.

Uighurs, along with Tajiks, Kazakhs, Uzbeks, Kyrgyz, Russians and the odd Hunza trader from across the border, gather in their hundreds from near and far to buy, sell and argue over thousands of livestock. Fat-tailed sheep, horses, goats, chickens and donkeys are all poked and prodded while their owners try to convince the crowds of their livestock's qualities. Covered stalls sell fatty kebabs, haircuts, spices and herbs, coat hangers, soap, pots and pans. The air is thick with the smell of animals, sweat and cooked mutton.

Kashgar is one of the few places in China to have entered the hardy independent travellers' lexicon of 'cool' venues. A legendarily laid-back populace, C. P. Skrine's 'fat and cheerful race', and a postcard-pretty setting at the end of an arduous journey has ensured its reputation amongst those who travel out of the way, a Shangri-La for the backpackers of the world. In China, all such destinations, Dali in Yunnan province, Lhasa in Tibet, lie outside Han areas amongst the minority peoples. We were thrilled to be here. A place that back in England, Beijing and Henan, I had only daydreamed about. Kassshhgarrrrrr – even the name was exotic.

It had been a gruelling final few days with oppressive heat in the day, and wind and rain at night. There was a general feeling of relief. I had fantasised that our arrival out of the desert would be greeted by an adoring posse of female backpackers. We would be welcomed, our conversation sought out. No bus for us. We were doing it for ourselves, under our own steam – true travellers.

Unfortunately, there were few other visitors around to be impressed.

We ate our first evening meal together in an open-air café traditionally frequented by Western backpackers. Everyone had made a special effort and we hardly recognised each other. Gone were the dirt, beards, filthy clothes and greasy hair. Instead, a shower, razors and a rummage around in rucksacks had produced a clean-cut, well-pressed sleekness. Dom's hair was a lighter blonde and seemingly massive. I wore a shirt with a collar. Fim wore a pair of green crocodile-skin shoes that none of us had seen before. He had bought them in Rome the previous year, he said.

But there was no one to hear our tales of desert derring-do. We ate in a subdued silence. We looked as if we were all on our first date.

'I thought Kashgar was supposed to be a honey pot,' said Dom.

'Melting pot,' said Ed.

'That's what I meant.'

'Melting pot and honey pot are two entirely different concepts.'

'Look, I know what I meant. Where are the girls?'

Despite the severe lack of adoring female company, Kashgar's reputation as an oasis is fully deserved. We idled our days away and ate under shady awnings. Now and then two of us would struggle with a game of chess. Some people believe Kashgar might be the place where the game originated. We wandered along to watch the faithful pour out of the main mosque after prayer. Uzbek women in medieval wimples waited outside. I bought some worker-blue long-johns for the mountains ahead. In a ramshackle beer garden, charming Uighurs placed impressive-sounding business cards in our hands: 'Mohammed Wang, President, Trans-Karakoram International Ltd.' They assured us that if we would only set up a partnership together we would become rich.

We repaired and cleaned the bikes and tried to anticipate any future mechanical problems. The town was the last place we could buy spare parts. Bits of metal lay strewn amidst splashes of oil as bikes were stripped down in anticipation of the next part of the journey. From Kashgar we would take the Karakoram Highway that would take us out of China across the Khunjerab Pass and into Pakistan. A thin ribbon of tarmac that reached a height of nearly 15,000 feet, it is squeezed between the two massive mountain ranges of the Karakoram and the Pamirs.

Yet despite the distance driven, I was still flailing with my bike repairs. The night before our arrival, on a windswept plain and in driving rain, I had tried with freezing hands to replace the steering bearings. With hands dipped in yak grease, I had attempted to grease each individual steel ball before replacing them in their little metal circular container. As darkness fell I was still at it; tired and frustrated I kept dropping them in the dirt at my feet. For every one I placed correctly, two seemed to escape my slippery and unresponsive grip and disappear in the darkness. Sensing my helplessness, Fim and Tim offered assistance. I retired to make tea and re-peg everyone's flapping guy ropes.

We stayed in the Seman Hotel, in the grounds of the old Russian consulate that closed in the early 1950s. Soviet influence here used to be strong, and many Kashgaris assumed we were Russian. When Peter Fleming travelled through he described staying at the British consulate (now a hotel as well) and playing tennis with Russian diplomats and advisors. Polo was organised by the redoubtable Mrs Thomson-Glover, the British Consul's wife, who, despite a shoulder wound from a stray bullet, galloped around with the rest of the riders. Later, Diana Shipton recorded an equally happy time amongst the dust and the donkeys as wife of the last British Consul in the 1940s.

The Seman is a large decaying structure with threadbare carpets, unsmiling staff and the ubiquitous brown fake-marble lobby. It was a surprise to read that we were staying in an unparalleled international oasis of luxury. According to the hotel brochure, 'Kashgar Seman Hotel was built in 1890 the former Russian Embassy headquarters. The Chinese Tourist Administration awarded the hotel a two-star rating. Though many people have ranked it as one of the top ten hotels in the world based on service and facilities.'

This was quite some claim as anyone who had spent a night in the state-run building would be able to verify. It was a tired half-empty establishment with staff who lived on site and viewed the guests as an inconvenience. It brought back vivid memories of the hundreds of nights spent in similar establishments across China. And the student quarters in Changchun.

The Uighur *fuwuyuan* were amongst the most fierce I had encountered. They had a limited grasp of Mandarin and this made their instructions all the more guttural and sharp.

'No hot water! Washing. Dirty, now!' (A command to immediately soil one's pants?)

Despite this we enjoyed their company. With market economics sweeping the land, they are an endangered species and reminded us of a civilisation we had left behind. Modern hotel design with individual magnetic cards for each room, plumbing that worked, lower levels of staffing and management that embraced a service culture are ensuring that the glory years of the surly and powerful *fuwuyuan* are effectively over.

In Henan I had witnessed the dramatic changes that these new forces with their alien creed of 'the customer is king' had wrought on the traditional *fuwuyuan* landscape.

In the hotel where I had lived, everyone had been trained

to say 'good morning' when they spotted a guest. It was a welcome change from the muttered refusals and evasion of previous hotel regimes, and also a contrast with the startled cries of *'waiguoren'* ('foreigner') which one still encountered on the city streets (something that had disappeared from the more cosmopolitan cities).

Yet in its own way, it was more exhausting. Someone must have taken guest awareness training to new levels of intensity judging by the relentless way that the 'good morning' regime was implemented. A typical day: Get up, walk down corridor, 'Good morning!' (from cleaner), walk across lobby to dining room, 'Good morning,' 'Good morning!' (one from reception and another from duty manager), enter restaurant, met by waitress, 'Good morning,' who shows me to a table. Another waitress appears to take my order, 'Good morning!' Ordering tea, I tell her that I will be taking the buffet. Getting up to go to the buffet that is near the entrance, another waitress thinks I am leaving, 'Goodbye!' No, no, I'm not going anywhere. I walk back to my table with some food, I am greeted with a 'Good morning!' by a waitress who thinks I have just arrived. Eventually I sit down while another waitress fusses over my cutlery. I snap, 'Look, please can you just leave me alone. I want to eat my breakfast on my own.'

Perplexed looks, whispers with colleagues. I feel guilty but relieved to have set the scene for fifteen minutes' reflective munching. Then suddenly, Bang! Bang! Bang! The glass window on my right shakes, I turn my head and see a window cleaner, merry eyes and mouthing something at me in an exaggerated dramatic fashion. Is this the imparting of some important information relating to my stay in the hotel? Am I getting in the way of her work? Is there a fire?

I peer closer as she mouths again, 'Good morning!'

In Kashgar we came across another familiar actor on the stage of China's hotels, the domestic business traveller. Not since Henan had I seen these voyagers of China's dull provincial hotels. They are a demanding lot and test the patience of the *fuwuyuan* and anyone else in the hotel to the limit.

The male business traveller in China follows a set routine. Discuss sleeping arrangements of your group in a loud voice whilst at the reception. On the way to your room ask the *fuwuyuan* lots of unnecessary questions about dinner provision. Enter room, but leave your door open and immediately turn on the TV, which should be at a volume loud enough to disturb others at the end of the corridor. Take a shower, then wander around room or corridor naked apart from a small vest and tiny towel wrapped around your waist. Occasionally slap your thighs and stomach as if in a health spa. Should really smoke and occasionally phone your friends and tell them in a loud voice what you are doing. Definitely wear the plastic slippers provided.

'*Wei*, *wei*, Wang?'

'I'm staying in a hotel.'

'Really?'

'Yes, I have just had a shower . . .'

Now and then the true business traveller strides to the door, or if really important, remains seated and shouts loudly (several times) for the *fuwuyuan*.

'Foo-woo-you-nnn!'

When she appears, simply place your order for tea, hot water, ashtray or soap as appropriate. This is also the time to point out the fixtures that fail to work.

As most travellers on business are in some delegation, the above picture should be magnified to a greater degree. Occasionally I would walk past an open bedroom door to see four or five men in a haze of smoke, all talking, TV at full blast, one of them on a phone and all wearing the obligatory tiny towels.

Like the *fuwuyuan*, this travel phenomenon is slowly disappearing under the weight of Progress as new architectural and service practices render such behaviour more and more difficult (bedroom doors that shut by themselves in accordance with fire regulations, plumbing that works, and no smoking regimes).

So it was with great joy that we were able to witness a business delegation in full hotel mode. They were from Qingdao on the other side of the country, and were on a visit to assess the local beer distribution situation. Whilst cheerful, they made it quite obvious that they felt themselves to be on a trip in an alien land.

Qingdao is a seaside resort town in Shandong, a province in the north-east of the country. It has the air of a place lost in time; dotted along its shoreline are the large villas of its former German rulers. Gardens with bougainvillea slope down to the sea and large bay windows look out on to the Gulf of Bohai. The Germans left behind a pretty town of which, despite the best efforts of the city planners, much still remains. There is a promenade, packed in the summer with Chinese holidaymakers, where you can buy an ice cream and wander with everyone else. Many of the villas are owned by work units. There is a more laid-back atmosphere than in other Chinese cities, and everything is kept pristine – a Bavarian Bournemouth on the shores of the Yellow Sea.

I went there once to sell beer. On the promenade, an old man came and sat down on the bench next to me, and after a few minutes' staring, tugged at my sleeve.

'Scotch on the rocks?'

It was my turn to stare. 'Scotch on the rocks?'

'Yeah! Scotch on the rocks, Between the Sheets, Screwdriver, Tequila Sunrise,' he rapped the cocktail list out with an American accent. There was a brief hiatus while he struggled to recall some other sophisticated concoction before he started talking in Mandarin.

'The last foreigner I spoke to was an American – in the 1940s.'

During this tumultuous time in China's history, for a brief moment, there was a US naval presence in the bay. Every night, hundreds of white bell-bottomed sailors would come ashore for the evening. He had been a barman in one of the hotels, now used as a department store.

'Great times, Americans were good fun. Very naughty,' and his face creased up in laughter.

As well as leaving their own character on a small part of China, the Germans laid the foundations of Qingdao Brewery, now the most successful national beer in China, and drunk in Chinese restaurants around the world. It was to this company that the travelling businessmen belonged. Every year, in acknowledgement of the central role of this medium-sized city in the alcoholic consciousness of the nation, there is the Qingdao Beer Festival, on the outskirts of the city. It is a big affair, not quite as central to the world economy as its organisers would like to make out, but nevertheless with dozens of participating brands of beer from home and abroad, and thousands of visitors.

It turned out that we had been at the same festival that had seen a group of Zulu dancers marooned amongst the tipsy crowd. The South African beer company that had flown them in had problems getting its beer through customs, and they had no employer to perform for. Finally coaxed to perform anyway, they were watched wide-eyed by thousands of uncomprehending Shandong peasants who clutched terrified offspring to their legs.

One of the business delegation decided to re-enact the Zulu song and dance in his small towel and plastic slippers in a sort of jerky shuffle around the room. His colleagues laughed uproariously in appreciation, and there was soon a rhythmic clapping. I excused myself.

We had the most beautiful drive from Kashgar through mountains and a maze of sunlit valleys. Towering slabs of rock topped with ice and snow dwarfed everything, and occasionally the snow would cascade down to the road, as if someone had overfilled a vessel. Narrow valleys opened onto broad shaggy grassland with lakes. The sheer scale of the scenery took our breath away. We stopped often to try and soak in as much as we could of the overpowering presence of pristine nature at high altitude. We passed the occasional camel or donkey with herdsmen attached, but there were no convoys of trucks ferrying goods as we had imagined. I doubt if there is more traffic now than twenty years ago. We passed Lake Karakul, 12,500 feet up in the Pamirs with the magnificent 'Father of the Ice Mountains', Muztagh Ata, in the distance, a giant slab of whiteness. We sat in awe of its size and brightness.

Later on, as night fell, my engine coughed and stalled. I

grimaced at the thought of breaking down here, so high up, so exposed. My regulator needed changing, which I undertook under Fim's long-suffering guidance. The air was cold and sharp and our tappings on metal echoed up the mountain. Two hours later, much to my delight, the problem was fixed. I was suffused with a warm glow, having moved one step closer to true bikerhood.

I lit a cigarette while surveying the replaced regulator. The wind had picked up, it was cold and too late to move anywhere. I had to be careful not to set fire to the oversized rabbit-fur hat I had bought in Kashgar. Its fluffy brim threatened self-immolation as the wind whipped cigarette sparks through the air. We were not in the Hunza Valley nursing milky tea and full up with dhal as we had expected. Instead we were nearly 20,000 feet up in the mountains. Black rock towered above our stony camp by the side of the road.

Tim scrambled around on the scree to our right, his nervous energy multiplied by a quirky decision to stop smoking the night before. It was quite obvious to all of us that his resolve would crack before the morning arrived. Searching for things to do, he made tea, offered biscuits around and even offered to put up my tent. As an intermittent smoker, I was torn as to whether to offer encouragement, enquire as to why now, or just tell him that success was extremely unlikely. Between us we offered a mixture of all three.

I was woken up in the morning by Tim rummaging through the bag at the end of my sleeping bag.

'What are you doing?'

'Just nicking a tab.'

I was secretly relieved. There is something depressing about superior demonstrations of willpower by one's friends.

Tashkurgan is the last town in China, the very western extremity of Chinese official influence. The customs post is a low squat concrete building with a red and white pole strung across the road. Behind, an afternoon sun lit up a wide, open plain ringed by mountains. A gate of promise. We rushed into the official building, desperate to complete formalities before they closed for the day. We were too late, but they had been expecting us.

'Are you or are you not the bikers from Beijing?' asked a uniformed man perched on a table.

We all looked with surprise and consternation at one another and then back to the customs official. He looked at us through a haze of cigarette smoke. Was this how it would all end? In the prepared calmness of officialdom, were we to be turned back at the final frontier? Were his colleagues going to manhandle us into a police jeep and back to Beijing? Were we witnessing the long tentacles of the central government in action, unamused by foreigners riding around China? None of us spoke. The official peered out of the window at our bikes. We followed his stare.

'Yes, you are. We read about you in the newspaper.' Shit, shit, shit. That was it. After nearly 3,000 miles we were to be turned back almost within sight of the Pakistan border. Perhaps there was even some sort of warrant out for our arrest? Would it all end like Steve McQueen in *The Great Escape*, with the other side in view? Paranoid to the end, we hedged our bets and pretended not to understand.

The official smiled, walked towards Tim and shook his hand.

'Congratulations! We read about you in the paper. We didn't think you would get this far.'

A small town, surrounded by mountains with an old ruined fort and tall poplar trees, nothing much happens in picturesque Tashkurgan. It sits in wonderful isolation. It has existed for centuries as a marker between shifting empires. The ruined stone fort, which gives the town its name, has remained empty since the 1920s when the last occupants, a troop of Cossacks, departed. The town seems to exist only for passing visitors. I parked my bike behind a large concrete construction with broken windows, in search of water and a useless final clean before the Pakistan border. For some reason this part of the trip brought out a previously dormant pride in the humble Changjiang 750. Maybe it was the surrounding mountains that demanded a greater effort, a formal acknowledgement of the majestic scenery. Was it the border or the height that impressed a feeling of being on display? I tiptoed through an open back door and entered an enormous kitchen with all the industrial-sized implements and tools required. On a greasy wooden table lay a skinned sheep, its head lolling just off the table and flies buzzing around its open stomach.

A woman entered in dark overalls with a white bonnet, and we exchanged pleasantries. She told me where to find the water tap and got on with slicing up the sheep with a huge blade. The simplicity of the transaction, the minimal interruption of each other's existence summed up the relationship of this lost town with outsiders. Cut off from the rest of China, from Pakistan, from anywhere, it inhabits a no man's land where the only things in common are shelter, food and water.

We spent the night drinking beer on the street with a group of travellers who had just come across the Khunjerab Pass by bus. Serge and Nell were French, and Lisa was an American. Serge was pleasant, Lisa was interesting, but Nell was gorgeous with enormous brown eyes and softly spoken English.

Serge warned us about everything on the road ahead in Pakistan. Heat, diarrhoea, no water – *'C'était très difficile.'* We all found this quite unwelcome news. Surely it couldn't be as hard or as unpleasant as the Turfan Depression, the Gobi or the Taklamakan Desert could it? Could it? I feigned indifference to his stories and leaned back in my chair. Perhaps he was engaged in an opening skirmish of that tedious traveller game, 'my-journey-was-worse-than-yours.' If so, he would be beaten tonight as we were puffed up and proud. The words of the customs official still rang in my head. Our epic travelling exploits had been recognised by the Chinese themselves; we were in newsprint.

The French couple had found a stray pup in Pakistan and brought it across into China. We were all amazed that they would bring a dog over the border. Nell's eyes became watery as Dom suggested that bringing a dog into China was a sure way to hasten its death. It would have to be watched night and day if it wasn't to be snatched up and boiled for supper by some Gansu peasant.

'Really?' she exhaled.

Why yes. And we delighted in telling a series of fabricated horror stories about the Chinese and their eating habits.

Fim and Ed went off to play pool with Serge and Nell, even though they were both exhausted. They were somehow hoping that Serge would disappear from the planet in a puff of smoke and they would be left with the magnificent, pouting Nell. When a man meets an attractive woman abroad, there is a pathetic male belief that anything can happen. The normal laws of reality are suspended and yes, she just might leave her boyfriend, walk across the room and whisper 'I want you' before dragging you off to bed. Every instance of eye-contact was meaningful, every proffered cigarette suggestive. It didn't matter that her boyfriend was good-looking, charming and intelligent – we were bikers.

I entered my room ready for sleep. Taking off my shoes and socks I hopped and skipped across the regulation burgundy carpet only to find my normal routine entering a slide. The floor was wet and it smelt of urine. Drying my feet on the thin curtains, I clambered into bed. I knew it was a cheap hotel and we were at the end of China, but I was quite sure that this was the first time that I could remember having a urine-soaked carpet in my room. I went to sleep, reminding myself to mention it to the unshaven manager in the morning. Perhaps he would offer a few bottles of beer as compensation – they would be appreciated later on in Pakistan.

Bang! Bang! Bang! The door shook.

'Time to get moving!'

Lying in the warm half-sleep of the morning, it was exhausting just thinking about the cold corridor that led to the showers. I could hear people moving outside, the hiss of the shower, taps turning on and the schoolboy yelps of Tim as he encountered the Tashkurgan plumbing system. Judging by his cries there was obviously no hot water available. I shivered in my warm bed. I wondered if Nell had got up and whether she would be braving the washroom. Maybe I would have that shower . . .

As I swung my feet over the edge of the bed, they made solid contact with the still-damp carpet. Damn! There was a faint knock at the door and Nell appeared, radiant and freshly showered.

'*Bonjour.*'

'*Bonjour.*'

'I just wanted to apologise for Fido.'

'Who?'

'Fido, the dog, and the mess on your floor last night,' she said laughing.

'*Pas de problème! Pas de problème!*' I cringed, laughing in return. With that the door shut.

'Pathetic,' said Dom from underneath his covers on the opposite bed.

We were allowed to complete customs that morning. Beyond the metal red and white pole a straight road dissected a grassy valley. I felt a bit sheepish in front of the same customs guys who we had played dumb with the evening before. After a dig around in our sidecars we were waved on and a guard pulled up the barrier. We were still officially in China, but from here on there was no authority. As we swept off without a backward glance, light drizzle fell. There was no one else on the road and we were caught up in the grand emptiness of the valley, excited at the thought of being in Pakistan by nightfall – only 80 miles to the border.

We passed through a wide-bottomed valley with the snow-capped Pamirs on our right, just out of sight behind low clouds. Gradually the valley narrowed and the road carried us upwards through defiles with large slabs of overhanging rock. We ascended through dark valleys, where the sun was blocked out by the sheer bulk of the mountains. The road opened out into a wonderful panorama of rock and grass, and then a lake. Domesticated yaks grazed on the grass with the occasional camel and the even more occasional Tajik herdsman. The higher we rose, the greater our field of vision. Each bend brought a more impressive sight than the last. Mountains, valleys, mountains, crevices, glaciers, more mountains. The softer rounded peaks of the Pamirs gave way to the black and jagged peaks of the Karakoram. The road looped back on itself as it snaked up a particularly steep incline.

The four other bikes were ahead of me and we were spread out, reduced to black dots in the huge landscape. Although summer, the temperature had plummeted and a biting wind cut coldly against us. My hands were freezing in thinly padded leather gloves. I rested my boots on the motorbike's piston covering to keep warm. The road is only open six months of the year as the weather is considered too severe and dangerous to make the crossing at other times.

The Karakoram are one of the world's great mountain ranges, running along the edge of China's border with Afghanistan, Pakistan and Kashmir, a length of 300 miles. They contain many of the world's highest peaks, with dozens over 23,000 feet, and the longest glaciers. Peaks are sharp and angular, like mountains in a dark fairytale. One waits for a flock of large ravens to circle.

Due to lack of oxygen my engine starts to falter and lose power as we climb the last stretch to the top of the Khunjerab Pass. The drive from Beijing has taken its toll and the bike is reduced to an elderly walking pace. We climb painfully up and up in a cold drizzle until we come across the last border post, an old olive-green truck body with a sign reading 'Frontier Defence of China' and a fluttering red flag. A couple of boys in uniform tumble out. We chat and have our photo taken. They look subdued by the surrounding landscape and certainly don't look tough enough to be living in such a wild and isolated place (Khunjerab translates as 'Blood Valley' in Tajik). There is general astonishment that we have driven all the way from Beijing, but also warm smiles, not so much at our achievement, but at the fact that we are driving Chinese-made machines.

After a stiff salute we crawl up the road until we reach the highest point of the Khunjerab Pass, a no man's land 15,500 feet high, a snowy stillness amidst rock, ice and mist. We celebrate with cigars and a bottle of hoarded Bulgarian wine that immediately gives us all headaches. Another photo, the click of the shutter muffled by the snow and altitude. I glance back at the way we have come and then forward at the black crumbling rock in front of us. We had done it. We had crossed China on the notorious Changjiang 750. No helmets, no back-up trucks, no deaths or mutilation. No falling out. I was in a state of pure happiness, perhaps exacerbated by the wine at high altitude. We grinned inanely at each other. The drive from east to west seemed one long goodbye to a country that had fascinated and infuriated for over five years. A therapeutic road trip that somehow justified the years spent in China. All those hours of straining at characters in the half-light, failed relationships, endless train journeys, tea and cigarettes, karaoke and alcohol, and a thousand and one pleasures and frustrations. It was over and somehow complete.

Epilogue

London, nearly three months later.

We did make it back to London eventually. Four months after leaving Beijing, we were seated in a shabby corner pub, just south of the Thames in the middle of the afternoon. We were the only customers. Traffic rumbled past outside on its way north as we anxiously nursed pints of bitter. The trip was over. Affected by the mild depression and the listlessness that greets all travellers on their return, we waited until it was time for an agreed appearance in Trafalgar Square in front of friends and family. I finished my pint and declined a third. Tim smoked Regals continuously. ('You get twenty-five in a packet.') Despite hot baths and scrubbing the night before at a friend's farmhouse, the drive into London plus months of ingrained dirt and weather-beaten clothes had us all still looking like hardened travellers. It felt strange to be back. Beijing and China seemed a lifetime away.

After crossing into northern Pakistan we had kept heading vaguely west, down through the Hunza Valley on the Karakoram Highway to Islamabad. A road of over 600 miles carved out of the mountainous banks of the Hunza and Indus rivers, it wound its way up to Peshawar and the Afghan border, before heading across the lawless desert and mountains of Baluchistan. Attempting a mountainous cross-country route to avoid the worst of the heat, we were detained by local police and brought before a weary district commissioner. Informing us that it was too dangerous a region for foreigners to cross on their own, he ordered bearded militiamen to sit on the back of each of our bikes. After four days in which we covered less than twenty miles we arrived at isolated Zhob, where a less understanding district commissioner promptly put us under house arrest. Escorted to the edge of town by the Zhob militia, the road to Iran was pointed out. We laboured under the preposterous heat of the desert to Bam and Iran, a country in limbo. Stranded in Tehran because of red tape, Dom and Ed, the two blonds in the group, had had telephone numbers and secret messages stuffed into their pockets by impressionable young Tehrani women. We trundled along north-west from Tehran and into a tense eastern Turkey under the gaze of Mount Ararat. Military personnel hunting Kurdish separatist fighters would appear and then disappear in a pastoral countryside as we drove towards Istanbul. We crossed the Bosphorous and into Europe. The impossibility of finding any spare parts once out of Asia meant we had arrived with balding tyres, broken lights and dangerously erratic engines. Apart from a punctured airbed, all the expedition equipment that I had so excitedly caressed outside Beijing had by now disappeared.

We only met two groups of Chinese once we had left China. We rushed to talk with them each time, a reminder of something we had left behind. One group was a delegation of light industry officials from Sichuan, sightseeing in Isfahan. In baggy grey suits and led by a man with a little flag, they were happy to talk in their own language. The other group were not so keen to see us. In a brothel masquerading as a discotheque on the outskirts of Bucharest, Fim and I overheard the distinctive tones of Beijing voices. A group of

Chinese men sat with women twice their size perched on their knees in flimsy slips. The largest woman, in a halo of peroxide hair and jutting breasts, urged the smallest Beijinger to take her home. We introduced ourselves, sat down and began a stilted conversation in Mandarin. They were officials in the Foreign Affairs Department and were embarrassed by our presence.

I was light-headed at the thought that we had driven from one side of the world to the other, more than 11,000 miles, and we had all made it without serious injury. In my case without a licence. More astonishing was that we had made it on motorbikes whose faulty mechanics and wiring constantly tempted fate. The limitations of our transport had shaped our trip as much as the route we had chosen and afterwards I would take a certain pride in the slowness of our progress. There is a Chinese phrase that says people often enjoy the journey more than the arrival. That was how I felt. I would have liked to have kept going. I didn't know whether to shout or cry.

Outside, Ed argued with a traffic warden who was trying to issue a ticket for one of the bikes. Pleading guilty, he pointed to the foreign number plates as an excuse.

'Where did you come from then?' asked the traffic warden. 'Don't tell me . . . China!'

Laughing to himself and shaking his head, he wrote out a ticket.

Bibliography

Aitchen, K. Wu *Turkistan Tumult* (1940, Methuen)

Becker, Jasper *The Chinese* (2000, John Murray)

Bond, Michael Harris *The Psychology of the Chinese People* (1986, Oxford University Press)

Cable, M., French, E. and French, F. *The Gobi Desert* (1984, Virago)

Fleming, Peter *News from Tartary* (1936, Jonathan Cape)

Hutchings, Graham *Modern China* (2001, Penguin)

Jenner, W. J. F. *The Tyranny of History* (1992, Penguin)

Lai, T. C. *At the Chinese Table* (1984, Oxford University Press)

Ma, Jian *Red Dust* (2001, Chatto & Windus)

Neville-Hadley, Peter *China: The Silk Routes* (1997, Cadogan)

Scotland, Tony *The Empty Throne* (1994, Penguin)

Segal, Gerald 'Does China Matter?' *Foreign Affairs* September 2000

Skrine C. P., *Chinese Central Asia* (1926, Methuen)

Study in China: A Guide for Foreign Students (1988, Beijing Languages Institute Press)

Things Chinese and Their Stories (1994, China Travel and Tourism Press)

Waley, Arthur *Yuan Mei, Eighteenth-Century Chinese Poet* (1956, Stanford University Press)

Wang, Shuo *Please Don't Call Me Human* (2000, No Exit Press)

Warner, Langdon *The Long Old Road in China* (1926, Doubleday)

Wood, Frances *Did Marco Polo go to China?* (1998, Westview Press)

Yang, Bo *The Ugly Chinaman* (1992, Allen and Unwin)

Yuan, Ke, ed. *Classified Anecdotes of the Qing Dynasty* (1986, Shangwu Yinshuguan)

Yule, H. and Cordier, H. *The Book of Ser Marco Polo* (1903, John Murray)

Empire of the Soul
by Paul William Roberts

£7.99 • -paperback • 1 84024 188 8 • 129 x 198 mm/352 pp

'An outrageously funny, brilliantly penetrating and deeply affectionate portrait of India.' *Martin Amis*

'India is a harsh mistress: she seems to appreciate individual sacrifice so little. Yet she has never wanted for lovers . . .'

India demands a passionate response. In 1974 Paul William Roberts embarked on the first of many trips that began a lasting affair with the country. Spanning twenty years of travel, Roberts paints a picture of a place of constant change, of polarities and extremes, of holy men and millionaire drug dealers, of desperate poverty and riches beyond compare. With characters as diverse as the founder of India's first pornographic magazine to Mother Teresa, *Empire of the Soul* is a seductive, witty and truly unforgettable book.

The Nomad

The Diaries of Isabelle Eberhardt

Translated by Nina de Voogd
Edited by Elizabeth Kershaw and introduced by Annette Kobak

£6.99 • paperback • 1 84024 140 3 • 129 x 198 mm/208 pp

The fascinating story of a strange, passionate life.

In 1904 and at the age of only 27, Isabelle Eberhardt drowned in the deserts of North Africa. Buried beneath the rubble and mud that crushed her were found battered leather journals containing the extraordinary tale of her life. The illegitimate child of aristocracts, a 20-year-old Isabelle travelled to Algeria with her mother, who died 6 months after their arrival. Reinventing herself as a man, embracing Arab nomad tribes and their lifestyle, she wandered the Sahara on horseback.

A controversial figure and equally loved and hated, Isabelle's diaries recount her sexual adventures and drug-taking, her conversion to Islam and the mysterious attempt on her life. Experiencing moments of both desperate loneliness and euphoric joy, Isabelle struggles to find her place, her voice as a writer and the true purpose of human existence.

Blue Cuban Nights

by Ted Ferguson

£7.99 • paperback • 1 84024 226 4 • 129 x 198 mm/320 pp

Poetry, politics and a pulsing Latin beat.

Ted Ferguson is in love with Cuba, a country that swings to rumba whilst embracing Communism: a country of contradictions. Breaking out of the tourist bubble and opening closed doors, Ferguson uncovers a cornucopia of colourful individuals and their idiosyncracies. He meets Roca, a collector of pig paraphernalia and Tony the jazz aficionado of bootleg Dizzy Gillespie tapes. He sees the mausoleums of the rich equipped with air-conditioning and telephones, and the poor who hunt the city's street cats for a decent meal. Ferguson's Cuba encompasses all that is sexy, vibrant and utterly alluring about the hotbed of the Caribbean.

La Bella Vita
by Vida Adamoli

£7.99 • paperback • 1 84024 220 5 • 129 x 198 mm/320 pp

An evocative, entertaining and poignant reminiscence of sixties and seventies Italy.

Southern Italy, 1960. Torre Saracena is an ancient Italian village, a huddle of shuttered houses and sun-baked streets perched on a rocky promontory above the sea. For centuries this insular community has closed its ranks against everyone outside its walls; even the inhabitants of the nearest town are classified as foreigners.

An 18-year-old Vida fell in love, married her Italian boyfriend and moved to Rome. Escaping from the bustle of the capital, she, her husband and two small sons immersed themselves in the apparent idyll of Torre Saracena. But from feuding and festivals through to murder and brushes with the Neapolitan Mafia, life is never dull. Vida's is a delightful story of twenty years living *la bella vita* with the villagers and bohemians who became her trusted friends.

Wild East
Travels in the New Mongolia
by Jill Lawless

£7.99 • paperback • 1 84024 210 8 • 129 x 198 mm/320 pp

'Engaging . . . a revealing and often amusing account of journeys through a beautiful country awakening from a tumultuous era.' *The Toronto Mail*

'I first glimpsed Mongolia from the air. The overwhelming impression was of space, beauty and a deceptive serenity; a gently undulating sea of rich grass, flecked with white felt tents, like aspirin scattered over a green bedspread.'

Mongolia conjures up exotic images of wild horsemen, of endless grasslands, of a ruthless Genghis Khan, and of weathered nomads – a mysterious land that time forgot. Jill Lawless arrived in Mongolia to find a country emerging from centuries of isolation beneath the shadow of its oppressive neighbours, at once discovering its Buddhist heritage and the trappings of the Western world. The result is a land of fascinating and bewildering contrasts.

Blue Road
by Windy Baboulene

£7.99 • paperback • 1 84024 234 5 • 129 x 198 mm/320 pp

A wildly funny story of life on the ocean waves.

'"You must be Norman," I smiled.
"And you must be Mistaken," he said, smiling back with a certain edge. "If you start calling me Norman, I shall set fire to you."'

After blowing up his school chemistry lab, 16-year-old 'Windy' Baboulene escapes the Old Bill by running away to join the Merchant Navy. Embarking on farcical rites of passage at sea, Windy and his mates work their way around the world, leaving a trail of destruction in their wake. After finding freedom, romance and a police cell. in Australia, Windy eventually begins the long voyage home to England, a fully-fledged, hairy-arsed 17-year-old veteran.

For a current catalogue and a full listing of
Summersdale travel books, visit our website:

www. summersdale.com